# TO GREAT YOHO AND BACK

*To my good
neighbors at Crowdcrest*

*'Bob' Singleton, Sr*

# TO GREAT YOHO AND BACK

## A WWII Biography of Robert Leon Singleton

Robert L. Singleton Jr.

**BEARCLIFF PUBLISHING**
WEST STOCKBRIDGE, MASSACHUSETTS

BEARCLIFF PUBLISHING
WEST STOCKBRIDGE, MASSACHUSETTS

*Library of Congress Control Number: 2001119900*

*ISBN: 0-9716843-0-8 (hard cover)
0-9716843-1-6 (soft cover)*

*Printed on acid-free paper in the United States of America*

*to*

*Norma Jane*

# Contents

# PREFACE

IT DIDN'T TAKE A BESTSELLER BY TOM BROKAW to convince me that something was special about the World War II generation. My parents were part of that group, and Dad was an Army Air Force veteran.

Like most of his contemporaries, he didn't talk much about the war. If the subject came up, it was triggered by questions from me or my sister after overhearing remarks made at gatherings of grown-ups. More often than not, it seemed that light got shed on this subject around Christmastime, when Dad set up my prized electric train in a miniature snow-covered village under the blinking scotch pine in our living room. The all-metal-and-wood functioning scale-model, crafted by a company called Märklin, was sent back to the states by Uncle Clayt, who was an Army officer in occupied Germany. The German train prompted Dad to talk about the time he flew bombing missions. I was absolutely fascinated by his stories, which were carefully meted out in the lap of our warm davenport and secure surroundings. Christmas was a magical time for us—a time when we got an extra dose of quality time from Dad, who spent most of his days at the family shoe store.

With each Christmas that went by we gleaned a bit more information about his experience as an airman in the war. As a young boy, I was particularly captivated by his scrapbook, which included a snapshot collection of daunting fighter aircraft with garish markings and photographs of B-17 formations dropping bombs on smoke-covered cities. Early on we learned that there was a right way, a wrong way, and an Army way to do things. I never understood how to do it the Army way, but figured it was something to avoid. As we got older, we learned that he sat in the best seat in the airplane—inside the glass nose bubble—where the view was spectacular and "bombs away" was called out. I gained further insight into his experience when I solicited his input for my sixth-grade social studies project on World War II. That's when he produced another worn, but well-preserved collection of loose-leaf pages containing an organized, neatly hand-written summary of each of his bombing missions, including yellowed newspaper clippings reporting the results of each raid. He also showed me some fragments of jagged-edged flak that had pierced his Flying Fortress and nearly struck him. I was shocked by the sharp edges and heavy weight of the metal chunks, which he casually dropped into the palm of my hand.

He tried to be nonchalant about his role in the war, but you could tell by the tone of his voice that it was something that had made a big impression on him. As time moved forward we learned about his buddy Johnnie Rutherford and the crazy bunch of guys he bunked with in a metal hut on the English countryside. If Mom got involved in the conversation it usually had something to do with a place they lived called "Zaraguzie" Street, where she supposedly smacked him in the belly with a frying pan. She said she was angry with him at the time of the incident, but the sparkle in her blue eyes betrayed her true feelings. It wasn't until I was older that I realized that he never intended to join the Army and become a bombardier. Rather than waiting to be drafted into the infantry, he enlisted in the more exciting aviation cadet program, but washed out of pilot training with most of his class, after which he was retrained as a gunnery instructor and got shipped overseas. That's where he volunteered to fly in the bombardier's seat so that he could accumulate more combat missions, thereby earning an earlier release and quicker return home to Mom.

As a boy, I was enthralled by airplanes and made a hobby of building and collecting models, some of which flew under their own power and others hung by string from my bedroom ceiling. I could identify any aircraft make or type on sight. As a young teenager, on snowy winter days I wore Dad's scruffy, fleece-lined leather bomber jacket, which I found in the olive-drab trunk in our attic. It had a faded Eighth Air Force patch and a pair of insignias with cartoon-like devils and bombs. It never occurred to me that it might have sentimental value or would be the fashion rage of the younger set two decades later. In college I majored in aeronautical engineering with aspirations of becoming an astronaut. While such dreams were not unusual among young males at the time, looking back I'm quite sure that I was influenced by Dad's stories and undisguised yearning to fly. Hence, when the war in Vietnam looked like it wasn't going to end—and I drew number 36 in the draft lottery—signing up for reserve officers training in the Air Force seemed like the natural thing to do. Indeed, my college flight training piqued Dad's interest, and before I had a chance to earn my wings he secured his private pilot's license.

Our common love of flying created a bond between us marked by cherished memories of flying together over the beautiful landscape of our hometown in Lancaster County, Pennsylvania—usually during my holiday visits. The day after Christmas 1971, when I was leaving for military pilot training in Arizona with new bride in tow, Mom and Dad were there to bid us goodbye. Dad was never one to get teary, but I distinctly recall how his eyes filled up and his jaw twisted as he tried to hide his emotions. This was certainly not the first time I had left home, but it was the first time I had ever seen him affected this way. Only later did it occur to me that our departure may have evoked poignant memories of something significant in his own life. The more I thought about it, the more obvious it was.

When I began flying military aircraft, I often thought about what aerial combat would be like and reflected on what Dad had written in his mission log 25 years earlier, when he was my age. The older I got, the more I appreciated his contribution as a young airman in a big war and the personal sacrifices he had to make simply because he came of age during that period. A remarkable thing about his war experience is that it was unremarkable among his own contemporaries, many of whom perished, were wounded, or came back with psychological scars that would never be erased. Perhaps it was because there were so many who fared worse that the average combat veteran—if there is such a thing—never talked much about it. They felt that war stories would only desecrate the memory of the dead and dishonor the wounded.

The most remarkable thing about Dad's war experience is how it meshes into the fabric of his life and influences the way he looks at the world around him. It's not his combat experience per se; but it's his total life experience, which includes this extraordinary period of history, and the character it engendered that makes it so compelling. Brokaw expresses this point so eloquently in *The Greatest Generation*.[1] It's why this book, which was originally conceived as a story about Dad's war years in England, blossomed into a story about his life, from his family roots to the present time—and his relationship with my mother, who made his life truly complete.

After Mom died, Dad and I returned to England to explore his wartime stomping grounds. It was his first trip overseas since his Army stint a half-century earlier. We located the King's Head pub at Great Yeldham and the meager remains of the aerodrome at Ridgewell. The ancient Ashen Church was still there, and we met some folks of a generation who remembered a base filled with Yanks, the unmistakable drone of a bomber fleet, the intermittent buzzing of the enemy's guided bombs overhead, and the terrifying mid-air collision and explosion on final approach of two bombers that returned from a successful bombing raid in January 1945. We found, renovated but still standing, the Garden House Hotel in Cambridge, where he met Uncle Frank, and visited the American Military Cemetery outside of town. I had seen pictures and read about the beauty of this place, which resembles the hallowed burial grounds in Normandy—long concentric rows of white marble crosses on lovingly manicured green lawns, surrounded by lush greenery and profound silence except for the intermittent chirping of birds. But it was a place that to fully absorb its significance you had to be there. I was caught off guard by its effect on me. We had to split apart to take it all in. I could tell that Dad needed to be alone. I know that I did.

THIS BOOK IS ABOUT THE LIFE of an extraordinary man, whose early years were interrupted by the Depression and a world war. Extensive research was conducted to learn about his ancestors and their circumstances. All historical facts other than common knowledge are documented. Information based on the memories of surviving relatives is also footnoted. While people, places, and events are all substantiated, with apologies to the deceased I have often taken liberties to presume motivations or feelings based on limited available facts defining the circumstances. By exploring my father's roots, the text speaks to the formation of simple values and strong beliefs that make him so special. Throughout the story he speaks to us through quotations from taped interviews—which for the sake of simplicity I have marked by quotation marks but left unnoted—and in excerpts from his mission log and intimate letters written to my mother during the war years—which are highlighted in both italics and quotation marks.

Some of the events described in this book may seem mundane or tedious to the casual reader. I have made no attempt to dramatize events or delete commonplace anecdotes for the sake of appealing to a mass readership; because, based on interviews with Dad and hearing many stories often repeated, these include his most vivid recollections, thus to a great extent describe what is important from his perspective —and as his grandchildren would most appreciate it.

For me, the project has been a labor of love and fascinating historical journey. Dad knew little about his grandparents and their world before I began this project. He never fully appreciated his role in the war until we placed it in the greater context of the accomplishments of his 381st Bomb Group, the Eighth Air Force, and his generation. But I always knew there was something special about my father and the war years. That's why I wrote this.

# ACKNOWLEDGEMENTS

I WAS MOTIVATED TO TAKE ON THIS PROJECT YEARS AGO by a loose-leaf collection of mission notes compiled by Dad when he was stationed in England and flying bombing missions from December 1944 through April 1945. This mission log is reproduced in the appendix. My inspiration was the simplicity of his hand-written comments, which have always struck me in the way they understate the significance of one young man's role in a gigantic war effort. I cannot find the words to overstate my gratitude for his preserving and sharing that precious, personal account of his experience in flak-infested skies.

A major challenge of a project like this is attempting to capture the thoughts and feelings of a person who is living in a war zone and experiencing the horror of combat. I used the medium of structured interviews and open-ended discussion to stimulate his recollection of those events long ago, but despite some success, he understandably has forgotten many details. My biggest surprise came when he made mention of "your mother's letters" during our third interview session. As a result of my follow-up, and thanks to Mom's faithful safeguarding of every letter that she received from Dad during the war years, her collection was not only saved from incineration, but it has served as a daily chronicle of his days in the Army. How can I thank her enough?

I would like to express my appreciation to Dad's Army buddy from Lancaster, John Rutherford, who served with him in England and was kind enough to spend several hours recounting his parallel experience as a gunnery instructor and toggalier. Thanks also to Jim Tennet, Curator of Ridgewell Airfield Commemorative Association, for his diligent search of microfilm records under difficult circumstances. And a special thanks to Chaplain James Good Brown, who offers the most insightful thoughts about the men of their bomb group in his exceptional book, *The Mighty Men of the 381st: Heroes All.* I would also like to acknowledge the *381st Bomb Group Memorial Associa-*

*tion*, whose internet site has been an excellent source for confirming historical facts and details.

In writing about family history, I first sought out relatives to help fill in missing information. Many thanks to Marian Medsger, Evelyn Singleton Thom, Mollie and Ed Singleton, and Audrey Diffenbach Hauser for their valued time and patience trying to recollect ancient history. I am also grateful to Dorothy Saylor for sharing her late husband's genealogical data on the Singleton branch of the family tree and to Richard Rhoads for his diagram which traces the Rhoads side.

Thanks to Paul and Shirley Risk, Dad's Willow Valley neighbors, I had early access to a private copy of the *Biographical Annals of Lancaster County* and Bridgens' *Atlas of Lancaster County*, which provided excellent information about the family during the time they lived in Drumore Township in the nineteenth century. Portrayal of life in the twentieth century was facilitated by Dad's collection of articles from Lancaster Newspapers' excellent millennium series on *Our Century*. I would also like to acknowledge the Lancaster County Historical Society, whose reading room provided an abundance of information from old newspapers, census records, county surveys, cemetery indexes, and city and county directories. And thanks to the kindness of Dick Bertrand, who let me borrow his *World War II* periodicals, I didn't have to visit the library while I was in Florida.

A special thanks to Kitty Axelson-Berry of Modern Memoirs in Amherst, Massachusetts for her advice and encouragement during my first book publication cycle and to her skillful associate Art McLean, who provided invaluable proofreading assistance.

# CHAPTER 1

# SCOTCH AMBROSIA

A SWEET, MOIST AIR hangs protectively above the gently rolling hills of southern Lancaster County, renowned for its rich soil and prolific summer gardens. It always smells organically fresh here, hinting of springtime fragrances on mild winter days and scented into late autumn with a lingering redolence of livestock, silage and tobacco. Groomed fields and corn rows follow natural contours of the terrain for as far as the eye can see. The texture of the landscape, tinted in verdant hues and earth tones, is unbroken except for clusters of leafy foliage, small streams meandering through uncluttered pastures, and rambling farm lanes accented by wooden fences, weathered barns, gleaming silos, and well-preserved stone houses.

Unspoiled since the first Scotch-Irish Presbyterians settled here three hundred years ago, the bucolic landscape of Drumore Township in southern Lancaster County is where the family took root: at the farm in the village of Liberty Square where Ambrose Singleton spent his childhood; on the Buck intersection, three miles to the northeast, where he started a family and career as a grocer; and in the Mt. Hope Methodist Church cemetery to the east, where he was laid to rest.

The serenity of this region betrays its historical prominence and commercial vitality. Organized in 1729 and named after a county in Ireland called Druim Miur, Drumore was one of the original townships in Lancaster. By the time Ambrose was born in 1854, it was one of the most populous and robust agricultural townships in the county. Fewer than a hundred people lived in Liberty Square, but the township had a diverse population of about three thousand, most of whom lived and worked on farms. Many also labored at one of six grist mills, seven saw mills, ten stores, and fifteen schools, or at the iron furnace and forge. Iron ore was mined in pits on the other side of Quarryville, four miles to the east of Buck, across the township's northeast corner.

The township is laid out like a nine-mile deep riverside lot extending to the northeast from a four mile stretch of waterfront on

Pennsylvania's great Susquehanna River. Liberty Square is situated in
the northwest corner of the township, a few miles to the east of
McCall's Ferry, a major shipping depot on the Susquehanna. The
Singleton farm, just north of the village of Liberty Square, is located
between two tributaries that wind on southwesterly courses to the
river. Muddy Run, a small creek which forms the northwest township
border, begins a couple of miles to the north of Liberty Square in the
hamlet of Rawlinsville and flows southwesterly along the west side of
the farm, powering two mills on its journey to the Susquehanna. Fishing Creek springs up a few miles to the east of Rawlinsville in the hills
north of Buck and wanders southwest along the east side of the farm,
servicing three other mills on the way to the big river. A third, larger
tributary, Conowingo Creek, also emanates from the Buck hills, but
diverges to the east then south by the old iron furnace and foundry
before crossing the township border. There it passes the birthplace of
Robert Fulton, continues through the township bearing his name, and
crosses the state border six miles further south, joining the great river
near the top of the Chesapeake. This border, which later became the
Mason-Dixon Line, was in dispute with Maryland for many years.

When the first permanent white settlers migrated to southern
Lancaster County in the early 1700s, the only people living there were
peaceful Native Americans and frontier traders, situated mainly along
the banks of the Susquehanna and its tributaries. The earliest settlers,
Swiss Mennonites, were followed by waves of French Huguenots,
Scotch-Irish, Welsh, English Quakers, and Germans. But most of
Drumore's early inhabitants were part of a second wave of Scots that
are believed to have been diverted to the area near the Maryland border by Pennsylvania's Quaker government, because Maryland squatters
could not be kept out without using force, a method inconsistent with
Quaker beliefs.[1]

The Scots arrived with a history of forced migration from Scot-
land to Ireland under English rule. Like persecuted Germanic people
from the Rhineland region of Europe, they were attracted by the religious toleration espoused by William Penn, founder of the colony.
They were viewed as belligerent due to their lax attitude regarding
property rights and contempt for Indians. But they were effective in
forming a strong line of defense against hostile Indians, Maryland
squatters, and French enemies in the early wars. "While German
speaking folks viewed Scots as 'indifferent' farmers, they also saw

them as devout in religion, active in politics, and determined to defend individual rights."[2] Scots may have been more wanderlust than settled in their habits, but they made good neighbors and shared important values, like a belief in God, a strong work ethic, and a practical, action-biased approach to dealing with problems.

Their Drumore neighborhood was diverse. By the 1800s, the pristine countryside was peppered with farms deeded to people with *Anglo* names like Hopkins, Kelly, McMichael, McPherson, Morrison, Penny, Phillips, Ramsay, Scott, and Watson; French names like Aument, Lefevre, and Rhinier; and a collection of Germanic, or Lancaster County "Dutch" (Deutsch), names like Eckman, Eshelman, Graybill, Groff, Herr, Hess, Kendig, Miller, Newswanger, Stauffer and Sweigart.

It's no accident that many immigrants settled in Drumore. Conditions were perfect for a rich rural life: temperate climate; fertile, limestone-rich soil; plentiful natural resources; and practical, God-fearing neighbors with quietly shared values. Security was insured by an ingrained work ethic, community spirit, burgeoning markets, and large population centers nearby. In addition to the local commercial infrastructure, the urbane port city of Philadelphia was a day's ride by wagon to the east, and the bustling port of Baltimore roughly equidistant to the south. Just as important, the city of Lancaster was located at the county center about 13 miles to the north. The oldest inland city in the U.S., Lancaster was the cultural and economic hub of the region. Its popular and vibrant public markets provided convenient outlets for Drumore's bounty—wheat, corn, oats, potatoes and dairy products—and prosperity for its hard-working families.

SURROUNDED BY THIS miracle, Ambrose's struggle, barely disclosed by skimpy family lore, is an enigma of sorts—particularly as it relates to his supposed drinking problem. Ambrose A. Singleton was born on September 11, 1854 to William and Rebecca (McFee) Singleton. A late bloom on the family tree, Ambrose was separated in age from his father by nearly four decades. Siblings John, Charles, and Ella were likely older, although their ages cannot be confirmed.[3] Like many children his age, Ambrose grew up on an average-size farm in a predominantly agricultural community. But something may have been missing. It's possible that Ambrose viewed the pastoral landscape of his childhood not for its serenity, but for the span that separated him from fulfilling interaction with friends of his own age, or perhaps even a youngster's attraction to a nearby killing war with the Confederates. Nobody will ever know whether it was just his Scotch-Irish blood that caused him to stray from farm life, or whether the opportunity simply did not present itself.

After the war, when Ambrose came of age, his father, by then in his 60s, sold the Liberty Square farm and moved with his wife to an easier, city life in Lancaster, where he apparently took up some work as a carpenter. The older children had already left the nest. John was a cabinetmaker in Lancaster, Ella was married, and Charles was a clerk in the grocery store up at Buck. Not surprisingly, Ambrose, suddenly released from the confining security of his childhood world, unattached and possibly aimless, took a job as a grocery clerk at the busy crossroads store where his brother worked and moved into a room above the store.

The village of Buck, with a population of a couple dozen in an area about the size of a small farm, years later adopted as its subtitle, "The biggest littlest city in U.S." The County Directory labeled Buck as "the most convenient shipping point on the L.&Q. [Lancaster and Quarryville] Branch of the P.&R. [Philadelphia and Reading] R.R." It was located on the intersection of three thoroughfares: the Lancaster Port Deposit Road, which was the main overland connection between Lancaster and Baltimore; the State Road, which ran east-west between McCall's Ferry and Quarryville, not far from where it connected to the Philadelphia Turnpike; and a third road, which ran northwest to Rawlinsville and southwest past the Conowingo Furnace to Mechanics Grove. In addition to the grocery store, Buck made claim to a post office, creamery, hotel and tavern, and it advertised a daily stage to Lancaster for an 80-cent fare.

While only a tiny village, Buck was a lively destination for young Ambrose. The hotel and tavern were popular stops for traders, dealers, and drovers, coming and going by horse and wagon between farms, mills, forges, rail terminals, river crossings, and the big cities. The busy little post office, creamery, and grocery store were regular and frequent stops for the locals. News of births, marriages, deaths, property transactions, and other local gossip passed through the highway hub like whiffs of newly cut hay on a humid day. Ambrose, the lanky-but-nice-looking, laid-back-but-sociable, and grown-up-but-unmarried grocery store clerk from Liberty Square would have been a willing, if not unwitting, participant in the friendly social exchange, rapidly developing a circle of acquaintances. Buck was the center of Ambrose's new world, and it was here that he made the acquaintance of his bride-to-be Emma, the landlord's younger sister.

EMMA MCMICHAEL, seven years younger than Ambrose, lived with her parents James and Anna on a big farm two miles to the east on the road to Quarryville. Her elderly father, James M. McMichael, was a prominent county figure with a proud lineage. For 27 years he had been the well-known superintendent of the James M. Hopkins ore banks in Quarryville, and since the Civil War he had been an active and progressive farmer in East Drumore. As one of the founders and builders of the nearby Mt. Hope Methodist Episcopal Church, James also served as a steward, trustee, and Sunday School Superintendent. Located just to the south of his farm, the Mt. Hope M.E. Church was originally organized in the home of his parents, Jonathan and Sarah.

The McMichaels came to Drumore from north of Philadelphia in Bucks County after Jonathan completed service in the War of 1812, following a military tradition started by his father, a Scotch-Irish immigrant who fought in the Revolutionary War. They settled on a homestead southwest of Quarryville, not far from where the church would be built. The Mt. Hope church was a family institution and the spiritual fountainhead for James's older brother William. Reverend William, who for over 50 years served as a Methodist clergyman in Lancaster County, ultimately filled a pulpit in Philadelphia, where he died as the oldest member of the Philadelphia M.E. Conference.

James, the third of seven children, was born around the time his parents relocated to Drumore. Unlike his parents, James spent his prime years during a generation of peacetime and fathered a prolific, if not heroic, lineage of his own. He had 17 children—11 boys and 6 girls—to three wives. Mary Garrett, his first wife, died at age 30 after bearing his first four children; Hester Phillips, his second wife, known as Hettie, gave birth to eight more before dying at age 37. Esther Ann Steele, his third wife, who was younger by 24 years and known as Anna, gave birth to Emma in 1861, the year after Hettie's death. After Emma, four more children were born, the youngest (Frank) when James was nearly 60 years old.

James undoubtedly led a full and productive life. According to the *Biographical Annals of Lancaster County*, he had a "genial and sunshiny" disposition and was known "always to look on the bright side."[4] According to his obituary:

> He gained his education in the hard school of experience, but as he was a great reader, he naturally became a well informed man. In politics he was early a Whig, later joining the Republican party....It was always his belief that John Wesley and Abraham Lincoln were inspired men, therefore he was a staunch follower of both these characters.[5]

The Annals also reported that "for years he was known as a professional peace maker, and some very knotty controversies were settled by him....Modest and retiring, he cared little for popularity but lived a beautiful life, in close accord with the Golden Rule."[6]

James's prominence notwithstanding, the McMichael clan, if only through their sheer numbers, were well known to citizens of Drumore and people who passed through Buck. As part of their military heritage the family boasted three Civil War veterans: Emma's uncle Samuel, who lived with his wife and four children at the old homestead vacated by his parents; and older stepbrothers John and Peter, a carpenter and railroad laborer who both lived in Drumore with their families. All were proud members of the Grand Army of the Republic (G.A.R.) veterans' brotherhood. Emma's older stepbrother Thomas L., after leaving the farm at age 21, became a drover, livestock dealer, and speculator. He owned a farm north of Quarryville and the property at Buck where the grocery store was situated. He was a member of the Free and Accepted Masons, Elks, American Mechanics, and Young Republicans. As "one of the most popular men, personally, in all of Lancaster County," Thomas eventually got involved in politics and was elected County Sheriff on the Republican ticket at the young age of 43.[7] Emma's next oldest stepbrother, Harry, graduated from the First State Normal School, a teacher training college in Millersville, and quickly advanced as an ambitious, young educator in Lancaster County. At age 29 he was enticed to the American West, taking a job as Principal of Schools in Wichita, Kansas; then at age 32 he moved to Indianapolis, where he studied law and was admitted to the Bar.

Following in Harry's footsteps, Emma seized the opportunity to study at Millersville State Normal School and practiced teaching for a couple of years before getting married. As the oldest child living at home, Emma may have run errands to the Buck post office or grocery store, but it was probably her gregarious brother who made the introduction. Ambrose, acceptably handsome, modestly self-sufficient, and ostensibly independent, was a good find for Emma. To the budding grocer, already familiar with some members of her family, Emma was a beautiful prize, and the prospect of marrying into the McMichael clan was not unattractive.

Emma's father James was in his early 70s when he agreed to give away his daughter to the happy grocer from Buck. At the time Emma's older sisters were living out of town with their families in Nebraska, Philadelphia, or Lancaster. Perhaps the elderly James, but more likely his young wife Anna, hoped that Emma would be the first of James's daughters to marry a man who would settle nearby. While the prospect seemed realistic, it would not turn out that way. Like many before them, Ambrose and Emma would eventually leave the hard rural life for the city, and it would be Emma's sweet, younger sister Jennie who would remain unmarried on the farm and devote herself to their aged Drumore parents.

AMBROSE AND EMMA tied the knot in the Mt. Hope church at the mature ages in those days of 30 and 23 years, respectively. Emma moved into Ambrose's apartment above the grocery store, and they eagerly started a family. Their first child Harry, named after Emma's respected older brother, was born in late 1885 and was followed the next year by James Herbert, who was named after Emma's father but referred to as Herbert. In 1888 their first daughter Ella Wanita was born, named after Ambrose's sister.

It may have seemed like a cozy existence for the young family of five in the undersized apartment above the small country store in the biggest littlest city in the U.S., but their bliss was short-lived. There was no electricity, indoor plumbing, or other conveniences in this rural outpost, unlike in the developing cities, which were beginning to look attractive to hard-working country folks. By this time a rail network extended from Lancaster to as far south as Quarryville, making the city more accessible and enticing. A noticeable population shift from the farms to the towns accelerated, and rural crossroads villages like Buck became less significant.

Ambrose was no doubt aware of this trend through the movements of his family and daily contact with crossroads clientele. After long, hard days minding the store, the walls on his second floor retreat could have seemed to become ever more confining. Three tireless infants and a new bride accustomed to a more advantaged life can be trying for any young man, let alone one used to taking quiet independence for granted. And, under the circumstances, the young family's social life was probably dominated by the Mt. Hope church and Emma's numerous, influential relatives. Ambrose no longer had his own parents or any siblings living close by; Charles had left Buck a few years earlier to open a general store in Mechanics Grove. Even if Ambrose had been in a position to leave Drumore, he probably felt root-bound. That's when Scotch-Irish wanderlust might have begun to get the better of him.

Ambrose began to find relaxation and affiliations outside the family. It was common in days before well-established life and health insurance companies that a breadwinner looked to one of numerous beneficial societies to help provide for the family in the event of a tragedy. Ambrose was no exception. He joined Kosicusko Lodge no. 374, Independent Order of Odd Fellows of Rawlinsville, which was a short ride by horseback from Buck, and Washington Lodge no. 156 of the Free and Accepted Masons of Quarryville, where his popular brother-in-law Thomas was a member. The latter club was conveniently located not far from his in-laws' farm. Unlike Emma, a devout Methodist, Ambrose probably enjoyed an occasional social drink at these retreats with his friends and acquaintances. Between fraternal societies in Rawlinsville and Quarryville, and comforting fellowship in the Buck Tavern across from the grocery store, he would have had ample opportunities to partake.

After the birth of his fourth child, William Leroy, named after his grandfather but known as Roy, it appears that Ambrose began to drift. He was listed in the 1892 Lancaster County Directory, no longer as a "clerk" at the Buck store, but as a "salesman" in Quarryville. It also appears that his family may then have been living at brother-in-law Thomas's farm in Martinsville, located to the north of Quarryville.

The following year, Ambrose's father, William, who was living in Lancaster but helping out at Charles's store in Mechanics Grove, passed away just short of his 80th year. And it appears that Ambrose benefited from his legacy. Shortly after William's death, he opened a retail grocery store at 33 South Queen Street in center-city Lancaster, attractively situated off Penn Square between the popular Central and

Southern markets. After the sale of his parent's residence at 516 West Walnut Street, Ambrose moved his family and widowed mother into a larger house on 322 West James Street—only a block away from where his brother John lived on Mary Street. It wasn't long before two more children were born: Ruth Anna, known as Ruthie, in 1893; and Jennie Pauline, known as Pauline, in 1895. They were named after Emma's mother and sister, respectively.

Ambrose's good fortune, if it ever materialized, unfortunately didn't last long. His new grocery store was across the street from the Lincoln Hotel, built by Lancaster's Sprenger Brewery as a prestige downtown outlet for its beer.[8] If that wasn't enough of a temptation, it was probably around this time that Ambrose joined the Keystone Chapter no. 73 of the Knights of Friendship, a fraternal organization housed at 26 South Queen Street, a few doors from the Lincoln. The grocery store lasted for little more than a year, and Ambrose once again became a "traveling salesman," according to the 1896 directory. With established watering holes in Quarryville, Rawlinsville and Lancaster, perhaps he was wandering more than traveling. Nevertheless, business was good enough; a seventh child, Edgar Ross, was born in 1896.

The next few years followed like a grim blur. Shortly after Edgar was born, second son Herbert died at only 9 years old. Relatives said the child was "bitten by a rat."[9] Perhaps he was a victim of an infectious disease like typhoid, diphtheria or scarlet fever, which were common in those days. A contributor to the problem could have been Lancaster's outdated water system, which supplied untreated water to city residents from the Conestoga River, into a reservoir on East King Street, and through wooden mains to the center of town. That system was believed to have been the cause of an epidemic a few years later, which began with a diphtheria outbreak on Cabbage Hill in the southwestern section of town, not far from their James Street home. In 1897 another son Arthur was born sickly, and Emma's mother died at age 61. To make matters worse, baby Arthur died the next year, and his death was followed by the stillbirth of their ninth child Raymond. For Ambrose and Emma the heartache must have been devastating. The strain of it could have partly motivated their decision to leave Lancaster for greener pastures in Philadelphia. For whatever reason, the James Street property was sold, and widow Rebecca was relocated to a room at 426 Mary Street, near brother-in-law John's home, where she died not long afterwards.

It's not clear exactly when or why the family decided to move. Certainly, nothing was keeping them in Lancaster. The grocery store had floundered. Emma's only living parent James, now in his 87th year, was being cared for by sister Jennie in the house on the edge of the Quarryville property now owned by brother Thomas, who had just been elected County Sheriff. Perhaps Ambrose needed his own space away from the omnipresent McMichaels. Brother Charles might have facilitated the move. He had left Mechanics Grove for Philadelphia shortly after their father's death; perhaps he found a job opportunity for Ambrose. Emma was probably willing to try anything. She also might have thought that she could develop a support structure among some of her relatives who had returned to the City of Brotherly Love.

The last years of the nineteenth century may have been a "gilded age" in America, but the journey to Philadelphia wasn't very luxurious. Many of the roads were still unpaved at the time. Ambrose's family of eight traveled with all their possessions by horse and wagon. The three youngest rode with their parents on the buckboard while the older kids Harry, Ella and six-year-old Roy had to walk alongside. Passersby criticized Ambrose for making the children travel on foot.[10] That must have been humiliating and hurtful for both parents. To make matters worse, the grass didn't turn out to be greener in Philadelphia. What happened there is not contained in family lore; but, less than five years later, they returned to Lancaster—after Harry, emulating his educated mother and eminent uncle, graduated from high school in 1903.

Fortuitously, the city of Lancaster was booming at the beginning of the twentieth century. Jobs and conveniences were in good supply. A rapidly expanding trolley network continued to draw population into the city. "By the early 1900s the telephone, electric railway, the wireless telegraph, and all the other innumerable inventions…wholly changed the condition of modern life."[11] One could travel by trolley to about anywhere in the county, as well as to Philadelphia or Harrisburg.

What motivated the family's return isn't clear. Patriarch James had passed away two years earlier at age 89…"after a long illness;"[12] however, a surfeit of Lancaster McMichaels survived him. Emma's relatives in Drumore included stock dealer Sam, farmer Jacob, and their large families. The family also had a growing presence in the city. Emma's youngest brother, Frank, lived with his wife Laura and their children on Ross Street at the North End of town. Frank was a trolley car conductor and seemed excessively proud of it. War veterans John and Peter McMichael had also moved into town with their large broods; they lived on North Lime Street and North Mulberry Street, respectively. Emma's sister Lucinda lived nearby with her husband Harry Webster and family. In addition, Sheriff Tom had moved with his new wife Margaret to East King Street, across Franklin Street from the County Jail on the East End. Emma's relatives were probably helpful in her family's relocation and may have helped Ambrose find a job and establish a residence at 803 North Plum Street in the growing northeast section of town.

Ambrose's first job in Lancaster was as a "time keeper" at the Stehli Silk Mill, one of Lancaster's newest and largest employers. The Stehli company had recently completed building what was known as "the longest mill in the nation" on Martha Street, which was about four blocks from their Plum Street row house. Paying about a dollar-a-day in wages, Stehli offered all the benefits of a blue-collar existence:

> Silk weaving was a thriving industry in America, and the Lancaster Board of Trade had been actively wooing silk mills to the town. In 1897, John Hiemenz, a wealthy local Realtor, donated land on North Marshall Street near Martha Street for such a factory. He even gave the foundation stone and bricks to build the mill and also promised not to make a similar offer to any competing silk company for at least five years. The Stehli company of Zurich, Switzerland, took the offer and built its huge mill on Hiemenz's land in 1898. Eventually it employed 1,200 workers, many of whom lived in homes built around the mill specifically for its workers. The new community was called Rossmere, and almost 90 percent of its homes were tenant-occupied in 1908.

> Workers often toiled hellish shifts, and most labor unions were still shadowy, quasi-illegal organizations. On the afternoon of November 4, 1907, over half the employees of Stehli Silk Mill—more than 300 men and women—walked off the job. That their union formed under the guidance of the anarcho-syndicalist International Workers of the World was a sign that the workers of Lancaster were far more radical than the county around them....

The financial panic of October 1907 had led to a brief, sharp recession, and Stehli had used the downturn as a pretext to lay off 35 workers–who happened to be the union agitators in the plant. The strikers sought a 10-hour workday, a 20 percent wage hike to bring their wages in line with other silk mills in the region (which apparently paid about 12 cents an hour) and the return of the 35 who had been fired.

But the IWW was stretched thin and riven by dissension and could offer little help. The local newspapers gave the strikers scant support. The recession also hurt them—three silk mills in York had shut down in November and Stehli simply hired their laid-off workers as scabs. By the end of the month, the pickets and their families faced starvation, and on Dec. 2, the strike collapsed.[13]

Ambrose, by now a resilient survivor, was presumably unhurt by the mill turmoil. Remarkably, the silk mill not only was a source of subsistence for him, but it provided jobs for five of his six children as they grew old enough to work and pay board. Only Harry, holder of a Philadelphia high school diploma, got a less menial job as clerk at the post office. Young Roy, eager to establish his own independence, left school after finishing the eighth grade and took a job as a "twister" at the silk mill, like older sister Ella. Getting his education the hard way, not only was a portion of his skimpy earnings drawn to pay board, but Roy would often hand over half of his dollar-a-day wage to help put food on the table when Ambrose went on drinking sprees.[14]

But for his drinking, Ambrose was a hard-working, upstanding family man. He joined First M.E. Church on Duke and Walnut streets in 1905, a year before Emma became a member. Roy likely had conflicting feelings about his father. In later years he would speak little about Ambrose, although he did share a few unpleasant memories. He disclosed that, as a young man, at his mother's insistence, he had to occasionally fetch Ambrose from the local tavern. It must have been a serious problem: Emma was said to complain that they could have purchased several houses with the booze Ambrose consumed.[15]

If Ambrose had a drinking problem, Lancaster was not the best place to kick the habit. "Turn of the century Lancaster was a rollicking, wide open town famous for its vaudeville halls, prostitutes and brewery."[16] The amusement business tripled in size during the first decade of the century, and beer-making in Lancaster was a huge business until Prohibition. The town claimed 200 saloons and 6 breweries, which included: Sprenger, the largest; Wacker, the oldest; Hafner Empire; and Rieker Star, who touted "the purest and the best."[17] Needless to say, beer and liquor were good, plenty, and cheap.

Ambrose likely renewed his membership in the Knights, which met on Tuesday evenings across from his old grocery store. He also might have accepted an occasional invitation from brother-in-law John or Peter to fraternize at one of Lancaster's 18 G.A.R. posts. It was easy to get anywhere in town by foot and trolley, and there were plenty of watering holes around the silk mill and in the north end. To acquaintances Ambrose may have seemed like a normal, happy, well-adjusted gentleman—a hard-working family man, quick to share the benefits of living in prosperous times. But his legacy also reveals a less attractive dimension. While the details remain a mystery, Ambrose's behavior, probably influenced by a combination of his Scotch-Irish heritage and troubled experience, would leave an indelible, reverse imprint on the values of his children and grandchildren.

Soon after the anxious period of the Stehli strike, oldest son Harry married his night school classmate Effie Eslinger and moved to a house nearby on Park Avenue, where their only child Evelyn Ellen was born 10 months later. Now that Harry had responsibilities of his own and ambitions to advance in the post office, the presumed burden of extra support for Emma probably shifted to Roy, the oldest son living at home. Ella, the oldest and ostensibly the most "pious" daughter, moved out the following June, marrying Vinson Saylor in a shotgun wedding.[18] Their baby Grace, born in September, would years later become a school teacher in the neighborhood.

Ambrose by this time was apparently turning over a new leaf in a job at Keystone Lock Works, owned by Edward T. Fraim, located on the second block of Park Avenue within easy walking distance of his home. This plant, which ultimately became part of the Fraim-Slaymaker Lock Company, was one of five padlock companies in Lancaster and another in nearby Columbia which together produced one-fifth of the padlocks made in the United States. Slaymaker was a progressive company, having the reputation of being the only white-owned employer in town that would hire skilled black workmen.[19] It was a successful company for many years, and Ambrose seemed to find a niche there. He became a member of the company's Beneficial

Association and faithfully worked in positions of time keeper and assembler for the remainder of his life.

Despite their tireless struggle, through good times and bad Ambrose and Emma can be credited with successfully managing a crowded household, selflessly sharing the meager fruits of hard labor, and predictably instilling Christian values in their offspring. After Harry and Ella moved out, they cheerfully took in Emma's 50-year-old sister Jennie, who, after the death of their aged father, moved into town, got a job at the silk mill, and temporarily lived with brother Tom on King Street. In addition to providing a home for Jennie, the Singletons also made room for Ruthie's and Pauline's new husbands, Amos Harsh and Sam Kendig, respectively. In a house this crowded it's a wonder that their youngest son never left home. But sadly, Edgar was diabetic and lost his hearing at age 22. He became a career clerk at Stehli, remained single, and resigned himself to boarding with his parents. Ambrose's ungainly brood of seven would live on Plum Street for 15 years, then move their belongings to alternative quarters on New Street, just around the corner, remaining there until Ambrose died at home…"of complications." [20]

# CHAPTER 2

# WILLYS KNIGHT

OF AMBROSE'S SONS, Harry seemed to have the most going for him. In addition to his Philadelphia high school education, he devoured books like his prominent uncle and grandfather, took correspondence courses, attended Lancaster Business College after work, and had a promising career at the post office. When he failed to win the coveted position of postmaster, he got a job as Secretary and Treasurer of the Quarryville Shoe Company and moved his family back to southern Lancaster County. Regrettably, the company went bankrupt, its owner shot himself, and they were back in Lancaster a year later.[1]

Not much was heard from Harry after that. Following Ambrose's death, he and his family moved to Baltimore, where he got a job with another shoe company. Daughter Evelyn said that she was dutifully tutored by her father in subjects like Latin, which helped her become the first of Ambrose's grandchildren to establish academic credentials (B.A. Goucher, 1930, and PhD. Johns Hopkins, 1933). This was noteworthy, because Baltimore may also have presented Harry with other after-hours entertainment. Relatives said that he developed an interest in horse racing, which had become very popular in those days. In 1919 a horse named *Sir Barton* was the first horse in history to win what years later would be called the Triple Crown—only to be beaten the following year by the famous horse *Man O' War*, who won an incredible 20 of 21 races before retiring in 1921. Family gossip alleges that Harry got wrapped up in the excitement and "lost his shirt on the horses." Perhaps each generation picks its own poison. Indeed, Harry was hit hard by the Depression, during which he spent two years in New Orleans working at a job created by FDR's Works Progress Administration.[2]

ROY, SIX YEARS YOUNGER than Harry, seems to have been at more of a disadvantage. He was exposed to harsh realities at a more tender age. As a child, he was faced with the death of three siblings, uprooted by three difficult relocations, and deprived of uninterrupted schooling. By age 16 he was conditioned to make accommodations for an alcoholic father while laboring in the agitated bowels of an unsettled company. The security of his first job at the silk mill was threatened by the recession of 1907 and the subsequent notorious strike. But despite this handicap, Roy was a member of the family who would make it to a better place, capitalizing on an agreeable personality inherited from his father, religious faith acquired from his mother, street smarts wrought through hard experience, and a work ethic motivated by desire to rise above a sweat shop existence.

At age 17 Roy confirmed his faith and strengthened his social standing by joining his parents' First M.E. Church. Within three years, thanks to his good looks, likable personality, and burning ambition, he landed a better job downtown as a sales clerk at Robert B. Todd Shoes, launching his career in the shoe business. Like his father, Roy would remain a bachelor into his mid-20s. While his disjointed childhood made it difficult to develop lasting relationships, he struck up a friendship with Charlie Rhoads, a contemporary whose family also had recently moved into the city from a tenant farm in southern Lancaster County. Charlie, an apprentice sheet metal worker, lived only a few blocks away on 1013 North Lime Street.

During non-working hours Roy and Charlie would "pal around together."[3] Times were good. The second ten years of the twentieth century have even been described as a "Happy Days" decade.[4] As a young adult seeking financial independence, Roy may have missed out on much of the fun; but he and Charlie would find time for recreation, and Lancaster had plenty to offer. His favorite pastime was bowling at the lanes in the Malta Temple building on East King Street or above the Arcade Market, located behind Todd's store on North Queen Street. On weekends he and Charlie could hop a trolley to visit the big amusement park at Rocky Springs, where kids their age would swim in the Conestoga or hang around the dance pavilion. During the summer of 1915 they took a camping trip to Fishing Creek in the part of the county where they grew up. Roy described the area as "wilderness" in a postcard sent to his girlfriend, Charlie's younger sister Iva. The postcard showed a picture of the ancient Drumore post office and general store, which probably brought back old memories. It was likely through Charlie that Roy got to know his future bride Iva Cathrine, known as "Ivy." After finishing high school, Ivy got a job at the silk mill, like Roy's sisters Ruthie and Pauline and their Aunt Jennie. She was four years younger than Roy, but they had a few things in common. Both were church-going Methodists from large families with roots in southern Lancaster County. And they both believed that life offered more than a job at the silk mill.

IVY WAS THE THIRD of seven children born to Aaron and Cathrine J. Rhoads. Aaron was a fourth generation descendant of Philip Roth, who arrived in Philadelphia from Germany in 1752. They were related through Philip's son Heinrich Roth, grandson Henry Roth, and great grandson Henry Roads, who changed the spelling of his surname to better reflect its German pronunciation.[5] Henry's son Aaron likewise wasn't one to be swayed by convention. He also changed his name's spelling, this time to "Rhoads," and married a girl 20 years younger. Her name was Cathrine J. Keesey, daughter of Jacob Keesey and granddaughter of Conrad Keesey and Fanny Dietrich. Aaron and Cathrine started their life together managing a tenant farm on the huge property of H. G. Rush, located below the village of New Danville, three miles south of Lancaster. They labored there for two decades before joining the migration to the city.

Aaron and Cathrine were genuine Pennsylvania Dutch stock. Both had heavy accents. Aaron chewed tobacco. While Ivy didn't take on her parents' thick accents, she adopted favorite expressions, such as "Ei-yi-yi," to express feelings of amazement, bewilderment, or disapproval. She was much closer in age to her mother, from whom she acquired extraordinary cooking skills. Cathrine prepared meals for both the family and the hired farm workers. She was said to have been "one of the best cooks in Lancaster County" and once received an award for her talent—a noteworthy distinction in the land of Pennsylvania Dutch.[6] Her culinary skills naturally rubbed off on both daughters, Ivy and Gertie. The three women had a surplus of opportunities to fine tune their art on the big-boned, highly spirited, and predominantly male members of the household: Aaron, Charlie, and younger brothers, Ray, Jay, "Aarnie," and Elwood.

Ivy's fondest childhood memory was playing in "Rush's Woods," a large cluster of trees bordering a stream which ran by the coal cellar of their stone farmhouse. She also recalled time spent at little Harmony Hall School in New Danville and century-old Boehm's M.E. Church below the village of Willow Street. Other memories were less pleasant, like being hired out to perform housekeeping chores for rich people (their landlord) or the time she spent at Stehli's silk mill. Years later those experiences would contribute to extreme modesty about her family's increasing middle-class affluence.

It was during her stint at the silk mill that Ivy was attracted to Roy, who like his father, was a soft-spoken but compelling salesman, facilitating his rapid progress in retailing. After spending four years with R. B. Todd, Roy was recruited to a more attractive position working for entrepreneur Herbert T. Wilbur, who operated the Wilbur & Martin Shoe Company. In 1915, to accommodate rapid growth of his shoe business, Herbert, known as "H.T.," moved his store from King Street to larger premises at 34 North Queen Street, site of the old Grape Hotel, which was built in 1742 and famous for meetings of revolutionary patriots in the 1770s. It was a prime retail location less than a block off Lancaster's bustling Penn Square. H.T. promoted his business in newspaper ads as "Lancaster's Largest Shoe Store."[7] It was a growth opportunity for Roy.

SOON AFTER LANDING his position with Wilbur & Martin, Roy proposed to Ivy, and on March 9, 1916 they were married by the Justice of the Peace in a double wedding ceremony with Gertie Rhoads and George Goldfus at the Rhoads' Lime Street home. The date was conveniently scheduled after a week-long "Big Clearance Sale" at the shoe store.[8] Their honeymoon was celebrated in glamorous Atlantic City. The event was recorded on a post-card portrait showing them in black bathing garb posed in front of a photographer's fake seascape. Upon returning to Lancaster they moved into their first home, an apartment on Marshall Street in the East End, considered the city's largest streetcar suburb. A daughter, Marian Pauline, was born just before Christmas that year.

Life was filled with hope for Roy. He was well-liked. An unsolicited offer of more money almost succeeded in enticing him back to his old employer, but he decided to remain with Wilbur & Martin's, where he was given a raise and promotion to the position of Manager. His situation also improved sooner than expected on the home front. Their Marshall Street apartment was located next to railroad tracks operated by Heidelbaugh Coal Yards. With the birth of Marian, Ivy complained that she didn't want to raise her daughter in coal dust.[9] Hence, for the tidy sum of $1,200, the confident 26-year-old shoe salesman bought a brand new three-bedroom house at 753 Franklin Street, only a block away from the Plum Street brood and two blocks away from the Rhoads gang. They were happy to be back near old friends and family, but privately felt they had come a long way since New Danville and the Buck.

While the blossoming young couple was discovering a comfortable place for themselves in modern society, an old world of which they knew little was coming apart. The so-called great war in Europe flared up around the time they had first met. It was a chronic event in the news, but one that had little relevance to them—an unfortunate distraction at most. The general attitude in the country was one of preparedness. Nevertheless, around the time they got married patriotic fever was breaking out. And by the time they moved into their new house on Franklin Street, the U.S. had entered the war under the Wilson Doctrine of making the world safe for democracy.

Lancaster County people greeted U.S. involvement in the war with mixed feelings; but, not surprisingly, anti-German sentiment was more pronounced in the city. Lancaster was not a cohesive town, but a collection of administrative wards, which functioned like adjacent villages, each having its own commercial, residential, and cultural infrastructure. Franklin and Plum streets were in the 6th Ward, a newer blue-collar section of town. It lacked a cultural identity, like the heavily ethnic and "colored" 7th Ward on the southeast side—or the mostly German 4th Ward in the southwest quadrant and adjacent 8th Ward on Cabbage Hill. With a war brewing, citizens in the latter areas felt they had to clarify their loyalties: German Street was renamed Farnum Street, and Freiburg Street was renamed Pershing Avenue. Victory gardens sprouted on vacant lots and business properties, including Slaymaker Lock works. In support of the war effort citizens were also encouraged to observe "gasless Sundays, meatless Mondays, and heatless Tuesdays."[10] The war got close to home when conscription was enacted in May 1917.

More than 5,000 young men from Lancaster would end up taking the oath, and 250 would make the ultimate sacrifice. Roy reported for his draft physical, but, ironically, was disqualified for "flat feet."[11] It's not clear whether his age, marriage, or paternal status also could have rendered his deferment, but it seems that he had finally won a place on the brighter side of fortune. In all probability he was diligently minding the shoe store on Armistice Day when "the church bells and whistles sounded, competing for the longest siren."[12] A month later, during the week before Christmas, his first son Wilbur, named after his boss and mentor, was born.

THE GENERAL EUPHORIA following the armistice was dampened by the 1918 Spanish flu epidemic, which was supposedly carried back by returning soldiers. The disease killed over a half million people in the U.S. and millions more around the world, shockingly more than were killed in the great war. Roy's younger brother Edgar, who had avoided military service on account of his diabetes, was struck by this invisible, new enemy. He survived with only a bad inner ear infection, but a drainage procedure performed by a local doctor caused his immediate and complete loss of hearing. Ambrose and Emma, no strangers to ailing children, appeared unsettled after Edgar's illness, evidenced by two changes of residence in quick succession: first down the street to 712 North Plum, then around the corner to 321 East New Street. It's also possible that Ambrose experienced some heightened anxiety and pesky cravings around this time. It was 1920, the year that Prohibition went into effect.

Across the country people believed that sanity would return, but attitudes and lifestyles were changing. With the end of the war a new generation had come of age. Among other things, the advance of the 1920s brought an increasing presence of automobiles—referred to as *machines*—although trolley *cars* remained the predominant mode of transportation. While socially conservative Lancastrians would not get caught up in the flapper craze or other outrageous behavior found in big cities, many could afford a machine, and booze was still accessible. On the surface Lancaster brewers were out of business, but in garages and back alleys they continued to produce, and their prolific output was surreptitiously transported in barrels through the sewer system. The law knew about it but looked the other way. Thus, as machines grew in number, driving accompanied by excessive drinking naturally became a serious problem. It was a recurring topic in the newspapers.

It probably worked out for the best that Ambrose would never own a machine. Roy, on the other hand, in understandable reaction to his father's problem, was a resolute teetotaler, but he couldn't afford the extravagance of an automobile. Every working day he would board a trolley on Franklin Street and get off at Penn Square, a half-block from Wilbur & Martin's. As he was being groomed to take on more responsibility at the shoe store, his boss spent increasingly more time engaged in extravagant hobbies like auto racing or the latest craze with flying-machines. It was a good arrangement for both of them. Roy was dedicated to the business; he treated it as if it were his own. A stanch Methodist like his mother and grandmother, he was likewise committed to the First Methodist Church, fondly known to its members as First Church, where he served in various lay capacities, including Treasurer, for many years. As a young man, he developed a disciplined habit of tithing, a practice that he embraced for his entire life. Truly a model citizen, husband, and father, Roy was determined to create a life for his children that was better than his own.

Outside family, church, and career, Roy found time to join the Lancaster Kiwanis Club, a popular service organization; Conestoga Chapter 23, Artisans Order of Mutual Protection, a close-knit beneficial association that met monthly; and the Knights of Malta. The latter organization was a vehicle for his favorite pastime, bowling. He also bowled in a weekly league with the Artisans, occasionally achieving scores in the high 500s and recognition in local sports columns. His children always observed that, when their dad set out to do something, he did it well. It was a strong attribute that he would quietly and modestly demonstrate many times and in many ways.

Roy's only vice was cigar smoking, which in those days was not understood to be a serious health problem. He loved cigars, frequently lighting up first thing in the morning. Locally manufactured cigars, like beer, were superior and plentiful. In 1922 Lancaster had more than 200 cigar manufacturers, 35 tobacco processors, and 225 leaf tobacco dealers.[13] It was a huge business, contributing to the wealth of the local economy, the sweet aroma throughout the countryside, and insidiously shortened lives for many. Indeed, cigars have always been appropriate for special occasions, and Roy had plenty of reasons to celebrate. His boss continued to reward him with more money and responsibility. When the business outgrew its premises, they relocated to a larger space at 118 North Queen Street. Greater opportunity loomed there, and things were stable at home. By the end of that year his parents and their boarders were comfortably resettled on New Street. But Roy had a special reason to light up a nice cigar: at the beginning of the new year his third child was born—a son, on January 27, 1922. It seemed appropriate to give the newest addition to the family a contemporary name: Robert Leon.

BOBBY WAS ONE of 1,433 babies born in Lancaster County that year.[14] Nobody would have predicted that these children, during the next quarter century, would experience the worst economic depression and most horrific war the world would ever see. The halcyon days of the early 1920s never would have portended it. The year 1922 was the founding year of *Reader's Digest*, which became a lifelong reading companion for Bobby. It was the first year of WGAL radio, a popular, new medium that would bring music, laughter, major league baseball, and world events into family living rooms. It also happened to be the year that Lancaster County women would vote for the first time, even though Bobby's mother would not yet be comfortable asserting her new privilege.

Surrounded by a traditional, loving family with a hopeful future, Bobby's early childhood was cheerful and vibrant. Younger brother Eddie was born in 1923. The presence of a large, extended family was so pervasive as to be taken for granted. Four grandparents, three aunts, seven uncles, and their families resided within short walking distances, a situation which led to routine pandemonium at family gatherings. Uncle Edgar was especially popular with the children. On his regular Saturday afternoon visits, he would present each of the kids with a nickel. At the sight of deaf Edgar strolling down Clay Street, the kids would dash outside and raise wagging hands with *five* fingers fully extended, signaling a combined greeting and solicitation to their bene-factor—behavior that would never fail to produce nickels from their uncle and a scolding from their embarrassed mother. Young Uncles Jay and Elwood were also favorites. Both were tall, lean, and full of nonsense. Jay was shaped so much like a bean pole that his heart struggled to pump blood from one end to the other. Family members joked that his blood pressure was so low that he would fall asleep while walking. Jay used to point out the telephone pole in front of the North Duke Street firehouse that one day "woke him up" in mid-stride. The story never failed to make the kids laugh.

While family dominated his early childhood environment, Bobby regrettably never had a chance to form a relationship with his grand-parents. He was only 4 years old when Grandfather Ambrose died. Emma passed away the same year. Both grandparents were buried at the Mt. Hope Methodist Church cemetery, next to Herbert, Raymond, Arthur, and Emma's deceased relatives. Roy saw to it that they had prominent, but tasteful headstones, closing the door on an era filled with memories that would be shared only sparingly with his children.

Two years later Grandma Rhoads, who had recently moved with Grandpa to Frederick Street, a side street near the hospital, died at the young age of 54. Perhaps she was overworked. Since 1918 she had been caring for her crippled grandson Georgie Goldfus, the physical burden of which had contributed to her developing multiple hernias. Georgie lost his mother to tuberculosis when he was less than a year old and was abandoned by his father soon after his crippling affliction was diagnosed. His 73-year-old Grandpa Aaron, well-fed and said to be a bit lazy, also didn't stick around long. Orphan Georgie ended up being institutionalized at The Good Shepherd Home in Allentown, Pennsylvania. Aaron moved to Dixon, Illinois to live with his son Ray and Ray's second wife. Ray had skipped town following his divorce and refusal to pay child support—and also not long after Roy had generously covered his bail. Aaron didn't return to Lancaster until just prior to his death in 1941; his final days were spent in Roy and Ivy's home. Ivy couldn't get over the irony of it: her mother had always advised against marrying an older man.

The deaths of his grandparents were not memorable events for Bobby. His home environment provided more than enough relatives and a surplus of affection. As soon as he was old enough to venture out from under apron strings, his childhood world progressively expanded beyond the confines of his home to the large, grassy lot behind the Franklin Street rowhouses and the vast 6th Ward neighborhood. His trusted guide was older brother Wilbur, fondly known as Wil, and his constant companion was younger brother Eddie. Six-year-older Marian, known to the boys as Sis, was never part of the street gang. To the boys she was just a studious, older girl who liked girlish things and more than her share of Daddy's attention.

The neighborhood offered everything a young boy needed or wanted: an abundance of other boys, wide-open lots, narrow alleys, and places to seek adventure or mischief. Number 753 was the fourth house from the corner of North Franklin Street, which ended at a junction with Park Avenue. The latter street ran from the southwest along the cemetery to the northeast past Franklin and Reservoir streets to the 6th Ward park. But Franklin met Park at "five points," because, north of the junction, Franklin—which ran northwesterly—became two streets: Ann Street, which continued due north from the five points, ending at Ross Street by the dairy; and Clay Street, which headed west past the elementary school and crossed Plum, Lime, Duke and Queen streets along the north end of town.

George Frank's grocery store was on the northeast point. George and his wife lived above the store. Ivy purchased most of her groceries there. She often sent one of the kids across the street with a detailed shopping list: a pound of Domino sugar, Fels Naptha soap, etc. It was a busy place; customers had to queue up to be waited on. George, who was trained at "the Acme" on Plum Street, ran the show, and Mrs. Frank was stationed behind the counter with him. They systematically gathered all the items from long wooden shelves, penciled a sales slip with the price of each item, cranked the noisy register, counted the change, and handed it over with the order.

Opposite Frank's on the northern point was a gas station owned by brothers Ed and Bernie Marion. Never married, Ed and Bernie lived next door to the station with their sister Elizabeth. Their garage had a shoulder-deep access pit for under-chassis repairs and a coal-fired stove that glowed in the winter. Wilbur loved to hang around the garage and watch the two mechanics execute repairs with their profuse collection of greasy hand tools. It seemed to be a popular spot for the older guys. Motorcycle cops Mose Weaver, Herman Boettner, and George Sandoe also congregated there. The kids got to know the cops well and enjoyed eavesdropping on their banter about baseball, burnt rubber, and bootleggers in the sewers.

Across from Ed and Bernie's was Clay Street Elementary School. The school and adjacent playground filled the large, triangular lot on the northwestern point, which extended west to Plum Street. The kids attended early grade school there, but seemed to spend more time in the seedy lot on the other side of Park Street at the southwest point. That lot was too small for a building, but large enough for a giant billboard, and just right for a makeshift basketball court. Lancaster Advertising plastered colorful murals on one side of the board, and the neighborhood kids nailed a basketball hoop to the other. Nobody complained. The kids kept the weeds down, and endless rounds of elimination and foul shooting contests kept the kids off the street.

People residing on the five points bore the brunt of a regular ruckus outside. The billboard, school, gas station, and grocery store were directly opposite their front windows and porches. The Brackbills lived in the first house on the corner of North Franklin. Mr.

Brackbill used to work at Armstrong Cork Company, the biggest company in town, but was now Manager of the Men's and Boy's Department at Watt & Shand, Lancaster's biggest department store. He dressed the part. Ivy always thought the Brackbills were a little snooty. Next to them were the Aments, who had a son Miles, known as Miley. Miley was part of the gang. Then came the Bairds, who lived next door to the Singletons. Mr. Baird worked for the railroad. He wasn't around much, but "Ma'am" Baird was a habitual fixture and an occasional pain. One day when she heard Sis complain about a noise on the back steps, Ma'am searched the house with a shotgun.

A pavement, about eight feet across, separated number 753 and the fifth house from the corner. Two single ladies, the Ott sisters, lived there. Miss Ethel worked at Armstrong; Miss Elizabeth taught school. They had a cat named Clippings, which they treated as their child. The neighborhood kids drove them crazy. One time Miss Elizabeth found a chewing gum wrapper in her yard and delivered it to Ivy, asserting that "one of the boys must have lost it."

The Sweigarts lived in number 749 on the other side of the Ott sisters. Mr. and Mrs. Sweigart were conservative Pennsylvania Dutch folks from the country. Mr. Sweigart was extremely strict with his two boys, Clayt and Don, who bracketed Wilbur in age. They were Wil's closest friends. Bobby and Eddie tagged along with the older guys, emulating and eventually becoming very close to both Clayt and Don. Roy and Ivy likewise befriended Mr. Sweigart and his wife, nicknamed Sweigy. On the other side of the Sweigarts were the Eisenbergers and Dillers. The Dillers had a couple of daughters. Sis occasionally played with them but felt they were a little strange. Their house completed the second row of four, which ended at Hand Avenue.

CLAY STREET ELEMENTARY SCHOOL, at its best, was a dreary interruption to the neighborhood fun. Conveniently, it was literally within a stone's throw from 753 North Franklin. Everyday during the school term Bobby arrived at the first bell and went home for lunch. Miss Geyer, an "old maid," taught the first grade. Miss Dorn taught second, and Miss MacElwee taught third. The Principal, Miss Eaby, also served as the fourth grade teacher. Bobby never forgot his embarrassment on the day she announced a substitute teacher. Miss Eaby came into the classroom to introduce a Miss Saylor. Bobby instantly recognized his cousin Grace, who had recently received her teaching degree. The sight of her made him squirm, and he desperately wished to become invisible. The young substitute, expecting to find her ally in a room full of skeptics, decided to call on "Bobby" first—by name no less! The blood rushed to his ears, and his mind went blank. During lunchtime recess he begged his mother to let him remain home. Of course, Ivy refused, although she may have been quietly empathetic. It was partly from her that Bobby inherited some of his shyness, a normally concealed trait that would occasionally surface as a surprising aspect of an otherwise ebullient personality.

By the time Bobby got to fourth grade, construction had just been completed at a new school on Reservoir Street, built to relieve overcrowding at Clay Street. Roy and Ivy naturally assumed that Bobby would not be one of the children assigned to the new school, because it was located seven blocks away. However, on the day it opened, their son was one of a few dozen students named to make the transfer. Their new principal entered the classroom, read the transfer roster, and instructed the chosen ones to follow him single-file on a trek to their new quarters. As the straggly line marched across Franklin Street, Ivy spotted Bobby among the commotion outside her window. Without hesitation she charged outside with apron waving, and at the top of her ample lungs, protested her son's transfer. Bobby, with memories of the cousin Grace incident still fresh, would now be totally embarrassed by this sidewalk spectacle, recalling, "I felt two inches tall!" He also remembered that his mother "won out....They pulled me out of the line, took me back to Clay Street, and we never heard any more about it." It wasn't until the fifth grade that he was required to make the transfer to Reservoir Street School.

Other than minor glitches, growing up was a wonderful experience for Bobby. The neighborhood kids were a large part of it. He had a large group of friends his own age, like Bob Geiter, Bob Randall, Stan Metzler, Dick Lander, and Johnny Frank, as well as older guys like Clayt, Don, Miley, Ed Sachs, Les Gerhart, and Joe ("Beans") Glacken. Then there was Peep Carson, who was a little younger. His given name was Walter, but he was popularly known by the barely redeeming nickname Peep, or Peepie, due to his distinctive looks and voice.

Peep lived around the corner on Park Avenue in the first of a new string of rowhouses built by Johnny Allen, a contractor who still excavated foundations with work horses pulling backhoes. Peep had an older brother and two sisters, but didn't seem to have much of a home life. His parents weren't close. Mr. Carson was said to be a bigwig at Keppel's Candy factory and a ladies' man. He was also known for his operatic voice and teaching his children to sing. On Saturday mornings he and his daughters performed on WGAL radio. One played piano and the other two sang. Peep wasn't a radio celebrity like his sisters, but he was a kind, gentle kid who had a trained, albeit bird-like voice of his own. In the summer he performed on the Singletons' front porch. Ivy "pitied" Peepie and treated him as one of her own.

Mr. Bannon lived a few doors down on the other side of the Carsons. He was the unofficial coach of the boys' neighborhood softball team, which played on a crude diamond carved in the grassy field behind their rowhouses. On summer evenings the boys' fathers occasionally meandered from their tiny back yards to watch the sandlot games. However, the kids practically lived there. During the summers they often set up tents and camped out next to the diamond, where a sloppy, hand-painted sign proclaimed entry to Tent City.

The neighborhood mayhem rarely simmered down. A noisy game of baseball, basketball, or kickball was usually always in progress. The paved street often served as the playground, especially Ann Street, which saw minimal automobile traffic in the 1920s. But every back yard, foot path, sidewalk, or alley was fair game—day or night. Sometimes the play got reckless. During a round of hide and seek after dusk one evening, Bobby, Eddie, and Dick Lander raced through a narrow walkway between the rowhouses on the other side of the billboard. Unfortunately, it was too dark to see the iron gate that a homeowner had recently installed across the passageway. Unlucky Dick, running in the lead, slammed into the hidden gate like hard rubber against metal and careened onto the pavement as the other two skidded to a stop behind him. When he finally crooked his neck to check on the other guys, his eyeballs were still quivering and his face was splotched with blood and tears. For some reason Bobby never forgot that close call; perhaps he knew about the gate. He wouldn't avoid contact, however, the time he got into a tussle with Bob Geiter, a much heavier kid. Fortunately, it was only ego that got bruised; the fat kid simply pinned his victim on the sidewalk next to Frank's store. Eddie also pressed his luck on more than one occasion. His scariest incident was the time he finally had to pay for constantly pestering the postman, a guy by the

name of Miles Messerman, who decided to lock his tormentor inside a
steel mail box on Franklin Street. Bobby never forgot the sound of
Eddie's muffled whimpers reverberating inside that metal container.

It's remarkable that there weren't more injuries. In the winter the
kids went sledding on a street that passed steeply under the railroad
tracks before taking a sharp, blind turn by the silk mill. An equally
popular thrill was hitching their sleds to the trolley cars that rolled up
Franklin Street from New Holland Avenue and stopped in front of
their house about every ten minutes. Just as a car was finished loading
and about to pull out, the kids would dash out, jump on their sleds,
and grasp the trolley's rear tailgate with one hand. The motorman tried
to chase them off, but generally submitted to the unwelcome presence
of snow parasites. The kids usually got a begrudged tow up Clay Street
and down Plum before peeling off. The motorman correctly figured
that an overreaction to the joy riders would only make his life more
miserable.

The little rascals never missed an opportunity to cause mischief,
and holidays provided a good excuse. On the Fourth of July they
would launch golf balls from tin cans set over exploding cherry
bombs. On Halloween nights they would sneak up behind a trolley
and yank its electrical connector post from the overhead power cable,
causing the car to stop dead in its tracks just as they'd take off a-hellin'.
The prank would infuriate the motorman and upset their parents. Few
neighbors were immune. Occasionally the pranksters stole doormats
from the front porches of irresistible neighbors, like the Ott sisters or
Ma'am Baird. A couple of days later they would return with mats in
hand and innocent expressions, asking "Is this yours?" They'd expect
to get a dime for the trouble and usually did. Ivy would get livid when
she learned about it.

But the fun was usually harmless, like taking advantage of "one-
arm Charlie." Charlie was a handicapped fellow who operated a
concession near the Reservoir Street School. He operated out of a
round shed with a domed roof next to the railroad tracks. The kids
called it the "roundhouse." Charlie sold a variety of penny candies,
soft drinks, newspapers, cigarettes, and who knows what else. He was
known for having large trays of chocolate-covered candies with white
peppermint centers—except for one or two candies that had pink centers. If a pink one was chosen, the picker got a prize, like a nickel
candy bar or small toy. It was such a popular spot that Ivy became

suspicious of the business conducted there. Roy never said much. The kids seemed attracted to the roundhouse like bees to honey. However, they rarely went there without Wilbur, because he was the one who could always pick the ones with pink centers. "Wil was noted for that." All the neighborhood kids appealed to him to work his magic for them. He would kneel down by the counter, squint intensely across the chocolate topography, and almost always come up with a winner! It was uncanny. Charlie never smiled when Wilbur showed up. It got to the point where the poor old fellow refused to let Wil pick for the other kids.

Growing up wasn't all fun and games, however. Roy and Ivy often had to remind the boys about their homework. The kids also had regular chores and were expected to earn their spending money. Bobby helped with the groceries. Lucky for him, most of their staples could be purchased at Frank's, "who had the food business collared in the five points area." But Ivy preferred the fresh produce from the Fulton Market, which was a few blocks away, and insisted on the *Louella* brand of butter, which was stocked only at the Plum Street Acme. She did it for Roy, who loved his bread smothered with Louella and dark molasses. The only place that carried the dark-colored syrup was Eby's grocery store, next to the market. Because this was the only item Ivy purchased at Eby's, she was embarrassed to go there. Thus, her reluctant emissary was Bobby, who toted an empty jar with a reflection of her guilt in his expression. Mr. Eby recognized the profile. When he spotted Bobby entering the store, he winked and tilted his head toward the basement, where the black syrup was stashed in a large barrel. On cue, Bobby would disappear below the floorboards, locate the drum, turn the heavy crank to refill the jar, scamper upstairs to deliver the exact change, and dash home with the black gold.

ROY WAS ENTITLED to his special brand of molasses and cigars. He worked hard, paid his bills promptly, and after tithing, spent most of what he earned on his family. Especially at Christmas. That was always a special event. During the holidays, he had longer hours at the shoe store; but when he got home, he would quickly get "wrapped up in the spirit." On Christmas Eve he stood a freshly cut scotch pine in the living room and built a small train yard around it for the kids. As the boys got older, they were permitted to set up a train yard for them-

selves in an allotted corner of the dining room. That was one of their
favorite activities, which usually began before the heavy aromas of
Thanksgiving had a chance to disperse. The trains were Lionel. Intense
hours were spent arranging the three-railed track, balsa wood bridges,
paper tunnels, and miniature metal houses bought at the five and ten,
which they illuminated with tiny electric lamps. Most of the wiring was
done by Wil. "He was very clever at that sort of thing."

The blissful times at home were interspersed with usual holiday
rituals: the Christmas Eve worship service and holiday morning visits
to relatives, who were all located within short walking distances. The
Saylors and Kendigs were a block away on Reynolds Avenue. Uncle
Edgar lived with Ruthie and Amos two blocks farther on Olive Street.
But the kids were always eager to get home. Continuously surrounded
by the delectable aromas of Ivy's baking, Christmas was a special time
at 753 Franklin. Peep usually came over to join in the festivities, as well
as Clayt and Don. Mr. and Mrs. Sweigart stayed home. Roy politely
attributed that to shyness; he explained that they were good, but
"backwards" people.

Things continued to go well at Wilbur & Martin's. Roy was a
natural shoe man. Eventually, H.T., who was spending increasingly
more time with extravagant hobbies, decided to sell the business and
offered his young manager the opportunity to purchase it. The offer
was contingent on Roy's bringing in a more experienced partner, with
the designated partner being Fred Hayes, Manager of Hanover Shoe
Store. Freddy was at least ten years older than Roy, who was 37 at the
time. But Freddy didn't make the best impression on Roy. Among
other eccentricities, his hands shook when he rolled his cigarettes. Not
that it made a difference. From the beginning Roy was determined to
buy the business as the sole owner and was ultimately successful in
persuading H.T. to agree.

It was a big deal for Roy—one that would put him deeply into
debt. While Wilbur & Martin's business was strong, competition was
fierce. There were a half dozen reputable shoe stores in town. The
dominant competitor was Shaub's Shoe Co., who had built their success over a period of 50 years and had earned a reputation for staying
open long hours to better serve rural county folks who only came to
town on market days. Nevertheless, Roy was determined, and he took
the leap. The consideration was $17,000, made up of $4,000 in bonds
at signing, a $5,000 mortgage on his house, and eight notes of $1,000

each, payable in January and July of each of the following four years. He was also obligated to pay H.T. $30 a week and half the profits until the end of the first calendar year. The deal was closed May 29, 1929— five months before the stock market crashed.

Fortunately, the October crash affected only a few people in the area. Lancaster people were generally self-sufficient and conservative to a fault. The city was one of the three most prosperous in the state, and local economic reports in late 1929 were optimistic, proclaiming the best business climate in eleven years.[15] Those directly affected by the crash probably remained silent. The only high-profile victim of the crash was Mayor Frank Musser, who was known to speculate in stocks. He retired at the end of 1929 and two years later was found dead in his garage on 716 North Lime Street. By then the impact of the Great Depression would be far less discriminating.

THE SINGLETONS CONTINUED TO PROSPER into the early 1930s. They modestly splurged on a few modern conveniences and gifts for the children. Ivy, who took great pride in her brilliantly white "wash," was the recipient of an electric washing machine. While she still had to manually crank wet laundry through a wringer, the old wash tub and scrubbing board became relics of the past. On the lighter side, a new Philco radio replaced the Victrola as their home entertainment center. It was encased in a glossy wooden cabinet and prominently displayed in the corner of their living room. The family would usually gather to hear *Amos and Andy* after supper on winter evenings, and they rarely missed tuning in to *The Shadow* on Sunday afternoons. They especially liked the ominous bass voice of the program's host, who unfailingly began with the now legendary words, "The Shadow knows...."

The Philco was a treat, but a subsequent acquisition was the boys' favorite source of year-round recreation: a beautiful, slate-top pool table. It just squeezed into their tiny cellar, barely leaving room for the visitors it attracted. Wilbur became the pool shark in the family. Roy was also a pretty good player and frequently challenged the boys. They organized family competitions, which grew into neighborhood tournaments. Clayt and Don came. Ed and Bernie Marion joined them after the gas station closed. Sometimes the cops showed up. Many of these guys were old enough to be the kids' uncles, but were accepted as just part of the gang. They generally entered through the outside cellar door, often while the family was still having supper. It wasn't unusual to hear the clacking of billiard balls during meals. The boys would rush through meals so as not to miss the action. Their patient parents never seemed to mind.

Roy and Ivy thrived in making a life for their children that was richer than their own. The kids probably never fully appreciated the commitment their father made in purchasing Wilbur & Martin's, but they knew things were different the day he drove home in a Willys Knight. The Knight was a used machine, but that didn't matter. What a glorious sight it was! Black and shiny. It had a massive hood, four doors, long running boards, and wide leather seats, front and back. Known as a "touring" car, the Knight was designed like a large, open carriage with a canvas-like fabric stretched over a metal roof frame and an oval-shaped isinglass window stitched into the rear panel. The sides were meant to be open most of the time. During inclement weather, flaps could be rolled down and attached to the door sills with half-turns of awkwardly placed fasteners. They didn't always attach easily, especially at the bottom edge; therefore, unsecured canvas would flap in the breeze like a sloppy shirt tail. The kids loved to ride in the Knight on rainy days just to be part of the spectacle.

The Knight was lovingly housed in a rented garage stall on Hand Avenue across from the Fulton Market. On Sunday mornings the three boys, dressed in their finery, followed Roy to the garage like black flies, competing for their turn to crank up the Knight before the family's drive to church. Roy would warn the designated crankster: "You be careful now. Don't let that crank snap back on you!" Bobby would painfully remember the time that it did. And Ivy never let them forget it when they headed for the garage. "Roy, you be careful with those kids!" she bellowed in her contralto voice.

After church and noontime dinner, afternoon pleasure drives in the Knight became a traditional Sunday routine. They visited family gravesites at the peaceful Mt. Hope and Willow Street cemeteries. They drove to Allentown to visit cousin Georgie at The Good Shepherd Home. Ivy was faithful to her nephew, who could always rely upon his Aunt Iva for letters, visits, and gifts of cash. Occasionally, the family stopped by Olive Street to pick up Aunt Ruthie and Uncle Amos, who were never able to afford a car. Sometimes they would drive to the grass strip on the Columbia Pike to watch the airplanes. A celebrity by the name of Jesse Jones performed aerobatics there in a plane that he had built from scratch. As flying grew in popularity, a new municipal airport was opened on the Manheim Pike. A greater variety of biplanes and the new Piper Cubs could be seen there.

On summer holidays like Memorial Day or Independence Day, after the traditional cemetery visits, the family would drive to one of Lancaster's parks, usually Long or Williamson, for a picnic and afternoon of fun. Sometimes they drove to a place called Sandy Beach, located off the Oregon Pike, known for its huge swings that soared over a little brown beach and the Conestoga Creek. Sometimes they would go to Mellinger's by the creek on Butter Road, an excellent place for floating in inner tubes. They also had a tiny beach with picnic tables and concession stand. The family typically went there when Mr. Mellinger was overdue on his charge account at Wilbur & Martin's. The kids could run up a tab for candy and ice cream, and Roy would simply deduct the total from Mellinger's balance.

The Knight added a new dimension and endless possibilities to their lives. The routine would never be exactly the same, but the family typically got home from their Sunday drives in time for *The Shadow* followed by supper. Sometimes after supper Roy and the boys piled back into the Willys and drove to Shultz's just off the corner of Lime and Chestnut streets. Mr. Shultz sold home-made ice cream from his house. They'd take their own containers, knock on his door, and place an order; their usual was a quart of vanilla and pint of chocolate. Without a doubt Shultz's was the best ice cream in town. And life was very sweet.

## Chapter 3

# Mrs. Smith's Noodles

By 1931 IT WAS EVIDENT that the economy was slowing, but Wilbur & Martin's remained very healthy thanks to Roy's business acumen. By religiously paying his bills early, he cultivated supplier loyalty and benefited from significant purchase price discounts, discreetly recorded in a separate account. This practice made it easier to manage profit margins as shoe retailers began offering out-of-the-ordinary sale prices in the face of weakening demand. Shoe suppliers like Florsheim spotted these trends and sent notices to all their retailers stating that discounted prices should be discontinued—a heavy-handed practice considered illegal today. Other suppliers, such as Jarman, announced price increases or restrictions on small orders to protect their margins. This, no doubt, frustrated Roy, who had successfully built his franchise by regularly "filling in" stocks to keep a full range of sizes and styles and by willingly placing special orders for individual customers.

His discipline and hard work paid dividends. One evening he drove home in a fashionable 1930 Studebaker four-door sedan. It was a like-new "demo" model purchased in cash on a trade-in deal from H. M. Vondersmith, the neighborhood dealer located on Lime Street. The Studebaker was modern compared to the Willys. It had an automatic starter. You simply had to pull out a choke knob, activate an adjacent starter lever, then carefully retard the choke when the engine transitioned from a rough cough to a deep purr. Unlike the old Knight, this beauty had glass windows all around that cranked up and down. The kids loved a ride on windy days just to experience how quiet it was inside. Even Sis liked it. It made them feel like rich kids.

As fate would have it, the economy deteriorated further in 1932. By 1933 symbols of the good old days disappeared like autumn leaves, and political events foreshadowed major change. Motor buses replaced miles of trolley lines that were now being dismantled between the city and county, including the old lines to Strasburg and Quarryville. In January ex-President Calvin Coolidge died suddenly, and ex-Mayor

Frank Musser was found dead in his garage. Al Capone was in prison, and Congress adopted a resolution to repeal Prohibition. In March an eloquent politician named Franklin Delano Roosevelt succeeded a beleaguered Herbert Hoover as the new President, and the recently appointed Chancellor of Germany, a controversial personality named Adolf Hitler, was granted dictatorship by the Reichstag. But, it wasn't these events that captured people's attention. It was the newspaper photos of bread lines and soup kitchens that weighed heavily on their minds. Too many people were out of work—even in Lancaster.

For many folks a new pair of shoes had become a luxury purchase. There were evenings that Roy came home dejected because Wilbur & Martin's had not recorded a single sale on that day. Shoe manufacturers, also feeling the pinch, were unyielding; and, to make matters worse, there were bank problems. The day after Roosevelt was sworn in he proclaimed closure of the nation's banks in order to halt massive withdrawals. Roy received a letter from a traditionally loyal supplier requesting money to replace a check for $21.75 that didn't clear. He anxiously wrote letters to his suppliers requesting that checks be held until the banking situation improves.[1] But Lancaster Trust was one of the banks that never re-opened, and the $1,500 in Roy's account was lost. He was in a bind. He had notes coming due with H.T., a mortgage on the house, and a family to feed.

The family had already begun to sense that something was different. Ivy scrimped with a reduced household budget. Their normal, well-known Pennsylvania Dutch feasts of roasts and multiple side dishes were replaced with casseroles and leftovers more than usual. Strawberry shortcake became a main course. Ivy started growing tomato plants in their back yard. Some of the neighbors noticed the difference; one of them, a wage earner who may have been secretly envious during good times, was callous enough to remark about it. Conversation at the kitchen table occasionally became strained and muted. Once, in front of the children, Ivy suggested to Roy that, as a way to shore up the food budget, perhaps they should consider "taking some money out of the tithing account." Roy, privately stung by the comment, would not reveal his true feelings; but, in his calm, quiet way tried to reassure her: "Don't worry, Mother, everything will be fine."

The children, largely isolated from financial torment by protective and loving parents, did not fully appreciate their plight and shared in the hardship without even realizing it. They helped their mother save a penny here and there. Rather than spending 10 cents for a block of ice from the ice man, Ivy would send them to the dairy at the north end of Ann Street to pick up chunks of ice that spilled from their delivery trucks. The boys collected the heavy chunks in her old wash tubs and hauled them home in their express wagons.

The kids also learned to make their clothes last a little longer than usual and become accustomed to not getting as many new shoes. Traditionally, and always at the start of the new school year and before Easter, Roy would take the kids to the shoe store after hours and fit them with the latest styles. Frequently, he toted shoes home with him. However, when the Depression hit, the evening store binges ceased, and the styles he brought home were not always in fashion, at least for the boys. Bobby once overheard Roy whisper to Ivy that his sons' back-to-school shoes were "1928 models." For years Bobby would conjure up visions of those shoes, "a style that I wouldn't be caught dead in;" and, as time went on, he naively teased his dad by asking that he not bring home any more 1928 models. What he would most remember, however, was the time his wounded father responded by harshly reminding his son that he was "fortunate to have shoes." If only we could take back our thoughtless remarks as children.

To earn spending money young boys often hauled market baskets at one of the city's five popular farmers' markets: the Central, Southern, Arcade, Northern, and Fulton. It was rare to find a homemaker in Lancaster who didn't shop at one or more of them. The Fulton Market, on the corner of North Plum and Frederick streets, served the growing northeast part of town and was nearly as active as the large, downtown Central Market. Market days were Tuesdays and Saturdays. On Tuesday mornings, even during the school year, Wil, Bobby, and Eddie got up at 6 A.M., and with express wagons in tow scampered down Hand Avenue to the exit side of the market, where they waited for the first ladies to emerge with their loaded, wicker baskets. Like taxis, the boys waited in line to work for tips, which usually amounted to a nickel, dime, or as much as a quarter, depending on the length of the haul and generosity of the client. On Tuesdays, each boy could haul three or four loads and still get home by 7:30, just in time to eat breakfast and still make the first bell at Reservoir Street School. On Saturdays they hauled baskets until noon.

Saturdays were the busiest. A half dozen or more boys waited outside the market entrance positioning for customers. Some ladies selected certain boys to haul their baskets, and each boy developed his regular customers. Two of Bobby's best paying regulars were Mrs. Doan and Mrs. Walton. They both lived on Reservoir Street, Mrs. Doan at the corner of Hand Avenue, and Mrs. Walton next door. The delivery route was only a few blocks down Hand. Bobby got 15 cents for each haul. It was a good amount. He always went out of his way to be polite and helpful.

There was another lady who lived several blocks away—way out by the George Ross School on North Queen Street. She was known to have paid one of the other boys a meager dime for her multi-block haul. After word got around, the boys learned to avoid her when she appeared on the curb with her heavy basket. But, never one to follow the crowd, Bobby offered to haul her basket one day and graciously accepted a quarter after lugging her basket the entire way, including up the steps to her front door. The kid who felt cheated became angry when he heard about the generous tip and had the nerve to confront his reluctant competitor. Bobby responded, "Maybe it's the way you handled the customer," but neglected to explain how he made polite small talk with his new client for the duration of the hike. He was a natural salesman, like his old man and grandfather he never got to know. On Saturdays he would easily bring in a dollar hauling baskets. During the Christmas season, like the paperboy and iceman, he would earn much more.

Through the worst days of the Depression Roy and Ivy never failed to provide clothes or necessities for their children. Bobby saved a little of the money he earned, but spent most of it on personal items and recreational pursuits. Movies were extremely popular, and westerns were his favorite. On Saturday afternoons the three boys usually hiked to one of the six movie theaters downtown. They most often went to the Hamilton Theater, which had the best cowboy shows. The Hamilton, opened in 1916, was festooned with dusty organ pipes, which in the old days resonated with accompaniment to silent movies. Of course, by 1933 feature length talkies had been around for over five years. It only cost 10 cents to get in, and kids could sit through a Buck Jones movie for as many times as they wished. Regrettably, buddies Clayt and Don normally weren't able to join in the afternoon fun, because their strict father would not allow it. Bobby observed: "The hurt was plain on their faces."

After the movies the kids would buy a soda or candy at one of the downtown confectioneries or drug stores. Then they roamed the city, often stopping at one of the five and tens to look at accessories for their train yard. On occasion they would seek out Harry the "candy man" at Penn Square, hoping for a free handout, since the old guy was a McMichael relative. Cousin Harry, in his late 50s, was one of six children to Emma's stepbrother, Uncle Peter, the Civil War veteran. He lived with his wife Sarah on East End Avenue and made a living as a candy maker. Unfortunately, the boys never managed to get a freebie. Times were tough.

The big Philco in the living room kept the family in touch with current events while helping them forget about the hard times. Amos and Andy made them laugh. FDR's aristocratic voice reassured them. Sports announcers agitated them with reports of Babe Ruth's $52,000 contract with the Yankees. The news of 300-pound comedian Fatty Arbuckle's death at age 45 saddened them. They paid little attention to reports about New Deal programs, outrageous events in the Reich, or the phase-out of Prohibition. It took only a couple of weeks for Sprenger's to start marketing their beer after it was legalized, but it was reintroduction of extra salty beer pretzels that got the kids' attention.

IN THE SUMMER OF 1933, baseball, as usual, was the main event. As the boys grew up, they continued playing ball at tent city, but increasingly developed an interest in the highly popular and organized city softball league, where the older guys, in their late teens or early 20s, competed. Each of the city wards had a team, and the teams had official uniforms adorned in bold colors with their sponsor's logo and player's numerals. Games were held in the evenings and drew noisy crowds of spectators, who perched behind the backstop on wooden bleachers, stood in haphazard clusters around the ramshackle dugouts, or cheered from lawn chairs arranged in straggly ranks along the baselines. Competition was keen, and local rivalries were intense.

The 6th Ward ballpark was on a carefully mowed field in a large, open lot across the street from the rowhouses on Hand Avenue, adjacent to the Fulton Market. It was the same lot where the circus set up tents, trailers, and animal pens when they came to town. The 6th Ward team was named after their sponsor, Mrs. Smith's Noodles, a local enterprise that sold their brand of pasta mostly at the farmers' markets. Despite the limp sounding name on the back of their shirts, the 6th

Ward team was good. They played high-quality, fast-moving, top-notch softball. The game had recently evolved from a 16- to a 12-inch ball. The Noodles played only fast-pitch softball, where the windmill pitch became legendary.

During the days, the boys played at the tent city lot, mimicking the pitching styles and batting stances of the league players. Bobby usually pitched if Wil wasn't around, or played second base. In the evenings, Ivy prepared dinner early so that the boys could be on time for the Noodles games at 6:30. The whole Franklin Street gang would usually be there—Clayt, Don, Sachs, Metz, Randall, and so on. Sometimes the kids were allowed to sit with the players. They knew most of the players by name: Pissy Weaver, catcher; Kissy Kissinger, one of the two pitchers; Bo Shenberger, first base; Kenny McMillan, second base; Donny Horst, left field; and Charlie Regar, short center.

Roy often joined the boys at the 6th Ward ball games. Not only did it give him time with his boys, but it was a relaxing and inexpensive diversion from Depression woes—something he looked forward to. But, when he would later reflect on that period of time, it would not be the financial strain, neighbors' gossip, or unprecedented world events that would first come to mind. It would be something much more personal, a heartbreaking episode which began during the summer of 1933 when his oldest son Wilbur fell and hurt his head.

WIL HADN'T YET TURNED 15. The boys were making their usual ruckus out on the front porch one day. Clayt and Don were there. From inside the house Ivy could hear the staccato of hard heels banging on wooden planks and concrete pavements. No doubt lanky Wil was demonstrating one of his favorite stunts: a running leap from the front porch, over and across the alleyway to the Ott's front porch, while negotiating the wide ravine and two, brick balustrades in the process. Only the taller guys, like Clayt and Wil, would dare to make it. Bobby and Eddie were still too small and afraid to try. Unfortunately, Wil came up short on this attempt. He tripped on the first brick wall and plummeted head first to the rock-hard pavement of the alleyway. The fall ended with a sharp thud followed by silence.

Fortunately, he regained consciousness, but the pain was enough to warrant a trip to the hospital, where he was diagnosed with a mild concussion. After a few days he returned to his normal routine but never seemed quite the same after the accident. When he was younger, his asthma had frequently slowed him down, but he was always considered the most agile, smart, and energetic one of the group. He was the best softball player and a terrific pitcher, who loved and emulated the Noodles. Everybody could see that he was clever with his hands. It's not clear if his mechanical skills were inherited or simply acquired from hours spent at Ed and Bernies' gas station; but, if anybody's bicycle needed repair, Wil was the one who could fix it. He also excelled in school, where he received the American Legion Award at the Lancaster Boy's High. It was an honor. Roy was proud, even though Ivy was uncomfortable about it. She still viewed the American Legion as a "drinking" organization. Regardless, the family felt nothing but love and pride for Wilbur. He was everything the oldest of three sons and brothers could be.

The vestiges of a record-breaking cold winter of 1934 rapidly melted with a warm spring and severe heat wave by late July. The country sweated through the national recovery program, and Wilbur & Martin's struggled to remain profitable. But baseball went on, as usual. Mrs. Smith's Noodles had a good season, and the boys remained loyal. Wilbur, the most ardent Noodles fan, was forced to miss some games late in the season, because he was getting frequent headaches. By September, when his pain became unbearable and his vision impaired, he was readmitted to the Lancaster General Hospital, where doctors confirmed that the problem was more serious than originally thought. Wil had a deadly brain tumor. The mass was situated directly behind his eyes and could not be treated locally. They recommended that he go to the University of Pennsylvania Hospital in Philadelphia, a teaching facility with access to more advanced surgical techniques.

Roy immediately tracked down the best surgeon he could find. He was given the name of a Dr. Duane of Chicago, whom he contacted by telephone. After conferring with the Lancaster doctors, Dr. Duane told Roy that it would be a costly operation with an uncertain outcome. He made it clear that the probability of a complete recovery was low. But, in response to Roy's insistence that it be done, "regardless of the cost," Dr. Duane replied, "If the operation is a success, all you'll owe me is my train fare."

Roy drove Wilbur to Philadelphia, a two-hour journey. Dr. Duane got there the following day and performed the operation. Thankfully, Wil survived the surgical ordeal but was kept in a recovery ward for a couple of weeks. It was rare for Roy to take time off from work, but every day during that period he drove to Philadelphia to be with his son. One of the treatments involved transfusing blood directly from father to son. There was a moment during this procedure when Wil cried out in pain. In desperation Roy pumped his fists in a futile attempt to accelerate the transfer of blood.[2] He would have done anything to save his son.

Wil's head was wrapped in a spiral mound of white gauze when they brought him home. Clearly, he was still experiencing pain, and parts of his body were paralyzed. Relatives, friends, and neighbors came by to visit. Ed and Bernie stopped by every day to share laughs. Despite the pain, Wil remained upbeat and optimistic. At one point he jokingly bequeathed his bicycle to his buddy Les Gerhart. Faithfully, Roy sat by the bed every night, talking continually while holding his son's hand. But Wil never got better. He held on a little longer, then died on November 11, 1934, 15 weeks after the diagnosis. It was the first time the children ever saw their father break down and cry.

Funerals in those days were typically held in the home of the deceased. Wil's casket was placed on a viewing stand in the living room. A black wreath was hung on the front door. Mourners crowded into the living room, dining room, and even on the stairs and second floor. Ed and Bernie closed the gas station to pay their respects. Dr. Witwer, minister at First Church, was there to officiate. Neighbors joined the family in the procession to the cemetery. It was the customary and natural thing to do; they were a close-knit community. The burial was at Willow Street Mennonite Church cemetery. Ivy selected the site, next to where mother Cathrine and her Keesey siblings were buried. Roy went along with her on this.

Wil's death was a devastating experience for the family. Of the children, Marian had the most time to prepare herself for the tragedy. She was working at her first job as a secretary for Roy Gump at Eshelman Feed when Wil was taken to Philadelphia. Uncle Vince stopped by her office on North Queen Street immediately after getting Roy's report on the surgery. He confided to Sis that "it would be a miracle if Wil lives." On the Sunday evening that Wil died, Marian was walking home from her Epworth League meeting at First Church and figured out what had happened as she approached the house. All the lights were turned on, and the blinds were completely drawn.[3]

It was more shocking for Bobby and Eddie, who were not yet teenagers at the time. Eddie could not be found for a few hours after

Wil died, until crying was heard coming from the closet. Bobby was also thrown off balance. In the days following Wil's death, Uncle Elwood and Aunt Ann stayed at the house to look after the kids while Roy and Ivy made preparations for the funeral and privately grieved. Elwood could always be counted on to keep the atmosphere light-hearted. He was famous for his comments, like the time they were in the kitchen and he asked, "How about a light lunch?"...after which he would flick on the light switch and let out a good belly laugh.

Uncle Elwood was in the living room on the morning of the funeral when Bobby and Eddie cautiously tiptoed down the stairs to view their deceased brother for the first time. Death for them was a new experience; they had no idea what to expect. With Eddie close behind, Bobby slowly descended, one step at a time. As they reached the final tread, the intensity of the moment was interrupted with a blood-curdling screech and clatter from the living room. Reflexively, they pivoted, and, nearly tripping over one another, bounded back up the stairs, gasping in terror. Their composure didn't return until they heard the guttural sound of Uncle Elwood's characteristic laughter. The nerve shattering racket that sounded like Wilbur's return from the dead was only a window blind that had overcome its catch and noisily retracted into its sprung coil. Interestingly, this would be one of Bobby's more vivid memories of his brother's irreconcilable death. Humor frequently allayed, but would sometimes hide, his true feelings.

It was much more difficult for Roy. Indeed, he took it even harder than Ivy. Having lost three brothers as a young boy, Roy had vowed never to subject his own family to the horrible and helpless fate of losing children. Privately, he never really got over it. That may have been why he seemed to make a greater effort caring for his remaining children—and years later doing so much to please his grandchildren. Incredibly, less than three months after Wilbur died, Roy's grief only intensified with the loss of his younger brother Edgar, who succumbed to diabetes at age 39. Roy bore the responsibility of seeing to it that Edgar was buried under a dignified headstone at the Mt. Hope cemetery next to Ambrose, Emma, and little Herbert, Arthur and Raymond.

AFTER WILBUR'S DEATH, Roy was more than ever determined to spend time with his sons—at Sunday afternoon park outings, tent city games, and pool tournaments. He also made a point to take them to father and son banquets, which were held at the YMCA, church or Artisans' club, where the boys were entertained by magicians and became Junior Artisans. During the first summer without Wil, he seemed particularly dedicated to his boys and to Mrs. Smith's Noodles. He volunteered as a scorekeeper, diligently posting tin numbers on the rickety scoreboard. Usually after the fourth inning, as a team sponsor, he would lead his boys, with their caps in hand, through the stands and among the crowds soliciting donations to help cover the team's expenses. The spectators, who were mostly neighbors and familiar faces, cheerfully gave what coins they could. They somehow knew that Roy was quietly giving a larger donation behind the scenes. It also became more apparent to Bobby that something was special about his dad. He would always remember the balmy summer evenings, the Noodles, Wil's death, and those poignant events as a young man when relationships with his father, family, and friends started to take on a deeper significance.

# CHAPTER 4

# CALIFORNIA TAN

IN THE AUTUMN OF 1935 young Bob entered the eighth grade and his second year at George Ross School on the corner of Ross and North Queen streets—a long, lonely bike hike up Clay Street from the five points. The school's claim to fame was its namesake, a signer of the Declaration of Independence who once lived a couple of blocks to the east on Ross Street. The only class that stirred Bob's interest was industrial arts. He didn't have Wil's intuitive mechanical abilities, but managed to acquire from his respected shop teacher Earl Koth the few carpentry skills that ultimately stuck with him. He also tried out for the basketball team; but, since he didn't play in any JV games the previous year, ended up opting for a spot as Manager of the varsity team. Clayt, the tallest and most athletic of the Franklin Street gang, played varsity ball when he attended George Ross; Bobby often went to the games to watch him and other billboard players. He loved the excitement of competition and, in particular, the popular school pep song, with which he would entertain and annoy his family for many years. It was an upbeat, but monotonous little sonata with contrapuntal segments:

> George Ross will shine tonight, George Ross will shine.
> George Ross will shine tonight, George Ross will shine!
> 'til the sun comes up, 'til the moon goes down…
> George Ross will shine!!

As sure as the sun came up, another summer arrived, along with another Noodles season, an invasion of seventeen year locusts, and a record shattering heat wave which sent the temperature to 106 degrees on July 10th. When Lancaster Sales Days were over, Roy took the family on a vacation to Atlantic City. They departed on a Thursday afternoon, when downtown stores were closed, and returned on Sunday night. The Saylors went with them—Aunt Ella, Uncle Vince, and their son Eugene, Grace's younger brother, nicknamed Gener by the kids. Gener, who was a few years older, added to the fun while making an effort to fill in for their missing brother. The families drove in a two-machine convoy with the Saylors' car in the lead. To relieve the boredom of a four-hour road trip with restless teenagers, Vince, the consummate joker, would hold up hand-scribbled signs outside his car window, announcing at gradually decreasing intervals: "50 miles to go!" then, "Not long now!" followed by "Only 3 more miles!" And so on. He probably stole the idea from Burma Shave.

They arrived by late afternoon, but not too late for the kids to run off to the beach. It was a scorching day. The sand was so hot on their feet they had to sit down before reaching the ocean. The adults straggled behind, unable to make it more than a few steps at a time on the blistering sand. The boys weren't discouraged; they spent all day—every day—on the beach. They called themselves beach bums. Lunch usually came from Ivy's robust picnic basket, and dinner was typically a fried seafood feast at one of the shore's many, popular open-air restaurants. At night they collapsed with full bellies and seared skin in rented rooms on the third floor of an off-Boardwalk rowhouse. They didn't mind having to share two rooms with a single washbowl and toilet. It was a vacation at the shore. They would joke about the hot sand for years. Summers weren't the same without Wil, but laughter was returning to 753 Franklin Street, and it was beginning to sound more genuine. The economic climate was also improving and the shoe business was doing better. Life moved on a day at a time.

As autumn arrived, things were brewing beyond the five points. A hurricane blasted the Atlantic coast. The New Deal was insidiously changing the relationship between workers and employers. Roosevelt was reelected by a landslide. Overseas, German troops occupied the Rhineland, a militarist regime had taken control of Japan, and Spanish civilians were being ravaged in a civil war. Concurrently, the Germans and Japanese were masterminding a global alliance.

But, despite these events, Main Street America concentrated on achieving full recovery from the Depression, which by 1936 appeared possible. The shoe business advanced steadily that year, thanks to Roy's rigorous attention to serving customers, managing costs, and paying bills promptly. By the next September, with debts paid off and business thriving, Roy splurged on a 1937 LaSalle, his first brand new automobile. He purchased it at Bomberger Cadillac-LaSalle Co. on 519 West King Street for $1,400—more than he paid for his first house. Nine months of accumulated early payment discounts covered the cost. Young Bob would always remember this, because earlier that year Roy had for the first time shown him the confidential business ledger, in which he recorded the discounts. "As soon as this column adds up to fourteen hundred dollars," Roy explained, "we're going to buy that machine." And that's exactly what he did.

It was quite a machine—rich, dark green in color. A LaSalle was considered a luxury automobile, the kind owned by affluent people. It had a powerful eight-cylinder engine, ornate hood, white-wall tires, large fenders, and very plush interior. Enough to embarrass Ivy. "What will the neighbors think," she muttered. Roy tried to explain: "Mother, we worked hard and sacrificed for this car." The kids, of course, were enthralled. It would be only a little more than a year until Bob was old enough to drive it.

At that time Bob was in the ninth grade at West Junior High School on Nevin and Walnut Street, his longest bicycle commute yet: southwest on Park Avenue, past the cemetery, west on James Street, across Prince, then south on Nevin for another block. On days when his shop class was scheduled, he had to pedal in the opposite direction to East Junior High on Ann Street, where the two schools shared shop facilities. After school he played intramural soccer and advanced to the JV team, coached by Mr. Thompson, an excellent soccer instructor and nice man. Outside school Bob's life remained centered around family, church, neighborhood, YMCA, movies, and last, but certainly not least, baseball. By now, the Noodles players knew the Singleton boys so well that they would greet them by name when they passed on the street. This was a big deal to Bob and Ed, but hardly significant in the scheme of things. A violent explosion of the giant dirigible Hindenberg had shocked the world that spring, and a pretty young aviator named Amelia Earhart went down somewhere in the Pacific that summer.

In the tenth grade Bob moved over to Boys High School on West Orange Street, between Water and Mulberry streets, not far from West Junior. He became interested in basketball again. It was exciting to play on a court which also served as a stage for the school auditorium. More importantly, in January he became old enough to be eligible for a student driver's permit. As a prospective driver, he was already fairly adept behind the wheel, because during the past year he had practiced handling the old Studebaker in off-road places like the parking lot of the Mt. Hope church, while family paid Sunday afternoon respects to deceased relatives. And occasionally, under the close supervision of his reluctant father, he had a chance to maneuver the stately LaSalle.

With his newly acquired, albeit restricted, degree of freedom, Bob understandably became a little restless and somewhat distracted 16-year-old. By this time Sis and the Sweigart boys had graduated from high school, and all had paying jobs. Bob's world was limited to Franklin Street and Boys High, where he felt lost on a small stage. He wanted independence, but his aspirations and horizons were limited. He would never give it much thought when Hitler moved military forces into Austria. He would pay only slightly more attention to the controversial, big event that June when Joe Louis decisively "kayoed" Germany's Max Schmeling in the first round. As always, he relied on the Noodles to pass the summer.

It wasn't until the autumn that the pace of his life accelerated. Bob was now entering his junior year at the brand new John Pierce McCaskey High School. The new school building, just completed the previous January, was gigantic, modern, and a little intimidating. It was known as one of the first "million dollar high schools" having "the advantages of spacious departments with up-to-the-minute equipment for every phase of high school education."[1] The super-school's namesake, "Jack" McCaskey, had once been a teacher at Boys High School until he won a race for Mayor against W. W. Greist, head of Lancaster's notorious Republican party machine. McCaskey was a political icon, and the new high school was his monument.

Going to school in a monument can be a bit disorienting. September passed in a blur of bright lights, long corridors, strange faces, and anxious minutes between classes. Early October was more of the same. McCaskey held graduations in both January and June. If everything went right, Bob figured he could complete his course work and be out of there by January 1940. To ease his restlessness, he started a routine of getting up at 4 A.M. to help a local dairyman named Leo Gottselig collect heavy metal containers of raw milk from local farms and transport them back to Leo's tiny processing plant on the corner of Franklin and Frederick streets. The idea came from Clayt and Don, who had also done this for Leo before graduating. Bob never got paid for the work, but he felt free and independent riding on the back of the big dairy truck. He also burned off some excess energy in Leo's hot, steamy processing shed. Roy and Ivy did not approve, which is probably why this senseless pastime lasted for less than a dozen gigs.

After that phase, he again sought refuge in the familiar: basketball and gymnastics at the Y; and big league baseball, which was now getting boring and too predictable. That October "Joe McCarthy's pitiless New York Yankees stamped the pitiful Chicago Cubs 8-3 for a fourth straight World Series victory that made the Yankees the first ball club to win three successive world championships."[2]

TEENAGE LIFE DIDN'T PERK UP until that unforgettable day in the fall of 1938 when Bob was presented with keys to his first set of wheels— a 1936 Chrysler convertible with a rumble seat! It was like a ticket to freedom and rite of passage to adulthood. A surprise gift from his dad, it seemed more like a gift from heaven. While slightly used, the car had stylish lines and was finished in a trendy color called California Tan. Roy knew how much it would mean to his son and was as proud as a father could be. He found the car on his own and announced the surprise a few days before it was delivered. On the big day he arranged to come home from work early to turn over the keys and tutor his son on the use of a "late clutch," the machine's only idiosyncrasy.

Bob could hardly wait for school to let out that day. He raced home as fast as his legs could pedal. Don Sweigart had heard the news and was there waiting for him. He wanted to share in the moment. Bob hadn't made it past the Diller's house when he spotted the tan glare sparkling in front of the house, right where the dealer had parked it. The doors were unlocked, but the ignition was empty. He rushed inside. Roy wasn't home yet. Ivy had the keys, and he begged her for them. "Don't you drive that machine until your father gets home," she declared. "Don't worry, Mom; I just want to start up the engine."

Back outside beaming Don was sitting in the passenger's seat with driver's credentials in his wallet. He knew that Bob still only had a learner's permit. Bob jumped in, anxiously inserted the key; and, the tan beast virtually started up on its own. It must have felt like sitting on one of Johnny Allen's tan work horses, full of energy and champing at the bit. Confirming in a sideways glance that his dad had not yet arrived, Bob cautiously eased out the clutch pedal. It wasn't a *little* late; it was a *lot* late. And it was impossible to resist the temptation any longer. With a squeak of the tires they were off. What exhilaration! Certainly, it wouldn't hurt to take one short and glorious spin around the block.

As they completed the victory lap, Bob spotted his Dad up ahead, stepping off the trolley. His outstretched neck made it obvious that he was looking for the tan car. As the approaching Chrysler came into his line of sight, he hesitated, then forced a smile. The disappointment was obvious. He never got angry, but it was clear that he was upset. Without a word Don jumped out, then Roy climbed in; and, after taking a breath, he calmly proceeded to play out the moment that he had so much looked forward to: proud father teaching eager son the fine points of operating a late clutch—an experience that Roy could never have dreamed about in his own youth. This special event also lingered as a bittersweet memory for the son and another one of life's hard lessons—the kind you desperately wish you could have learned another way. Bob would never forget the look on his father's face. "It was so unfair of me," he reflected. "It just hurt Dad to the quick."

Fortunately, youth rebound quickly from their clumsy stumbles over bumps in the road. Bob got his driver's license in the Chrysler and, for the first time in his life, felt liberated and sensed his emergent manhood. Soon thereafter, he began to reengage and look outward. The girls even seemed to pay more attention to him. It must have been the California Tan.

With a prospering shoe business, the Singletons were quickly moving up the economic ladder. After the addition of the Chrysler, Roy was determined to buy his family a nicer home in one of Lancaster's new housing developments, an upscale community known as Grandview Heights. It was on the east side of town, far enough on the other side of the railroad tracks and the old silk mill. The land was originally owned by Frank McGrann, a wealthy businessman who raised fine horses on an immense farm in the area. McGrann sold a large tract of the property to a developer named Shufflebottom, who was one of Roy's good customers. Mr. Shufflebottom subdivided the land and built high quality, custom and spec homes on meticulously curbed and tree-lined streets.

Roy chauffeured his family in the elegant LaSalle to explore the swanky new neighborhood and inspect some model homes. Ivy was still uncomfortable. "Roy, we can't afford this," she implored.

"Don't let it worry you, Mother," he replied.

"But, Roy, people will think we're showing off," she went on. The children always felt that their mother's conservatism had some effect on Roy, but not enough to change his mind on this decision.

That autumn—for $9,000—they purchased a simple but elegant, three-story red brick home at 927 Martha Avenue, a side street off McGrann Boulevard. The house had wide, white-painted trim around its large, paned windows and a distinctive, arched lintel over the front door. Situated on a half-acre plot with vacant lots on one side and across the street, the property looked like a country estate compared to 753 Franklin Street. The children knew that their mother liked it, regardless of her remarks. Ivy would never admit it, but she probably felt liberated in her own way—free from Franklin Street neighbors who were good friends, but a little too close and judgmental for comfort. She loved hanging her famously white laundry on the long wash lines in their spacious, new back yard—out of range of critical eyes.

Bob was not yet acclimated to McCaskey High when they decided to move to their new home, which was situated just outside the northeast city limits in a corner of Manheim Township, one of the city's largest suburbs. He would have to transfer to a smaller school, which housed grades 5–12 in a more traditional, formal-looking structure. Suddenly, the big city school didn't seem so bad after all. Manheim Township High School, called MTHS or Township by the locals, was located three miles north of the city, way out in a farm village called Neffsville.

Prior to their transfer, Roy escorted his two sons to the residence of Mr. Griffiths, Principal of MTHS, who lived in town on James Street. During their introduction Bob learned that his course credits in the city school system put him nearly a half semester ahead of his Township peers. Unfortunately, Township scheduled only June graduations. Therefore, he would be held back until his new classmates caught up. For the remainder of the fall semester he would have to report to class but would be excused from regular course work until January, when he would continue as a regular second-semester junior.

Needless to say, the good-looking kid—with a tan convertible—from the big, city school—probably entered Township with a bit of an attitude. His parents properly counseled him to ride the school bus until the other students got to know him. So, for the first few weeks he rode in the back of the bus, and for the remainder of the fall semester he sat in the back of the classroom reading daily newspapers. His first impression of Township was that the kids there seemed to have those distinctive Pennsylvania Dutch, Mennonite, or farmer names. But his attitude would eventually change.

An attractive, blue-eyed brunette in his homeroom caught his eye. He didn't have any classes with her, because she was enrolled in the commercial, not the academic course curriculum. But she did ride in the same school bus from Grandview Heights. She and her talkative, blonde, younger sister Mollie lived around the corner in a Tudor style house on McGrann Boulevard. Their home could easily be seen from Martha Avenue. Her name was Norma Jane Diffenbach. Despite her surname, "she didn't look Mennonite." But, although he was a city kid, he was still too shy with girls to make an approach.

That winter he found a familiar outlet in basketball and played with the junior varsity. Foster Ulrich was the coach. He developed friendships with teammates, like Don Rothfus, Dick Kreider, Ray Myers, Johnny Witmer, and Clair Lefever. Occasionally, the JV's scrimmaged with the varsity team, which was made up of mostly seniors, including Chet Grille, one of the top players. Bob was intensely competitive, and, thanks to his experience growing up across from the billboard, held his own fairly well on the Township court. In scrimmages with the varsity, he did particularly well, surprising Coach Ulrich with his fast breaks around Chet Grille. The coach commented how he liked the new kid's footwork. Chet wasn't impressed.

The assimilation process at his new country school was going pretty well with the other guys. While the girls seemed attracted to his good looks, tan convertible, and pleasant personality, he still hadn't gotten up the nerve to ask any for a date. Hence, it was fortuitous when he was invited to his first big Township social event by a pretty girl in the senior class named Anna Emich. It would be a private party—an outdoor cookout—held at a farm on Butter Road in a prestigious section of the township. Since mostly upperclassmen would be there, Bob wanted to make a good impression. Therefore, he talked his father into letting him borrow the LaSalle for the evening. Roy consented reluctantly but was glad to help out his son on his first date. The only condition was that he be home by 11 o'clock.

On party day bashful Bob anxiously picked up his eager date and managed to navigate his way to the site, where he proudly positioned the LaSalle in an open field with the other parked cars. A noisy group was already gathered, mostly made up of happy-go-lucky seniors and their dates. Bob recognized many and knew several by name, particularly the popular athletes, like Chet Grille. While the new kid felt a little out of place, he found the group to be friendly. Rapid fire introductions, small talk, wise cracks, and laughter transitioned to a relaxed, spring country barbecue; and, as the sun disappeared behind the trees, the crowd dispersed into smaller clusters of couples with the girls snuggling radiantly under the arms of their dates.

Eleven o'clock was approaching, and the evening would soon be scratched up as a success—if only his exit from the scene could have been less conspicuous. The LaSalle must have been too tempting a target. At some point during the evening a couple of guys, including Chet Grille, had sneaked out to the LaSalle and disconnected four spark plug wires. After bidding their friends goodbye, Bob and Anna returned to the big car, anxiously anticipating the final leg of their first date. Of course, the machine wouldn't cooperate. The starter motor functioned, but the big power plant just wouldn't kick in. After several attempts, the straining engine finally turned over on its own, but the entire body just rumbled and shook. What a mess! Bob knew he couldn't rely on his mechanical skills to get out of this embarrassing predicament. It was already past 11 o'clock.

The rest of the evening seems to have been blanked out of his mind. On four straining cylinders he somehow managed to return his exasperated date to her home and the green machine to its Martha Avenue garage. Any thought of a romantic encounter that night was overshadowed by dread of his father's expected reaction. Of course, the anticipation is always worse than the reality, and Roy's expression was all that needed to be said. Anna was understanding when they next talked. They had one more date. She was a pretty girl and very nice person, but this relationship was clearly never meant to be.

The spring of his junior year Bob went out for the track team along with his brother Ed, who was in the sophomore class. To polish their skills they set up a high-jump bar and sawdust pit in the vacant lot next to their house. Mollie often came by on her bicycle to watch Ed perform. She and Ed had already struck up a friendship and could frequently be spotted riding their bikes together. Sometimes Norma came along with Mollie. By now she had her eye on Bob, but he would pretend not to notice. Coy Mollie prodded Ed to encourage his shy brother to make a move. But that would take a little time.

Bob's track career was short circuited when he was asked to play on the tennis team by Arthur Ott, an assertive coach who years later would become the high school principal. Bob had never played tennis before, but the team needed to fill a roster. His classmate Dick Kreider was on the team, but it was Bob's best friend, a Jewish boy named Gene Epstein, called Eppie, who convinced him to give it a try. Eppie lived nearby on Janet Avenue. They had become friends playing table tennis at the YMCA and in the basements of their Grandview Heights homes. Eppie was an excellent tennis player. Bob turned out to be pretty good as well. This sport, which he began as a lark, eventually led to a varsity letter and reemerged years later as a constant and enduring passion.

Bob's social life remained active thanks to further invitations from girls in the senior class. Despite the LaSalle incident with Anna, his popularity remained unscathed. Nevertheless, he decided to stick with the California Tan; it attracted girls like flypaper. He went with a girl named Nancy Sabo on one or two dates and escorted a warm and attractive girl named Ruth Rote to her senior prom, getting the latter to agree to make it a double date with Eppie and a girl from another school. Eppie rode in the rumble seat and could be relied upon to keep the atmosphere light. Before the dance they went to dinner at a clubby, grown-up place called The German Village on Chestnut Street. Afterwards they went to Hostetter's Play Barn on the Old Philadelphia Pike, a popular dance hall at that time. Thanks to Eppie, bashful Bob minimized awkward moments alone with his enticing companion in the front seat. But as a result of this pattern, Bob fell short of developing intimate relationships—at least until he finally went out with Norma.

IT'S NOT CLEAR WHO made the first approach, but that was all it took. Their first date was in the autumn of their senior year. It was in late September, during the farm show season in Lancaster. Farm shows were a big deal in Lancaster. In the old days it was a single, huge event at the Lancaster County Agricultural Fairgrounds on the Harrisburg Pike in Manheim Township. But that county fair was discontinued in the early 1930s "because its managers felt that sideshows of questionable morality compromised the integrity of the fair and because numerous county communities held fairs of their own."[3] As a result, one could attend a series of farm shows in little towns like Ephrata,

New Holland, or Mt. Joy or visit the strictly agricultural fairs, in places like Lampeter or Southern Lancaster County. Bob asked Norm to the popular, big farm show at Ephrata, and she eagerly went along.

As usual, it was set up as a double date; Eppie by this time was dating a good friend of Norm's, Lynn Lapkin, nicknamed Lappie. As usual, Eppie and his date rode in the rumble seat. The chilly, open-air journey prepared them for the Ferris wheel ride, which most young couples looked forward to at the farm show. But when they arrived, Norm had to be coaxed to climb on the giant wheel; she wasn't much for amusements. Her trepidation made it easy for Bob to get his arm around her as they were smoothly lifted into the heavens. She relaxed after a few revolutions. Then it was dreamy. Silently and blissfully, they soared above the world through clear autumn skies, mildly scented with aromas of hay, popcorn, and cotton candy. They would see each other frequently after that evening, and the Ephrata Farm Show was a venue to which they would return regularly in the coming years.

The summer before his senior year Bob earned spending money by helping out his father at the shoe store. In the fall he continued working part-time after school. Norm also had a part-time secretarial job at Lancaster Newspapers. She worked for Doug Armstrong, a young editor who years later would rise to the top job. It was a convenient arrangement: after school Bob would give Norm a ride into town and drop her off at the newspaper office on his way to the shoe store. It was during this period of time that he taught her to drive. After several tries, she learned to relax behind the wheel of the Chrysler and mastered its notorious clutch. It wasn't long until she passed the test for her driver's license in the tan convertible.

Bob and Norm dated regularly. On special dates they usually went to dances—places like the Valencia in York or the Starlight Ballroom in Hershey. Big bands played there, led by celebrities like Jimmy Dorsey and Count Basie. They double dated with couples like Peck Stauffer and Polly Yeagley, who worked with Norm at the newspaper office. They also went to the movies, usually at the Colonial Theater on North Queen Street. The Colonial was known for having a band, which performed in the orchestra pit between shows. After the movie or dance they'd usually stop for a root beer on the way home, trying never to be late for their 11 o'clock curfew.

Norm's parents were very strict about this, especially her mother. Martin and Violet Diffenbach, nicknamed Mart and Vi, were self-sufficient, conservative Lancaster people. They were members of the St. Paul's Reformed Church on Duke Street, although Mart was from a traditional Mennonite family. He changed his church affiliation after meeting Vi, who was from the Troop family, a happy-go-lucky bunch who lived by the railroad tracks in Gordonville, a tiny farm hamlet in Paradise Township. Bob genuinely liked both of them, despite their strictness about the curfew. Mart was usually leaving the house around the time Bob brought Norm home. He was proprietor of a successful produce business in town known as Mettfett's, located at the Northern Market on North Queen and Walnut streets. Every day, long before the sun came up, he drove to the Philadelphia waterfront to purchase specialty produce and fresh seafood for his market stand. Mettfett's was well known in Lancaster for the quality of their goods and their downstairs oyster bar. Mart purchased a new Chevy every year, which he drove on the tiresome commute to Philly. He was followed there by his big Mettfett's panel truck, driven by a black employee. They brought the fresh goods back before the market opened and worked there until mid-afternoon. Then he would go home, eat dinner, grab some sleep, and repeat the cycle. It was remarkable how he managed this grueling schedule for so many years. Norm and Bob would often be necking in the sun parlor when Mart descended the stairs to leave on his nocturnal journey. He often had to remind Bob that it was time to go home.

Norma Diffenbach was a modest, attractive, and well-liked girl. She didn't get involved with the so-called popular girls who hung around together in cliques. She was a little shy and reserved, but had a sincere, friendly smile for everybody, without exception. Bob was probably luckier than he realized. On a few occasions he dated other girls, but it was evident to friends that he was especially fond of Norm and that she was no longer available since meeting him. Bob's competition resented that. One evening on their way home from a date, he pulled the Chrysler into a popular, secluded parking spot along the Conestoga for an intimate interlude before their curfew. One of Norm's jealous suitors and a companion, who happened to be prowling in the area, discovered the tan convertible. The intruders sneaked up to the car, directed a flashlight beam through the window, and howled with laughter as they caught the couple in a harmless embrace. Needless to say, Norm was totally embarrassed by the incident and worried that her reputation would be tarnished.

This too would pass. Their senior year was filled with good times and happiness. Bob was now too preoccupied with his social life to get involved in sports, and he liked his work at the shoe store. He was confident that he could have made the varsity basketball team as a senior, but it wasn't on his list of priorities. He was impressed by his father's success in the shoe business and saw a future there for himself. Roy had always encouraged him to pursue a college-preparatory curriculum in high school, but Bob had no interest in further schooling. Most of his friends felt the same way. He was eager to establish his own independence. The idea of military service was never a consideration. Although Hitler by this time had taken Poland and destroyed several British ships, one of which had over 200 U.S. citizens aboard, the prospect of the U.S. entering the war, let alone his own involvement, never seriously entered his mind.

The excitement in the spring of his senior year centered around Norma. As in the prior two years, by a vote of the student body, she was selected to be a court attendant and contestant for the school's May Queen, who was crowned at the annual May Day event. May Day was a big affair at Township. The festivities were usually held on a Friday before graduation on the big lawn in front of the school. A stage was set up for the Queen and her court. There were balloons, banners, a Maypole dance, and formal processional in advance of the crowning ceremony. The girls of the court were decked out in flowing spring pastels, and the spectators, including students, parents, and teachers, were also dressed up for the occasion. Selection of the May Queen was determined by student votes, with the faculty having an influence on the final outcome. The name of the winner was kept secret until the end of the ceremony, when a little flower girl, chosen from the elementary school, promenaded back and forth on the stage in front of the hopeful, beaming candidates until finally stopping, turning, then curtsying to her new majesty.

In the weeks and days prior to the big event, the atmosphere was thick with gossip and speculation about the possible winner. An attractive, popular, but somewhat pompous and flamboyant girl named Marilyn Fleming was confident that she would be named Queen. She shared her insight with Norma and said that she would be honored if Norm would assist in positioning the crown on her head at the ceremony. Norm, always wanting to please, could be counted on to be accommodating. Norm's mother received an unexpected call from Mrs. Fleming, who also not too subtly intimated that Marilyn was known to be the one selected as that year's Queen.

Bob played the role of Norm's escort on the big day but would remain in the audience during the ceremony. Standing by himself off to one side, he was nearly as nervous as Norm, although she looked more at ease. Just prior to the crowning Bob was approached by Miss Pottiger, a teacher who was involved in the selection process and one of the few who knew the outcome. Whether motivated by joy, empathy for the nervous-looking escort, or simple inability to keep a secret any longer, she approached Bob and whispered, "I've never done this before, but thought you should know that Norma's the one who's been selected!"

Bob could barely disguise his elation. When the little flower girl stopped in front of the new Queen, Norm was equally surprised and overwhelmed. Marilyn, ostensibly in shock, quickly disappeared after the ceremony. A large, close-up photo of the May Queen, with her radiant smile, sparkling crown, and triumphant bouquet of red roses, appeared in the Lancaster *Sunday News*. No doubt Norma's friends and proud boss at the newspaper office had some influence on the prominence of this news tidbit. Bob felt that, even if Norm had not garnered as many votes as Marilyn, the teachers would have lobbied for the same result. Everybody loved Norma. The experience had an effect on one friendship, but Marilyn, almost too magnanimously, stayed in touch with Norma for many years.

The excitement of graduation paled in comparison to May Day, but there could not have been two happier graduates commencing their adult lives. Bob went to work full time at the shoe store, and Norm at the newspaper office. After work they were generally together and continued to frequent movies and dances on weekends. During the summer they went swimming at the big pool at Brookside on the Harrisburg Pike or at The Willows on the Lincoln Highway. That's where Bob became acquainted with lifeguards Charlie Baile and Diz Daniels, who later married one of Norm's cousins, Betty Troop. During the winter Norm and Mollie often watched the guys play Saturday evening basketball at the YMCA. They played for First Methodist in the church league. Clayt played in the same league; and, another Troop cousin, Gloria Van Dyke, known as Glo, often joined the girls. She would become Clayt's future bride. The whole gang typically went to a place like Hupper's drug store for ice cream sodas before going home.

Bob and Norm were an item. They were securely employed, deeply in love, and plainly hopeful for a future together. The tan convertible and rumble seat started to feel too youthful and outdated. Bob decided to trade the aging Chrysler for a 1940 blue, two-door Chevy sedan. His dad loaned him part of the $846 that he paid for it.

FOLLOWING HIGH SCHOOL GRADUATION Bob continued to be subtly prodded by his dad to continue his education. Motivated by a father's pride and practical experience in a competitive and unpredictable world, Roy was disappointed that his son spurned suggestions to consider further schooling. But with only the leverage that comes from being the boss, he prevailed in convincing Bob that it would make sense to begin accumulating credits toward a college degree.

Roy's prodding was not the only thing that influenced his son's decision. Since that spring Hitler's armies had marched into the streets of Paris, and the Germans were bombing England. It was becoming increasingly apparent that the U.S. could not remain isolated. During the summer of 1940 a National Defense Tax on gas, oil, cigarettes, and amusement tickets became effective. That September, in a campaign speech, President Roosevelt insisted that "your boys are not going to be sent into any foreign wars."[4] Instead, the U.S. would lend overseas military bases to the British. However, on September 16th, he signed the Selective Service and Training Act. The following month over 6,000 young Americans holding draft serial number 158 were the first group to be called up in an unprecedented peacetime conscription.[5] Since it was understood that the selective service process would grant draft deferments to college students, Bob reasoned that it wouldn't hurt to reactivate his student status. He saw an advertisement in the paper for Pennsylvania State University Extension Courses, which were being held during evenings at Franklin & Marshall College, and sent for an application.

Bob was admitted into the Penn State program and started classes in January. He elected business-oriented courses, probably at Roy's suggestion. But, intellectually, he never really engaged. School was an unwelcome interruption to his new life style. He found himself just going through the academic motions, three nights a week. Outside his job and night school, he spent most of his time with Norm, except during baseball season.

That summer he and Ed formed a softball team to compete in the city league. They called it the Shoe Ten. The team consisted of shoe store employees, including Dick Ashby and Charlie Adams, Roy's senior employee. They also recruited Clayt Sweigart, Peep Carson, Bill Harnish and Zeta Kendig. Bill had limited athletic ability, but Zeta was an outstanding pitcher and undisguised ringer. Roy also played—to Ivy's dismay. Games were held in their old neighborhood at the 6th Ward Park. Thanks to Zeta, and in spite of Bill, who was always relegated to right field, the Shoe Ten had a respectable season.

Throughout this period Norm and Bob continued bonding, and both sets of parents approved of the relationship. It seemed natural that the parents, who were already neighbors, would also become good friends. Besides the fact that the Singleton brothers were courting Diffenbach sisters, the families had a lot in common. Both fathers were self-made and successful businessmen, although Mart, a product of Mennonite farmers, was more conservative to a fault. He refused to entrust banks with his hard-earned money, and, to his credit, sailed through the Depression intact. Vi was a lovable product of the Troop family. Like Ivy, she was a fantastic cook, and her rotund physical stature was complemented with great levity. As they both possessed characteristic Lancastrian modesty regarding conspicuous affluence, Vi and Ivy would openly joke about their social standing, addressing each other in self-ascribed nicknames, Dubonnet (pronounced without the soft French *t*) and Boscobel (with emphasis on the *bel*). The latter happened to be the name of the country estate of George Washington Singleton, an American politician of the Civil War era, but God only knows where Vi came up with the nicknames. There was never a dull moment when the two mothers were in the same room. Their children were always happy to have them around. On Thursdays, after the store closed, Roy and Ivy occasionally joined the kids at the swimming pool. Their 1920s style bathing suits always added a humorous flavor to the occasion.

The families soon became close enough to be comfortable taking weekend trips together to the Jersey shore. A weekend at the shore was always a treat for the Singletons, and spending summers there had been a tradition for the Diffenbachs when their four daughters were younger. The group convoyed in the Chevy and LaSalle and usually rented two large rooms at a boarding house on Pennsylvania Avenue. Depending on the accommodations, Vi assigned beds and carefully positioned privacy screens to separate parents, boys, and girls. Oldest daughter Ellen, known as Becky, came along, and her date joined Bob and Ed in the guy's section, identified by bed rolls spread on the floor. One doesn't need much of an imagination to envision the fun they had on these trips. The kids were blessed with parents who were good sports. It was better than summer camp. They were like one big happy family, which was a special and unique phenomenon, even by 1941 standards.

Sadly, their world would lose some of its innocence after the summer of 1941. They probably saw it coming. The situation overseas was grim: parts of London were bombed out, and the Germans had pushed through Eastern Europe into Russia. National defense efforts were picking up at home: several Lancaster factories were ramping up production under federal defense contracts for munitions, naval equipment, and silk parachutes. Raw materials were being diverted from non-defense businesses, causing peacetime jobs to be lost. The Red Cross set up an office on West Orange Street. Regional gasoline stations were ordered to close between 7 P.M. and 7 A.M. in an effort to conserve supplies and counteract the effect of a shortage of tanker ships.[6] On December 7th Bob was with his family returning from a Sunday afternoon visit with cousin Georgie in Allentown when they heard the shocking news of the attack on Pearl Harbor. The image of Georgie's twisted body and contorted, but joyful, face was still fresh in his mind. Bob must have wondered on that day if it would be only a matter of time until his number came up.

Once the U.S. declared war, it was difficult for a young man to plan for his future. Fortunately, Bob had a secure job at the shoe store, although suppliers were making it increasingly difficult by attempting to manage retail prices under the banner of patriotism. Both he and Ed, who also worked at the shoe store since graduating, were given encouragement by their dad to make it a career. In 1942, after significant alterations to the storefront, the name of the business was changed from Wilbur & Martin to Singleton's Shoes. Probably because he had managed to avoid being drafted in 1917, Roy took some comfort in assuming that his boys might also be passed over.

Bob was in love with Norma and had already considered the idea of marriage, which until Pearl Harbor would have improved his draft status. However, on January 1st the local Selective Service Board announced that men married after December 8th or in the future could not use dependency of their wives as a cause for deferment.[7] Student deferments would also carry less weight. Bob couldn't help but notice that many of his friends and acquaintances were either getting drafted or ended up enlisting in last ditch attempts to avoid the dreaded fate of an infantryman. Both Sweigart boys signed up: Clayt by this time had completed basic training and left for Officer Candidate School; Don had recently departed for basic training in preparation for paratrooper school. Ed, at age18, was the ripest for selection; he was immobilized with worry.

IT WAS A FULL SCALE WAR in the Pacific in the spring of '42. American soldiers were getting killed. President Roosevelt, reelected in a landslide, continued to confidently assure citizens that the enemy would be crushed, but the mood of the country was somber. It was impossible to do anything without being reminded of war. A ration card was now required to purchase gasoline. There were local drives for the collection of rubber, then for cooking fats and greases, which could be used in the production of explosives. And Ed was notified to report for his draft physical that summer.

Bob had made his decision before that. Not long after Pearl Harbor a newspaper advertisement placed by the Veterans of Foreign Wars caught his attention; it was recruiting applicants for Aviation Cadets. Without a college degree, an aviation cadet could become an officer and pilot in the new Army Air Force, which had recently changed its name from the Army Air Corps. Bob wanted to control his destiny and liked the option of choosing a branch of the military service. In addition, he had heard that it could be up to several months between the dates of enlistment and active duty. That would mean more time with Norm and the chance of serving less time before the war ended. But he was also tempted by the exciting prospect of flying. He had flown only once in his life—with Paulie Schlothauer. Paulie owned the Pennsylvania Hotel next to the shoe store. He was a swashbuckling character who loved flying—and women, according to Charlie Adams. Paulie owned a Piper Cub and invited Charlie to go along for a ride one afternoon. Charlie declined the offer; but, Bob, overhearing the conversation, expressed an interest. That's how he got his first ride. It was something he would never forget. Paulie even showed him what was called a slip landing. It was opportune that he got the flying demonstration when he did. For security reasons private pilot licenses were temporarily suspended after Pearl Harbor. Hence, by the time Bob picked up his cadet information kit at the Post Office, he had already experienced a savory taste of the wild blue.

Notice of his physical examination didn't arrive until summer. The instructions said to report to the Lancaster Post Office on "10 September 1942." It felt very strange. The prospect of serving in the military couldn't have been more foreign to him. And his father could offer no advice. Bob had no idea of what to expect beyond the stories told by the Sweigart boys. During a short visit home following basic training, Clayt entertained his Franklin Street buddies with overworked Army tales and the "twenty-one dollars a day, once a month" tune. Like the George Ross pep song, it was the one thing that stuck in Bob's mind. When Don came home on leave that summer, he stopped by the shoe store. Bob was in the display window doing his best to help Charlie Adams make it look good for the back-to-school season. It was hard to get enthusiastic about selling shoes with a war on, and business had been sluggish ever since Lancaster Sales Days were canceled in support of government efforts to stabilize prices. Bob happened to glance up from his work, and there outside the window stood handsome-as-ever Don dressed in his pressed uniform and shiny plain-tip oxfords. He could have passed for the character on the Army's recruiting posters. Military experience clearly did him no harm, and Bob secretly envied him. The Sweigarts were the extent of Bob's exposure to the military. Hence, his feelings wavered between excited anticipation, fear of the unknown, and yearning for a blissful life with his beloved that seemed to be slipping further into the future. But he had at least one date nailed down now, so he would begin to map out a revised future.

September 10th arrived in a flash. Bob reported to the post office, where he was ordered to join a group of recruits on an olive drab military bus that transported them to Camp Hill, near Harrisburg. Once they reached the Army base all further movements were surrendered to uniformed NCO's (noncommissioned officers) who barked instructions and herded their subjects like cattle through a series of examining stations, each of which had its own hurry-up-and-wait protocol. They quickly learned that an Army physical made no provisions for modesty or individuality. Bob just went with the flow, ostensibly at ease until the blood pressure test, which exposed his nervous tension. Having had his blood pressure taken in the past, he explained that his high readings would settle down after a few minutes; and, to his surprise and relief, the nurse cooperated, suggesting that he lie down on a nearby cot. True to her word, she returned after several minutes to repeat the wrap, pump, and read routine. Unfortunately, the numbers were still too high. It turned out to be nearly a half-hour before his pressure dropped into the acceptable range and he could proceed to the remaining stations. By the time he passed through the gauntlet, the other recruits were waiting at the bus, grumbling and ready to depart. While it was too close for comfort, he passed his first hurdle that day. Robert Leon Singleton, Serial Number 13 091 828, was officially sworn into the United States Army Air Force and assigned to Aviation Cadet Class 44-A. In typical Army fashion he was told that he would receive a notice in the mail informing him when training would start.

ALL THINGS CONSIDERED, signing up for aviation cadets seemed like a good decision. As anticipated, he would have several weeks or a few months before being called up. However, the Army being what it is, exact timing was uncertain until the last minute. Therefore, sitting on the drab bus on the way home from Camp Hill, he made another big decision: he would propose to Norm right away. He knew that he loved her, and she loved him. Of that he was certain.

Ivy accompanied him to J. Clark Houghton Jeweler to help select a diamond engagement ring. Bob never divulged where he proposed to Norm, but the Ferris wheel in Ephrata would have been a likely venue. As expected, all parents were thrilled, and they agreed to keep the news secret until an announcement could be made at a private gathering of their closest friends. Norma started the detailed planning. That autumn was especially beautiful, and, except for a big cloud on the horizon, their future looked bright. They basked in the moment.

The formal engagement was announced at their gathering on October 16, 1942. In attendance were both sets of parents; Mollie and Ed; Lynn Lapkin and her current beau Jack Belsinger; Clayt, who was dressed in his officer's uniform and accompanied by his latest flame; Polly Yeagley and Peck Stauffer; Eleanor and Dick Stauffer; and Sis with her new husband Harry Medsger. It was a quiet, semi-formal dinner party at the Diffenbach's home. The surprise was held until after the final course. The news was contained in a party favor at each place setting: a hand-painted silver walnut wrapped in a blue ribbon. Norm made them herself. Like a fortune cookie, each hollowed-out shell contained a sliver of paper with the hand-printed announcement. It was so typical of Norm to go out of her way attending to little details that make events special for everybody. Robert knew that he was one lucky guy.

It would be almost five months before Bob had to report for duty. More than ever, he was living a day at a time. But true to form, he followed a strict routine at work and night school, all the while dreaming of a future with Norm. With the passing of each day, the inevitability of their separation, while more imminent, seemed less real. Was there really a war? Would he actually fight in it? In an airplane? Many questions went through his mind, but the thought of not making it through the war never occurred to him—at least not until the following month when they received the terrible news:

> Technical Sgt. Donald K. Sweigart, 23, U.S. Army Air Forces, was killed November 11, 1942 when an Army paratroop transport plane crashed near Union S.C. The plane was on a training flight from Mobile, Alabama to Pope Field, N.C.[8]

It seemed like only yesterday that he and Don had shared the victory lap in the California Tan convertible.

# CHAPTER 5

# SAD SACKS

ORDERS DIDN'T ARRIVE until after Christmas. The scheduled report date was exactly five months after the date of his swearing-in at Camp Hill: March 10, 1943. On the morning of Bob's departure Roy did not want to risk losing composure in a face-to-face farewell. He waited until he was leaving for work before shouting up the stairs something to the effect of "Have a good trip! Good luck! I'll write!" And he could be counted on to keep his promise. It was more difficult for Ivy. Eddie had departed for basic training a few weeks earlier. Now she followed her remaining son out the door and just stood there wringing her hands as he climbed into the Chevy, backed out of the driveway, and headed down the street. Bob would never forget how upset she was and how hard she struggled not to show it. He could see that she was still standing there when he pulled into Diffenbach's driveway at 915 McGrann Boulevard.

The plan was for Norm to drop him off at the post office on her way to work. She would have exclusive use of the Chevy during his extended absence. She was waiting outside when he pulled into her driveway. Vi hustled out to deliver tearful hugs and kisses. Mart by now was at Mettfett's, halfway through his 15-hour daily routine. When they arrived at the post office, other girlfriends, wives, and parents were peeling off one-at-a-time as the recruits gathered in a haphazard cluster. Bob and Norm hurried their farewells, and Norm drove off in the shiny blue Chevy. As happy and proud as they both were that the car would now be all hers, other emotions took over as she pulled away, waving into the rear view mirror so that he couldn't see her eyes. Then, suddenly, it was emptiness.

All 17 recruits were properly dressed in jackets and ties. Bob didn't know a soul. State Inspector Frank Bonesky, Chairman of the VFW enlistment committee, shouted their instructions. Each recruit received a pat on the back, a motivational book, and a gift box of sundries from the women's auxiliary. That was all they were allowed to take with them. A photographer from one of the local newspapers captured the scene on film. Bob was in the center of the photo. Most recruits were intent on the guy barking instructions. But not Cadet Singleton. His blank expression and unfocused stare clearly revealed that his thoughts were in a different place.

The group was delivered by bus to the institutional granite of Lancaster's Pennsylvania Railroad station where, after a military wait, they boarded a train headed for Tennessee. Final destination was Fort Berry Hill, a basic training and screening installation for Army recruits. Bob struggled with mixed emotions during the long trip. He knew the military would not be "his kind of life," but was cautiously excited about taking on the challenge of something new and different. While the possibility of failing or getting hurt might have occurred to him, that was never a consideration. Such thoughts paled in comparison to his hopes and dreams for a future with Norma.

IT WAS RAINING when they arrived at Berry Hill. Bob couldn't believe how ugly and uninviting the place was. It was certainly nothing like home—and downright depressing for a guy who never gets depressed. Each cadet trainee was assigned a barracks and issued a duffel bag full of GI uniforms. They were ordered to pack their civvies in another bag, which the Army shipped back to their home addresses. It was like being transplanted on another planet. From there on the Drill Sergeant looked after them, so to speak.

The daily routine included reveille, PT (physical training), marches to the mess hall, quantities of food that they were usually too tired or hungry to gripe about, barracks inspections, classroom instruction, examinations, and endless sessions of marching, drilling and parading. Six weeks of this. In the minimal free time allotted Bob read and wrote letters. During the entire stint he never even saw the nearby town of Nashville. But he wrote letters every day, and, except for Sundays, also received one from Norm. That routine would continue for as long as they were apart.

He also corresponded regularly with his mom and dad and often with Mart and Vi. While one wouldn't know it from the Army's daily fare at Berry Hill, it was clear from letters that rationing was becoming a way of life at home. Meats, cheeses, and edible fats had been added to federal rationing lists along with shoes, canned goods, sugar, coffee, gasoline, fuel oil, typewriters, tires, and motor cars. Roy's regular weekly letters updated his son on the shoe store's weekly sales and business challenges, like the freeze on all prices and wages that was announced in April by the Office of Price Administration.

Bob didn't develop close friendships at Berry Hill, but got along well with most of the guys. His main associates were barracks buddies, whose last names began with the letter *S*. "Everything's alphabetical in the Army," they said. And people spoke in abbreviations or acronyms. Occasionally he went with a group of S's to see a movie, but instead of joining them at the bar afterwards, he returned to the barracks to write letters. On Saturday nights the USO (United Service Organizations) held dances on base, but he never bothered to go. Not without Norm.

Near the end of basic training they were subjected to a battery of aptitude tests to determine the MOS (Military Occupational Specialty) they would be suited for, which for aviation cadets was either pilot, navigator, bombardier, or armament. Bob listed as his preference pilot, even though the aptitude tests pegged him for navigator or armament. Luckily, since pilot slots were still available, he got his first choice—in a welcome freak of wartime. Rumors circulated that demand for pilots was beginning to decline, but he didn't want to miss the chance to pursue his secret dream, which was likely stimulated by the slip landing in Paulie's Piper Cub.

Berry Hill was never considered to be the best of camps, but Bob couldn't have imagined any place more miserable. Fortunately, after six weeks the sun came out, but better yet, he and other remaining pilot wannabes were shipped out by troop train to Army Air Force Pre-Flight School (Pilot), Group 13, Squadron 2, Flight C of San Antonio Army Air Cadet Corps (SAACC). There they be would become affectionately known as sad sacks, a name derived from the school's acronym. It was the equivalent of boot camp for the air corps. In other words, it was like starting over again. The ground program would last another six weeks, half-way through which most cadets would advance to upperclassman status and prepare for basic flight training.

THE WEATHER WAS BETTER in San Antonio and living conditions were improved. Bob sent Norm the first of a picture post card series, which revealed the interior of SAACC sleeping quarters. He wrote: *"Here is exactly what the inside of my barracks looks like."* It showed cadets lined up at the ends of their tightly-made metal beds, which were perfectly positioned between uniformly organized personal storage shelves. Everything was regimented in SAACC. PT was held twice a day, and it was stressful. Obstacle courses were a routine part of the regimen. They were taught how to properly stand at attention in a rigid pre-flight brace, with "head up, eyes front, chin in, shoulders back, chest up, gut in, etc." The upperclassmen, known as U-C, would scream, "Rack 'em back!" if a subordinate's posture wasn't perfect, or even if it was. Hazing by U-Cs was constant. It was all part of the game—a competitive screening process. The prize was a chance to fly.

The second picture postcard sent to Norm showed a marching band and cadets-in-review on a large parade ground. In addition to his affirmations of love and pining for the next time they would meet, he included in each piece of correspondence a brief description of a part of his day. This card was no exception:

> *...These devilish U-C made us change uniform 5 times tonite after mess. They gave us about 4 min. to change from one outfit to another. Each time had to hang up & button up the previous outfit. Said they were putting us in shape. The devils! Then they ran us around the block in between changes. Did I sweat! I can take it O.K. Some can't....*

The next card showed a rifle drill formation with personalized caption: *"I've been doing this."* It was funny to both of them, because guns were totally foreign to a shoe man from Lancaster. So was Morse code. The card reported:

> *...I took Code today & I think I'm doing O.K. You certainly have to be on the ball though. The U-C had another nice time with us tonite ...Received your letter & one from Dad today. Thanks a million. My faithful Honey still. Love, Bobby.*

Cards that followed showed mass calisthenics formations, Aircraft Identification classroom scenes, and military aircraft parked on the flight line. The SAACC postcard series continued through most of May, but the interval between mailings stretched out to a few days during the exam period later in the month. Bob mentioned that studies were getting harder, expressing surprise and delight that he got a perfect score on the *"Naval Ident."* exam. His confidence seemed to increase with every little success. On May 23rd he wrote:

*It is now 4 P.M. Sat. afternoon. Myself & 7 other fellows, out of the whole squadron (approx 100), passed 10 words per min. in Code today and are excused from Code classes until further notice. I feel pretty good about it. I can do anything I want to do during the Code periods now. Today is "Turnabout" day...instead of the U-C "racking" us, we rack them, etc. Talk about laughs, and fun! We're throwing a party tonite. Am an U-C in a day or so. Have open post Mon. Love, "Bob"*

This was not only a turnabout but, more importantly, it seemed like a turning point for Cadet Singleton. He was fully engaged, full of confidence, and ready to fly. Around this time the cadets were advised by their instructors that pilot slots were filling up and it was probably going to get harder to complete the program. They were warned that students in pilot training classes 43-11 and 43-12, which had graduated in November and December, suffered more wash-outs than normal. That didn't discourage Bob. He was still slated for pilot. It's why he was there.

He and some other new U-Cs celebrated by taking a weekend trip into San Antonio, where they visited Brackenridge Park and enjoyed a restaurant meal. The group consisted of barracks buddies, William Showers, Floyd W. Shultz ("Shultzie"), Donald E. Smith ("Smasher"), "Randie" Smythe, and Dick Stewart. Smasher, known also as Snuffy, occupied the lower level of Bob's bunk. Thank heavens none of them spoke with a lisp.

As the end of May approached the first part of the SAACC curriculum was drawing to a close. Only a few exams were left before the cadet corps would split up and remaining pilot candidates would advance to pre-flight school at Mustang Field in El Reno, Oklahoma. The final opportunity to blow off some steam before starting the next phase of training was Memorial Day. Bob, Shultzie, and Smasher took the opportunity to secure an overnight pass to San Antonio, where they got a room downtown at the Gunter Hotel. Bob and Smasher decided to take in a movie and dinner, but Shultzie had other plans. He was always a bit more carefree than the other guys and ostensibly not tied down to any girl back home. All the guys liked him—even if they didn't share his tastes for heavy liquor, cheap cigars, and chronic carousing. And they envied his extensive civilian flying experience. Not surprisingly, when they arrived that evening in San Antonio, the more-reserved two of the threesome took off for the movies, but Shultzie set out in search of something else.

He apparently found what he was looking for, but it was hard to tell. When Bob and Smasher returned to the hotel around midnight, Shultzie was passed out on the bed and an empty liquor bottle was on the floor. This presented a problem, not because of their sleeping arrangements, but because they were required to report back to base by morning reveille. It wasn't a pretty sight. And it took some time. Over the course of the next several hours, the sober twosome managed to get their friend into a bathtub full of cold water, back into his clothes, out of the hotel, on a bus, and back to base. With one on each flank they held him upright as they shuffled through the gate and past security. It would have been laughable if they weren't so relieved and worn out.

The next week, about 40 aspiring pilots shipped out by train to El Reno. Primary flight training at Mustang Field was a nine-and-a-half week program, but during the first few weeks they wouldn't see the inside of an airplane. The San Antonio cadets were sequenced with a group of more than 200 student pilots, which included many from other enlisted and officer training programs. They lived in clapboard barracks in the middle of a dusty field adjacent to the flight line. As usual, billets were alphabetical. Singleton, Shultz, Smith, and Smythe shared barracks with M. W. Ramsey, Frank Romanoski, Rick Sessi, Al Siddall, "Slim" Shirley, Frank Sprague, Dick Stewart, Bob Stump, Ed Stumph, "Thumper" Steumpfle, Jerry Tagliavia, and C. M. Taylor. In the beginning the program consisted of PT and classroom work focusing on aircraft systems, aerodynamics, and navigation. As the first flight approached, their anxiety and excitement increased.

Bob's group made their first visit to the flight line in early July. They toured the control tower and the flight operations center, where they were briefed on what to expect and what was expected of them. The daily schedule, laid out on a large, intimidating scheduling board behind the flight operations counter, drove everything. Each student would be assigned an instructor pilot, who in the primary training phase could just as likely be a civilian as a military man. They also got an up-close up look at the training aircraft, a Fairchild PT-19B.

PT, in this case, stands for Primary Trainer. The PT-19B Cornell was built to meet a 1939 Army Air Corps request for a new primary trainer. They wanted one that was more challenging than the old

Boeing-Stearman PT-13 Kaydet biplane trainers, which had recently been phased out. The newer design would help ease pilots' transition to higher performance fighters, like the P-47, P-51, and P-38, which at the time were still in development. The Cornell was a relatively streamlined, low-wing tail dragger with tandem open cockpits and dual flight controls. It had a wooden wing structure, a partially-fabric-covered steel-tube fuselage, and an aluminum cowling over its 175 hp Ranger L-440-3 inverted 6-cylinder inline engine. It was nearly 28 feet long and had a wingspan of over 35 feet. Nearly 8,000 PT-19 derivatives were built by Fairchild and three other companies between 1940 and 1944. Up until May 1942, they were painted in a traditional blue/yellow scheme; but, by the time Bob's class arrived at Mustang Field most of the planes were new and painted a dull silver-gray color, except for a long black-matte glare shield in front of separate front and rear windscreens. Only a few of the old blue/yellow jobs were out on the flight line. The gray PT-19 was sleek looking; it had a top speed of 124 mph. It also had a relatively high stall speed, which resulted in more difficult low-speed handling characteristics, especially for student pilots.

FLIGHT DAY FINALLY ARRIVED. The thrill of the experience would have been more memorable except for the fact that students were preoccupied with overwhelming lists of procedures that governed every phase of operations before, during, and after the flight. From day one, they were under pressure to perform to a minimum set of standards or get washed out at the whim of a check pilot on a scheduled or unannounced check ride. All things considered, Bob thrived on the challenge. His learning never got bogged down by worry about failing. He took to the air like a duck to water, pumping hard below the surface to absorb the details, but reasonably comfortable and always excited in his new surroundings.

Operations were pretty basic. They learned how to start the engine by manually spinning the prop. Main controls were throttle, stick, and rudder. Biceps made the airplane go up, triceps made it go down—something like that. Instrumentation was simple: airspeed indicator, altimeter, oil pressure gauge, and needle-ball indicator. To get oriented to the strange new cockpit environment students initially rode in the back seat, and instructors flew up front, where the visibility was better for landing. After a couple of flights they switched. Student and instructor communicated by intercom, but even with earphones held tightly against their heads by leather helmet and goggles, the crackling of the intercom and whistling of the air stream made it extremely difficult to hear. That was Bob's biggest problem.

His assigned instructor was Captain H. E. Frye. Bob was glad to have a military instructor. Some of the civilian instructors were known to carry a chip on their shoulder and occasionally take it out on their students. Bob was lucky. He found Captain Frye to be "a heck of a nice guy." Early in the program he had to apologize for not hearing all his instructor's commands over the intercom static, but Captain Frye was surprisingly understanding. After a few flights Bob was taking off and landing the airplane on his own, and he was complimented on his smooth touch downs. They flew two or three times a week. Turns got steeper and progressed to lazy eights and rolls. Stalls were practiced on every flight—with power on and power off. Soon they were learning how to enter and recover from spins.

Spins were wild. Extreme control inputs were required for entry and recovery. In a spin the landscape whizzes by in a horizontal blur. It's an unnatural maneuver. Some students couldn't handle the disorientation, and anxiety exacerbated nausea. Airsickness could ruin a flying career. If those prone to sickness couldn't get over it after a few flights, they either washed out or quit. It caused embarrassment, but never shame. Fortunately, Bob never had that problem. His skills and confidence improved with each flight. In his letters he told Norm that he was doing well and half-jokingly suggested that he was an "H.P." (hot pilot). He looked forward to his next phase of training in the faster, more powerful, all-metal basic trainer, the Vultee BT-13 Valiant, and after that the higher-performing and fighter-like AT-6 advanced trainer.

The first check ride occurred after about five hours of flight time; subsequent checks were at intervals of around ten hours. Check flights were relatively short, but every action on the ground and in the air was evaluated and graded. A typical student pilot had to pass five increasingly difficult check rides before successfully completing about 40 hours of primary flight training. Check rides were usually unannounced. Students were notified by a red tag posted next to their names on the big scheduling board. Every day four or five tags would typically be posted on the board.

Bob's first check ride was the hardest. He tensed up right from the start. Fortunately, his blood pressure settled down in time to execute a greased-on landing, and he passed. Although later check rides were tougher, they seemed more routine. Toward the end of the program, checks became more frequent. But more students were washing out, including some of Bob's good buddies, like Smasher Smith and Dick Stewart. They were now relegated to GDO status, which stood for something like general duty orders. The abbreviation was being used as a verb. What do you say to friends who GDO'd? Should a survivor feel special or just lucky? Rumors were still floating around that the Air Force needed fewer pilots.

The week after his check ride at about 34 hours into the program Bob eagerly arrived at the flight line only to find a scheduling board covered with red tags. He had never seen so much red on the board before. Nearly two-thirds of the 60 students were scheduled for check rides. His heart sank when he spotted that he was among them. It was like "writing on the wall."

His assigned check pilot was a civilian, and not a very friendly one at that. Nevertheless, he remained calm and took it one step at a time. By now he was familiar with the routine. After a perfect take off, the check pilot gave him an altitude and heading to one of the practice areas. When they arrived in the assigned area, Bob executed each maneuver after it was gruffly ordered through the crackling intercom. They started with some lazy eights and chandelles. Between each maneuver the unwelcome guest barked, "Knock it off!" Despite the tension Bob felt things were going reasonably well, although a student never really knows what the check pilot is thinking.

Soon he was directed to climb to a higher altitude and given a heading that would position them in the center of their airspace. They leveled off, and the back-seater called out for a two-and-a-half-turn spin to the right. This was a tricky maneuver, but Bob had practiced it many times. He concentrated on getting each step right: power back, stick back, full right rudder approaching the stall, then—suddenly— the nose rapidly falls off to the right, and the airplane transitions into a flat, but slightly-nose-down spin. The geography races by at about a rotation per second. He tried to remember the landmark on the horizon when the maneuver began: What was it?—the hilltop?—or that long road next to the ranch on the face of the hill? Was it the one that just whizzed by? Yes! Hurry, here it comes again off the right shoulder. Now, recover, to the practiced rhythm of "son-of-a...*bitch*!:" full-left-rudder, then, in a single, hard movement, *push* forward on the stick and kick the left rudder to the center position. Whoopee! His stomach jumped into his throat as the nose bucked over into a vertical dive. Then, as he carefully eased in back pressure with his biceps, the nose gradually came up and the airplane regained flying speed. Not too bad, he thought.

The relief was short-lived. His antennae went up when he heard the next command: "Let's take it back up and try another spin." This time the check pilot called for two-and-a-half turns to the left. And that's when Bob started to get nervous...and lose his concentration. As he quickly tried to analyze where he might have gone wrong on his first spin, he focused on the complex sequence of control inputs, and perhaps overlooked the simplest part: picking out a clear ground reference in advance of the maneuver. Bob executed the second spin, but with less confidence than the first. As they leveled off, the check pilot said the magic words: "Return to base." He never spoke again on the way back, and Bob didn't dare make any inquiries. He knew that his pull-out on the second spin had been slightly beyond two-and-a-half turns. But it was a smooth recovery. He should pass.

After a routine landing, he taxied the gray bird back to the ramp, shut it down, and climbed out. As he followed the check pilot back to the debriefing room, he thought about hauling market baskets and trying to initiate small talk. That's when the check pilot finally said the dreaded words: "Well, I'm sorrow, but I can't pass you." Bob sheepishly asked what he did wrong. He couldn't recall if the guy looked him in the eye when he said it, but he never forgot the terse response: "That last spin. You went two-and-three-quarter turns!" Those were the last words he heard from that son of a bitch.

Captain Frye was waiting outside as they walked to the operations center. He was smiling in expectation of a successful outcome, but his expression quickly changed as the stone-faced civilian approached. Bob stood back, welcoming the intervention. He could see that Captain Frye was extremely agitated. The check pilot was cornered by his instructor for several minutes until finally turning his back and walking away. Frye, looking dejected, approached Bob and apologized: "Cadet Singleton, I'm terribly sorry. This guy must have had a bad day. I tried to talk him out of it, but I can't overrule him. As far as I'm concerned, you've been doing fine. I'm awfully sorry." That was also the last Bob saw of Captain Frye.

Before that terrible day about a dozen of Bob's SAACC classmates had washed out at Mustang Field. By the end of that day, there were less than 20 left. Of Bob's friends Shultzie was the only one who made it. A competent and experienced pilot, he certainly deserved to. Shultzie acknowledged that he never would have made it without the "assistance" from Bob and Smasher, but that was a small consolation. Bob loved what he was doing and knew that he was doing well. Of course, there were some better pilots who had washed out that day. But the process seemed arbitrary and unfair. In truth, he understood that they were just unlucky victims of a bigger game plan and that overreaction was the typical Army reaction. But that didn't make it easier to accept. Bob was never so disappointed in all his life. He vowed to get back into the air someday.

The atmosphere was morbid around Mustang Field. The GDOs felt like a hopeless bunch. Bob's personnel records listed armament as one of his specialties, and the Air Force needed gunners. Thus, like a number of other guys in his situation, he was assigned to gunnery school at Sheppard Field in Wichita Falls, Texas, popularly referred to as "the asshole of the world." There wasn't much solace in news that they would report as more privileged members of the Regular Air Force and that their records would identify them as "OCS material." Bob had the lowly rank of private and he hardly felt privileged. His heart had been set on flying BT-13s at Winfield, Kansas, but instead, he was being shipped off to the asshole of the world with a bunch of sorry guys. He and Smasher often commiserated, but Bob shared his deepest feelings in daily letters to Norm. That was his outlet. Unlike some guys, he was fortunate to have a soul mate with whom he could share disappointments, as well as hopes and dreams. That, more than anything else, would ultimately see him through the war years.

A telegram sent to Norm confirmed his arrival at Wichita Falls at 7 P.M. on August 9, 1943. They reported to camp the next morning. Sheppard Field was a facility where new recruits went through basic training before being sent to gunnery school. For the Mustang Field contingent it was simply a place to camp out while awaiting orders to their next station. As such, they were supposed to be treated with a little more respect than basic trainees. Unfortunately, some of the

Sheppard NCOs didn't get the word. The contentious atmosphere this created caused it to be one of Bob's dreariest experiences in the Army.

WITH HOPES SHATTERED, Sheppard seemed worse than Berry Hill. The Mustang guys were required to participate in PT and military drills every day. None of it made any sense, including their policy on passes. Since orders to be reassigned could arrive at any time, passes to go off base were prohibited, not that Wichita Falls had much to offer. As a result, Bob's beleaguered bunch spent much of their time feeding each other's misery, which must have been plain to see. Some of them would naturally be inclined to get into trouble.

One evening Bob was in the barracks playing cards with a new acquaintance, a good-natured and somewhat reserved fellow from Quarryville, Pennsylvania. He was also at Sheppard for reassignment. His name was Carroll Baker, but to his buddies he was known as Bake. It was another typical evening at Sheppard—a miserable bunch of GIs sitting around the barracks, telling bad jokes, reading cheap books, writing gloomy letters, and playing repetitive card games. Suddenly, out of the blue, a sergeant barged into the room and roared, "Ten-HUT!" Instantly getting their attention, he continued: "Gentlemen, you've had your little joy ride. Tomorrow the entire barracks is as-signed to KP! You'll report for duty at zero-four-hundred!" At first, they thought it was a joke. Bake couldn't believe it. But, sure enough, at zero-three-thirty the next morning they were awakened and marched off to the mess hall.

Their group was turned over to the chief cook, who made the work assignments. Bob and Bake drew "pots and pans" along with a few other guys. It was one of the messier jobs. Scraping hardened fried eggs off charred metal was no picnic—it was a hot, steamy chore. But it was no worse than working at Gottselig's dairy, so Bob managed to take it in stride, as usual. Making the best of it, he tried to get Bake to laugh, but Bake was quietly fuming. The well-mannered guy from Quarryville felt that he'd done nothing to deserve this kind of treatment.

After the regular troops had breakfast that morning, the KP detail was ordered to "stop working, have some breakfast, then get their butts back to work." Bob and Bake didn't rush, knowing that they would just have to wait in a long chow line. So they kept working. The kitchen boss observed this and marched back to make sure they had gotten the word: "Gentlemen, you can take your break now. Have something to eat, then you'll feel more like working." Perhaps it was the tone of the guy's voice; but, something struck a raw nerve with Bake.

He exploded: "What! Feel more like working?! What the hell do you think we've been doing back here all morning?!" Slamming a pot down like a gantlet, he continued: "I resent that!" Bob shot a glare at Bake and grimaced, as a signal to stop. He had never heard Bake swear or lose his temper. Now he had gone too far. Bob feared they were both about to get seriously disciplined. But for whatever reason, the NCO maintained his composure, pivoted, and walked away, leaving Bake blustering and Bob sighing with relief. When they were alone again, Bob couldn't help breaking into nervous laughter. "My God, Bake," he scolded, "you could have had us both put in the brig!"

Bake didn't care. He was still roiling. "I meant what I said," he sputtered, "and don't you forget it!" Neither one of them ever would. That was Bob's most memorable event at Sheppard Field.

Guard duty was less exciting, but safer and more relaxed. In a post card to Norm he wrote:

*Hi Hon,*

*Am now on guard detail and just came off my first tour of duty. I really struck it good this time…all I do is sit in the little guard house by the railroad gate & open the gate when trains want thru (which is very seldom too!) I also have to phone in a routine report, one time during each tour of duty. I really like the job, no kiddin! I put this card in my pocket so that I could drop you a few lines…will write a letter tomorrow as usual. By the way, tomorrow, after 11 AM, I'm off for the day. Lots of Love, "Bobby"*

The post card showed a cartoon of a cowboy on one side of the Rio Grande and his donkey at the end of a rope on the other side of the river. The caption read: "I'm in Texas, but my Ass is in Mexico." Fortunately, the layover at Sheppard Field lasted for only about five weeks. The experience there was definitely not character-building, and it was clearly time to move on. Buck Private Singleton, along with Smasher Smith and a few other sad sacks, were ordered to report to the 4th Student Gunnery Squadron at Lackland Army Air Force Base in Laredo, Texas. There he would be closer to the border than he could ever have imagined.

GUNNERY SCHOOL was a month-and-a-half course, which consisted of learning everything one could possibly need to know about a fifty-caliber machine gun, firing on a gunnery range, and practicing air-to-air target shooting at the climax of the program. The .50 caliber M-2 Browning machine gun, also loosely referred to as a caliber-fifty, was the primary element of the armament system used to defend heavy bombers against fighter attacks. It fired half-inch diameter rounds at an ear-splitting rate of 700-800 per minute. The Boeing B-17 Flying Fortress, America's main strategic weapon in the European theater at the time, was equipped with 13 of these killing machines. Knowing how to operate one was serious business.

Bob didn't know the first thing about guns when he joined the Army. He had never laid his hands on a gun. Roy never kept a gun in the house. At gunnery school, not only were students taught how to fire a machine gun, but in order to graduate they had to demonstrate an ability to take apart a caliber-fifty gun and reassemble it *blindfolded*. More than a hundred component parts would be randomly spread on the floor in front of a gloved and blindfolded student: sear springs, pins, clips, barrel, etc. Most students found the challenge to be difficult and frustrating. But, for some reason, despite a lack of confidence in his mechanical skills, Bob readily developed a knack for this exercise and became one of the best blindfolded assemblers in his class. He also performed well on the firing range.

Gunnery couldn't compare to flying, but at least he was engaged in a satisfying activity. And it was more than just a game. By mid-1943 U.S. air forces in Europe were executing mass high-altitude daylight bombing raids over German territory. Aircraft losses were high, since the range of fighter escorts was limited and bombers had to rely on machine guns as their primary means of defense. Losses of air crews were even higher, requiring a steady flow of replacements. Odds were against an airman's finishing his tour, which required completing 25 combat missions. Bob and his classmates understood this and knew that they would most likely receive combat orders after completing gunnery school. Thus, despite a fascination with airplanes and flying, their feelings about the program were mixed.

As he had done so many times before, Bob went with the flow, taking a day at a time and not worrying about the future. He took his training seriously, but with no specific goals in mind. Daily letters kept him connected with a strong support structure back home. His overriding aspiration was a future with Norma, which after the disappointing SAACC experience, became even more paramount. Around this time Norm left her job at the newspaper office to work at the shoe store. With both sons in the Army Roy was short on help; thus, he was thrilled when his future daughter-in-law agreed to leave the newspaper and assume the burden of his business correspondence. In her letters Norm told Bob that she was happy working at the store.

Marriage, however, was the main topic of their correspondence. They had previously discussed the wisdom of delaying their marriage plans until after the war was over, but quickly abandoned that option. Now they were focussed on setting a wedding date and arranging to get together before that. Soon after arriving in Laredo, Bob identified the Hamilton Hotel downtown as a good place for Norm to come for a visit. It was a nice hotel, considering that there weren't many choices in Laredo. Just before the 16th of October Bob sent a lacey greeting card to recognize the first anniversary of their engagement. In it he eloquently confirmed his feelings:

> ... *You can't realize what you have done to my way of living, ever since that first nite. Honest Hon, you changed it so completely! I only then found out what "true happiness" was, and hope "will be" with me forever! As I said hundreds of times before, I think I'm the luckiest guy in the world, having you. I hope and pray that our life together, as one, will soon begin...*

Time at gunnery school passed quickly enough. Bob did well on the firing ranges in both daytime and night exercises. The real test came in air-to-air training, where students learned to fire a machine gun from the back seat of a specially-equipped AT-6 training aircraft. They were transported to the nearby base at Eagle Pass, Texas for a week of aerial training. Eagle Pass was also an advanced training school for student pilots. The smell of the dusty, oil-soaked tarmac must have evoked bittersweet memories for the GDOs.

Gunnery students flew a sortie about every other day. They sat in the gun-mounted open rear cockpit. They fired their machine gun to one side of the aircraft at a white, cylindrical target, which was towed several hundred feet behind an AT-6 or BT-13 aircraft flying parallel to the gun ship. The gun mount was installed with azimuth limits to prevent gunners from shooting the wing or tail section of their own plane. To test a gunner's ability to adjust his aim point, target speed and angle varied from pass to pass. Normally, two gunners in separate ships fired at the same target. Colored ammunition was used to distinguish between gunners. Hits were recorded, sorties were scored, and results were posted after landing. Bob's scores were satisfactory. On days when they didn't fly, students were assigned a ground duty, like loading ammunition. According to one of his post cards from Eagle Pass, Bob developed a combination of *"heat and wind burn ... esp. on face."*

The last training segment prior to final exams included firing machine guns from platform-mounted Sperry gun turrets and shooting 12-gauge shotguns at clay birds from the back of a moving truck. During the latter exercise, students fired from a standing position on a flat-bed truck, while it rumbled over a bumpy obstacle course. It was more challenging than skeet shooting, in which Bob was only an average scorer. But, from the back of the truck, he was one of the best, typically hitting 18 or 19 out of 20 targets. "Now, you figure that!" he would exclaim.

COME GRADUATION DAY, Bob not only graduated, but he finished second in his class. As one of the top graduates, he was given the opportunity to take an assignment as a gunnery instructor, which would allow him to remain on base for a year-long tour. It was a deal that he didn't have to think long or hard about. This would enable him to get married and remain stateside for a year. The war might be over after that. While not wanting to appear overly enthused, he accepted the offer. He couldn't wait to tell Norm.

Needless to say, Norm was overjoyed. The fact that he got promoted to PFC (private, first class) was no big deal. The icing on the cake was the part which required him to attend gunnery instructor school for a month in Florida—the perfect place to rendezvous with Norm and plan for the wedding! The orders read: "Flight Gunnery School (C.I.S.) 1178th FGTS, BAAF Ft Myers." The Central Instructor School was located at Buckingham Field, just outside of town. He immediately began making plans to meet Norm in Fort Myers.

He bid farewell to Smasher and his other buddies, who were on their way to bomber crew training at various places in the states. Then he departed on his own journey, a sweltering three-day trip by troop train across the deep South. On November 12th PFC Singleton finally arrived at Buckingham Field, and within a few days he sent a telegram to Norm confirming that he had made hotel arrangements for her visit to beautiful Fort Myers.

Since they were not yet married, Bob's mother would come along as chaperone. That took some doing, because Ivy had never traveled outside of her state without Roy, let alone on a thousand-mile journey from Pennsylvania to Florida. But, Bob's best friend worked behind the scenes to make it all happen. In one of his weekly letters Roy told his son that, if Norm's parents could not accompany her—he surmised that conservative Mart wouldn't want to spend the money— he would convince Ivy to go along. He would also see to it that Norm got the needed time off from work. Of course, Norm didn't need any convincing or advance notice. It had been eight months since she had seen her hubby-to-be.

The trip to Florida was a great adventure for both women. In those days trains were extremely crowded with military troops, and traveling conditions were less than comfortable. They would have to sleep upright if they managed to get a seat at all—a technique that Norm and Ivy perfected after the first few stops. Norm would politely say, so as to be overheard, "Mother, are you getting tired?" Then, some good soul would usually give up his seat to the heavyset lady, and most of the time Norm would get an adjacent seat. The little scam seemed out-of-character for two nonassertive women from Lancaster. They would forever giggle about their boldness on that trip.

The pair arrived for a week's visit on Saturday, November 20th. A taxi delivered them to the Bradford Hotel in downtown Fort Myers, which at the time wasn't much of a town. But, the hotel was the best in town. Their room, which Bob reserved for five dollars a night, was set up with a double bed for the women and a cot for him. It was better than Jersey shore accommodations. Bob arranged passes to spend two weekends in town and make visits on weekday evenings.

It was a wonderful eight days. They spent a lot of time relaxing in the sun and enjoying soft drinks from the beach concession. Ivy did not hesitate to pour her full figure into an extra large bathing suit and join the kids on the beach. She enjoyed listening to music on the radio, especially a popular tune of the time that was played over and over, "How Much is that Doggie in the Window."[1] The girls mainly went shopping when Bob was on base. When he phoned to check in on them, it seemed like they were never at the hotel. They were usually out buying gifts—loads of gifts—including some that Bob would send home to relatives for Christmas. He was glad that Norm had company, and pleased to have his mom there as well. Ivy was having the time of her life and happy to give the kids the space they needed. There was always plenty to laugh about.

Bob wasn't sure if he could get off base at the time they were scheduled to depart for the train station. He told them that, if he didn't get there in time to see them off, they should leave, and he would know they were on their way. As expected, he didn't make it on time; the women had already checked out. He was only a little disappointed; an extended goodbye would have just been more difficult. Returning to base, he smiled to himself as he visualized the two of them "loaded down like a bunch of gypsies," maneuvering for seats on the train, and singing that stupid doggie song. He missed them already.

Final exams at instructor school were on December 12th. It was three waves of testing: morning, afternoon, and evening. The next day Bob was informed that he had passed and received orders to return to regular duty as a gunnery instructor assigned to "Headquarters Squadron, 2nd Flight Gunnery Training School, Lackland AAF, Laredo." On December 15th he instructed Norm by telegram to stop sending mail to Fort Myers. He traveled for four days with stopovers at Montgomery, New Orleans, and San Antonio, confirmed by post cards sent from each stop. On December 21st he arrived in time to spend a lonely and dusty Christmas away from home —with plenty of quiet time to write letters.

At least he "felt like a person again" at Laredo. He was no longer a sad sack at the bottom of the pecking order. He was now a Gunnery Instructor in the Regular Army. He knew his business well and could tell right away that he was treated with more respect. Every few weeks a new group of students would pass through, and many of the students outranked him. Nevertheless, in class he was the boss, and it was his responsibility to make sure each student measured up. The Army made it clear that they didn't want to send any gunner into combat who was not fully qualified. Bob took his responsibility seriously.

Since Mustang Field, this tour of duty was Bob's most satisfying in the Army. The weather was pleasant, if not warm; in Laredo summer weather arrives in February. He worked long hours, but found time to enjoy himself with new friends, like PFC "Shorty" Otterman. Outside activities included playing softball, going to late movies, and making trips across the Mexican border to see the bull fights. He admitted to becoming a "runny-gate" in one of his post cards to his fiancée. But during his trips off base he was also checking out places where he and Norm could set up household after they got married. One of his more colorful post cards showed a streetscape of Laredo, "population 41,200;" the adjacent Rio Grande River; and Nuevo Laredo, "population 19,406."

The marriage was tentatively set for March 26, 1944. When PFC Singleton passed his one-year service anniversary in early March, he was double-promoted to buck sergeant and added two more stripes to his chevron. He would look sharp at the wedding.

# CHAPTER 6

# ZARAGUZIE STREET

SETTING A DATE FOR THE WEDDING was not all that simple. Bob was eligible for some leave, but it was hard to pin down a date that could be guaranteed. The nation was at war. Although he was stationed behind the lines, his assignment was considered critical. Gunnery school schedules were subject to change, and members of the training staff could be called up at any time as operational replacements. At home, his family preferred to have the wedding on a Sunday so as not to conflict with shoe store hours. In the end, everybody agreed to mark their calendars for Sunday, March 26th, even though timing would be uncertain until the last minute.

Bob admitted that Norm was the one who did all the worrying for both of them. She carried "ninety percent" of the burden of planning and making arrangements for the wedding. Vi and Ivy were involved, but Norm did most of the work and all of the worrying. Her job was complicated by the fact that it was wartime. Many of their close friends were in the service and far away from home. Ed and Mollie had arranged a last minute wedding in Colorado, where Ed was stationed before being shipped off to the Pacific. Mollie would stay there until he departed. Norm had to recruit her wedding party from other Lancaster relatives. Besides that, she was worried that her conservative parents would be reluctant to pick up the tab for what they might see as an extravagant reception. She insisted on helping to pay for an appropriately tasteful event, but her concerns were hardly justified. Mart and Vi felt nothing but affection for Norm and Bob. They would do their best to make it nice. Norm was just a worrier.

As fate would have it, when the third week of March rolled around, Bob's leave was put on a temporary hold. He didn't have the nerve to share this news, optimistic that his situation would change, which somehow it did. He sent a wire to Norm informing her that he would be a little later than originally scheduled then ended up arriving the night before the wedding with less than a week before having to report back to Lackland. When he got there it was obvious that Norm had been worried and upset, but his close call would be forgiven. The wheels were in motion, and nothing could get in their way.

They were married at First Methodist Church. The glowing bride was adorned in a long, flowing gown, and the groom was braced in his dress uniform. It was a mid-size wedding—mostly a family affair—having a typical wartime flavor, marked not only by the groom's uniform, but also by the noticeable absence of some close friends and relatives: siblings Ed and Mollie; Becky's husband Frank Powl, who was an AAF ordnance officer stationed near Bedford *England; and Clayt Sweigart, who was somewhere in Europe with Patton's army. Mart gave away the bride, and Roy served as best man. Becky was maid of honor. She was disappointed that her hubby, known as Butch, couldn't be there, not just for the wedding, but also to see their new baby daughter Diane, who was born after he left for England. Bob had a chance to hold baby Dee in Butch's absence.

Other bridesmaids were Norm's cousin Glo Sweigart, sister-in-law Marian Medsger, and childhood friend Gladys Swanson, the married daughter of John and Julia Zell. The Zells were Diffenbachs' good friends from Philadelphia. For years John and Jule regularly traveled by train from Philly to Gordonville, to purchase their meats at Hiram Troop's butcher shop, located next to the train station. Vi Troop, who worked at her father's shop, took a liking to the Zells, and their friendship survived long after her marriage to Martin Diffenbach.

Ushers were Sis's husband Harry Medsger, an industrial engineer with a draft deferment; Bill Feller, a draft-exempt utility company engineer married to one of Norm's old newspaper office friends; Clair Shenk; and Clair Hershey. The two Clairs, coincidentally of the same name, were married to Norm's cousins, Dot and Becky Mellinger.[1] They had avoided military service due to their wartime occupations or possibly their status as conscientious objectors. Both were devout Mennonites who in later years served as lay ministers in their church.

A conservative, but tasteful reception was held at the Iris Club, a beautiful Victorian mansion on the opposite side of Duke Street that served as a clubhouse for a sophisticated ladies' organization. Harry drove the couple from the Iris Club directly to the train station, where they would depart for a two-day honeymoon in New York City. They didn't have the time or money to go much farther. Typical of most newlyweds, they tried to remain inconspicuous. They would feign the repose of a typical military couple, loaded with bags and connecting by train. The only possible giveaway was the elaborately wrapped gift that Harry had given them with instructions not to open until reaching their destination. The gift was an alarm clock; and, just as Harry had planned it, the alarm went off while they were on the train. So much for being inconspicuous. It seemed like all eyes were on them.

They blended into the crowds when they got off the train at Penn Station in New York, although the masses of people and scale of things were somewhat intimidating. It was Norm's first trip to the big city, and Bob had been there only once at a shoe show with Roy. Their taxi followed a slalom course through fumes, noise, and mayhem to the Pennsylvania Hotel, where, thankfully, Bob had secured advance reservations, confirmed by mail. As they walked into the hotel lobby, they were confronted with long lines of restless GIs waiting to check in, a common sight in those days. New York harbor was the principal embarkation point for soldiers going to Europe. Temporarily stationed at nearby bases, they scrambled into the city on overnight passes in last ditch efforts to enjoy themselves or drown their sorrows.

Sergeant Singleton jumped into line with his confirmation slip in hand, and Norm patiently waited until he returned with a bellhop. On the packed elevator, no sooner had they begun to think about their imminent bliss than the bellhop nonchalantly turned around, held out their room key, and pointed out that their room was only a single. "What about it?" he asked. The thought of getting back into that registration line and the possibility of coming up empty-handed made Bob see red. Norm initially turned red; what were people thinking? But, like a woman on a mission, she resolved the problem, sweetly asking the bell man if he would allow them to first inspect the room. He did, and of course, it would do. While their honeymoon was short, it was cozy. They saw a little of the big city the next day and returned to Lancaster on Tuesday.

BOB LEFT FOR LAREDO on Wednesday. Norm would join him a week later. They timed it so that he would arrive a day before his scheduled reporting time. The extra day would be used to seek suitable off-base living quarters, which was not an easy task in this border town. Decent housing for military wives was scarce-to-practically-nonexistent. The Hamilton was the only hotel in town, and their wartime policy limited stays to three nights. Non-permanent-party military personnel were confined to base at night and plainly discouraged from bringing their wives with them. Try to explain this to newly married twenty-one-year-olds! Few followed the rules.

It took Bob longer than he expected to find housing. For nearly a week he searched Laredo streets after regular duty hours. The best he could find was a ramshackle apartment on 719 Zaragoza Street, a dirt road which ran parallel to the Rio Grande. The back yard stretched to the river, if one could call it that. The illustrious waterway appeared to be less than knee-deep at its center. Customs officials could be seen patrolling its sun-dried banks looking for wetbacks. The dusty street, clapboard apartment building, and littered back yard were virtually out of a scene from *The Grapes of Wrath*. That didn't bother Bob. A single room on the second floor was where they'd make their little nest. He couldn't afford more, anyway. Four bucks a week was half his pay.

Norm had an enjoyable trip. Despite hot, smelly conditions on the crowded trains, time flew by quickly. She was excited about her new life. On the train she met and became friends with another young military wife named Gwen Parsons, who was toting a tiny baby. They leveraged their profile to obtain the best seats. Norm felt like a veteran traveler by now. In St. Louis they went their separate ways, but Norm would forever speak fondly of Gwen and her baby, and they would faithfully exchange cards, photos, and letters for the rest of their lives. Norm couldn't stop chattering about Gwen and the baby when Bob met her at Laredo station.

She got noticeably quiet, however, when they pulled up to the apartment on Zaragoza Street. The rickety, wooden building had no exterior doors, so the center hallway featured a view of the crusty back yard and river beyond. It contained four apartments, two on each floor, separated by a common hallway. Each floor had a bathroom for use by its residents. A door at the end of the second-floor hallway led to a balcony overlooking the river. Their tiny one-room apartment had a tall wooden bed with ornately carved posts, a rocking chair, a straight chair, a little table, and a cubby hole that served as a kitchen. It was equipped with a steel sink and hot plate. Her first impression was that the kitchen looked like a broom closet and the bed looked like an "ark." Not exactly what she had dreamed about.

Of course, she would try to make the best of it. Norm was never one to complain. Their neighbors were also military types. Across the hall lived Bill and Jean Butts, farm people from Wichita, Kansas. They were nice people, but definitely from the farm. Bill was a mechanic assigned to Laredo AAF base as permanent party. He and Jean seemed to live on a diet of cornpone and milk. Bob called it "mush and milk;" he couldn't understand how they ate the stuff. Jean left their food uncovered in the ice box and graciously welcomed reluctant Norma to share in any of it. Not a chance. Norm's preparations were covered and labeled. She could tolerate sharing bathroom facilities, but co-mingling in the ice box went too far for a Lancaster girl. Bob knew how much she hated that. Frank and Margie Hall lived downstairs. They were nice people from a strange sounding town in Kansas called Olathe, with the letter *e* pronounced as an *a*. The other occupants of the building had six legs. Monstrous cockroaches. Norm tried her best to maintain a sense of humor about it. She always joked that she could hear them at night sneaking around "on stilts" but secretly prayed they would keep out of the ark.

Bob was permitted off base only three nights a week on passes. But it didn't take long to figure out how to circumvent this restriction. Love is a great motivator. Bill Butts owned a convertible with a rumble seat, which he used to commute to base every day. He offered to smuggle Bob through the gate if his stowaway could find somebody to vouch for him during nightly bed checks. No problem. It was easy to enlist somebody to conjure up an excuse for an empty bunk when the CQ (charge of quarters) passed through. His barracks ally would typically hang a towel over the edge of the unoccupied bunk, indicating that the missing body was in the shower, or would concoct some other little fib. It wasn't hard to get away with.

Bill had an earlier morning start time than Bob, so getting back to base by reporting time was also not a problem. A few blocks before reaching the main gate Bill would signal a heads up. Bob would then move to the back seat, squeeze down on the floor of the rumble seat, and pull the seat back down over himself. From this cramped hiding place he could get a glimpse of the MP's hand reaching for Bill's ID card when they stopped at the gate. At Bill's request Bob usually held his breath during this procedure. They both could get into serious trouble if his presence was detected. Fortunately, they had only a few close calls, once when the MP detained Bill longer than usual with routine questions. Bob broke into a sweat that time. Afterwards, they laughed about their little ruse in front of the wives. Bill, the jokester, usually exaggerated the story. But Norm didn't laugh. Unlike Bob, she worried a lot.

Bob would always remember the time Bill suggested they play a little joke on Norm. Bill would show up at Zaragoza Street without his regular passenger and tell Norm that her hubby got caught at the gate and was thrown in the brig. Knowing how Norm worried, Bob knew it would be a dirty trick, but decided to go along with the fun. When they parked at their apartments, Bob hid in the car while Bill climbed the stairs to break the news. From his usual hiding place Bob could hear Norm's shocked reaction; she swallowed the story, hook, line, and sinker! He rushed upstairs in an attempt to spare her more despair. When he got there Bill was already walking away, grinning. Teary-eyed Norm spotted Bob and reacted with surprise and relief, but there was no humor in it. It was the first time he saw her get mad. In the process of preparing supper, she was holding a frying pan; and, before he knew what hit him, Bam! He was smacked in the gut with the flat side of the pan. He never forgot it. Neither did Norm. But they would always put a slightly different spin on this episode. Of course, Bob blamed it on Bill, who constantly kidded him about it: "You really got the frying pan that time, didn't you Bob?"

Nobody could say that Norm wasn't a good sport. She made the best of difficult circumstances. Lack of normal cooking appliances didn't discourage her from trying to bake a cake soon after they moved in. Her first attempt was a flop, but she didn't give up. She indignantly threw the burnt oversized cookie over the balcony rail and down to the river bank dogs. On a more typical day she walked to a grocery store in town called the Jitney Jingle, where the produce was reasonably fresh—not like Mettfett's, but good by Texas standards. Then she returned to Zaragoza Street to prepare a home cooked meal for her new hubby. Occasionally, by herself or with Jean, she walked into town to relax in the peaceful shaded park next to the Hamilton Hotel, where she would sit on her favorite bench and write letters.

BOB WAS GENERALLY SATISFIED with his work at Lackland. He wasn't involved in aerial training, but he was a fully qualified gunnery instructor in the classroom and on the range. Army standards were rigid, and he had a strict curriculum to follow. He often compared notes with fellow instructors in an effort to improve his teaching techniques. He taught his students how to take apart and assemble the caliber-fifty blindfolded. He was conscientious, and his students succeeded. He proudly recalls having to hold back only one student.

Once weekly during the three-week course, students were taken by their instructors to the firing range, normally in groups of four. The range was about 500 yards long. Everybody in the area was required to wear ear plugs as protection from the relentless, piercing noise generated by the machine guns. Assigned shooters were positioned at gun mounts while those waiting for a turn stood back. Firing sequences lasted 10-15 minutes, followed by breaks of silence and a rotation of shooters. During breaks the guys generally milled around, chewing the fat or drinking coffee, while targets were collected and replaced. One day during a break, Bob was resting next to a gun mount with his ear plugs removed, and a sadly misguided student, for whatever reason, felt like firing off a few rounds. Unfortunately, the gun barrel was only a few feet behind Bob's head, and the shocking concussion practically caused him to lose his footing. Needless to say, he screamed bloody murder at the student. The dumbstruck delinquent apologized, but it was too late. The damage was done. From that day on Bob suffered from a constant ringing in his left ear. Even at the quietest times of the day or night he would never again experience complete silence. But he made up his mind that he would learn to live with the condition, which others would find intolerable. True to form, he put aside feelings of self-pity and moved on.

On weekends he and Norm regularly managed to get away. Once they took a bus tour to Las Cruces. Frequently, they went shopping in town or across the border—usually doing more looking than buying. Twice they went to the bull fights. Seats cost the equivalent of about two dollars on the shady side of the ring and a dollar on the sunny side. Norm preferred the shade, but they couldn't afford the extra two bucks. That was nearly a quarter of a week's pay. It didn't make much difference anyway. On the second visit their seats were near where the dead bulls were dragged out of the ring. The odor was so repulsive that Norm had to leave early.

During their stint at Laredo they developed a circle of friends and joined in social gatherings with other enlisted folks. Most were in Bob's group of eight gunnery instructors. They were from all over the country. A guy from Georgia nicknamed Peaches and his wife invited Norm and Bob to their house. Another time they were invited to a barbecue at a local ranch. Norm brought some of her Pennsylvania

Dutch potato salad, which everybody raved about. They met a lot of nice people, although lasting relationships would not be developed. Despite their address, Norm and Bob had a tendency to feel that they "lived better" than most of the people they met.

Without question they were young, in love, hopeful, and truly happy. Their Laredo apartment became fondly known as "Zaraguzie" Street. For years it was like a private code word for shared memories of an extended honeymoon, a life filled with promise, and the unfailing power of love and simple humor to overcome temporary discomfort and minor inconvenience. As miserable as the place was, their eyes would always sparkle when they talked about Zaraguzie Street. Their time there seemed to pass so quickly.

Bob knew that his instructor job was not a long term assignment, but he was hopeful that the war would be over by the time his tour was up. Following the D-Day invasion in June 1944 an end to the war looked to be a real possibility. But that was too much to hope for. By September General Eisenhower announced that the war in Germany was about to begin, and he cautioned U.S. citizens that families should expect GIs to be reassigned to the Pacific after the war in Europe was won.[2] During their regular staff briefings, Bob began hearing talk about his group being shipped overseas. Sure enough, it was only a few weeks before they received marching orders.

Sergeant Singleton's military occupational specialty was "MOS 938: Gunnery Instructor." He knew this would define the nature of his job overseas but had no idea where he would be stationed. Assignments for gunnery instructors were administered by the Central Instructor School at Buckingham Field. The latest series of assignments were classified as "projects," which were designed to set up gunnery schools at the overseas air bases. It was becoming apparent that gunnery instructors were needed in the field to provide refresher training and improve substandard shooting performance of air crews. Their orders were to report to Camp Kilmer, New Jersey; thus, they surmised that they would be embarking for Europe. But their destination would not be disclosed. Orders were issued to pack their gear and be ready to ship out on October 15th.

Norm was obviously unhappy about this turn of events, but her attention now had to be focused on the flurry of activity involved in packing and planning. While she wasn't allowed to accompany her husband overseas, nothing could stop her from following him to the embarkation point, while they sought every opportunity along the way to spend their precious remaining time together. It was not uncommon for military wives to follow their husbands on troop trains, which shared the same route structure and often hooked up with commercial trains going in the same direction. Those who could afford would try to reserve a Pullman berth for their wives. But most couples, including Bob and Norm, weren't flush enough for that. They were thrilled just knowing that their trains would be connected on the first leg of the journey from Laredo. It was uncertain whether they would remain connected after the first leg, which ended in New Orleans. Army folks became accustomed to "taking one stop at a time."

A couple dozen GIs, some with wives, gathered at Laredo station. Bob and Norm mostly stuck with three other couples, which included friends Dick and Tommie Stewart and Jack and Lois Wilson. Dick was a laid back but solid guy of good character; Jack was a nice guy, but a bit of a complainer. They were less familiar with the third couple, a know-it-all braggart and his wife, who was carrying an infant and clung to the two girls who constantly raved about her baby. When their train arrived the wives climbed into the civilian cars, and the GIs crammed with gear into the troop cars. After leaving the station, the married guys would hustle back to visit their wives or meet them between—a typical routine for military couples. Later in the day, the officer in charge of troop movements advised the group that there would be an overnight layover in New Orleans, and, aware that wives were tagging along, said that troops could get off the train as long as they reported back by eight in the morning. He made it very clear that, if there was any question about making it back by "oh-eight hundred," they should remain on board. He had to be kidding; this was New Orleans. Bob and Dick had spent the last part of the journey scurrying back and forth between cars and conductors, trying to find out if the civilian cars would remain attached on the following day. They felt compelled to have this information, which was crucial in planning these precious few days with their wives before an indefinite separation. The best they could determine was that, in all probability, they would remain together. "Both trains were heading north," they were told.

Bob was a stickler for being on time. Thus, he was concerned about not having an alarm clock when they went into New Orleans. He'd had enough close calls in the morning. His first inclination was to play it safe: go into town and return that evening. Stewart felt the same way. But the other guy pressed for staying in town, so they agreed to go and decide later. Six of them, plus baby, got off the train, crammed into a taxi, and headed for town. On the way in they explained their tight schedule to the cabbie, who, on the promise of an overblown tip from the big talker, agreed to pick them up in the morning and get them back to the train on time. He even recommended a convenient place to sleep: "Mrs. Kelly's" boarding house. He said that it wasn't as plush as the downtown hotels, but it was near the train station. He would take them there to see if three rooms were available.

Mrs. Kelly's was a three story clapboard house in a residential section of town. Their driver sauntered inside to check on vacancies. He probably had some kind of arrangement with Mrs. Kelly. An old lady waddled outside, ushered them in, and took their names. Norm and Bob had to climb two sets of stairs to reach their assigned room on the third floor. They were used to living in the penthouse. This one had only a bed and a wash basin. The bathroom was shared, as usual. They'd seen worse, but Bob studied Norm's expression. Of course, she said it was fine, but he knew what she was thinking. He made light of it with his often used expression: "Well, it's only one night; we're not buying the place...." And it's dirt cheap, he added to himself. At that point his main concern was the reliability of the taxi driver's promise to be there in the morning.

With such a low room rate they decided that a lavish night on the town was an option, so one of the guys ordered a different cabbie, who would be relied upon to make a dining recommendation. They were dropped off at the Roosevelt Hotel, a real swanky looking place. Bob thought it looked like the Ritz Carlton, a place he had seen in pictures. While the others basked in the glittering opulence of the lobby, the Lancaster couple discreetly reviewed prices on the menu posted outside the dining room. She whispered that it was too expensive, but he mentally counted the cash in his wallet and suggested that, under the circumstances, they should splurge. The others agreed, forcing the big talker to put his money where his mouth was.

It was marvelous. Facilitated by a tip to the maître de they were seated at a large, round table in a majestic hall with crystal chandeliers, expensive-looking china, and white linen table cloths. They felt like big deals. A small jazz combo and singer entertained them throughout the evening. Over dessert Norm excitedly whispered that the famous actor Van Hefflin was seated nearby with his back to Bob. Too late they spotted the celebrity signing a few autographs on his way out. After dinner they took a little stroll, but opted out of a visit to the French Quarter. Most of them didn't drink, one couple had a cranky baby, and it seemed like an good time to downshift to reality. They were back at Mrs. Kelly's by 10 o'clock, and it was morning before they realized it. They didn't get much sleep, not because of the accommodations, but mainly due to worrying about whether the cabbie would show up.

The next morning they rose early and grabbed coffee and donuts at a stand-up place within walking distance. Bob would rather have waited to eat after they were securely back on the train. He felt that they were cutting it close. But amazingly, the cabbie showed up at the agreed time and hustled them to the station. The good news was that they made it back by 0800. The disappointing news was that troop and civilian cars were scheduled to go separate ways when they reached the next stop in Greensboro, North Carolina.

After a short layover in Greensboro, Bob would continue to Camp Kilmer in Brunswick, New Jersey, and Norm would return to Lancaster on a different train. Bob promised that he would phone her when he arrived in Camp Kilmer and would try to arrange for a rendezvous in New York City. Norm could barely speak. She had always understood that parting was a possibility; they had talked at length about the eventuality. She had agreed that, when the day came, she would be a "good scout." But she was never really prepared for it. It just didn't seem right. Their future suddenly seemed uncertain. She would have given anything to return to Zaraguzie Street. So would he.

CAMP KILMER in New Brunswick, New Jersey, served as the main embarkation point for troops headed to the European Theater of Operations (ETO). Hordes of GIs processed through this facility to receive immunizations, equipment, and information needed to operate in an overseas combat zone. Bob spent his first evening sewing stripes on new winter uniforms. Jack Wilson and Woodie Wehrkemp, part of the group from Laredo, were assigned to KP duty. Luckily, Bob was exempt from that, because he was part of a CIS project team, which had more seniority than regular gunners in the Army's sacrosanct pecking order. But like the others, he would have to attend refresher courses on aircraft identification and Morse code. There were also classes on security and censorship procedures, which would impact the way all correspondence was written from then on. One would think that dealing with huge masses of transient soldiers would be a difficult logistics challenge. The hurry-up-and-wait routine was expected. However, the process was surprisingly well organized, and restless GIs were kept busy during their indefinite, but brief stay. Because troops could be mobilized on short notice, liberty passes were heavily regulated. They had to be managed carefully, as Camp Kilmer was only an hour's bus ride from New York City.

A little regulation never suppressed a GI's determination to take care of personal business. More often than not, depending on embarkation timetables, passes could be obtained to leave base after duty hours. Overnight passes were occasionally issued, but when they were, the runny-gates had strict orders to report back by 0800. It wasn't long before Bob was on a bus headed through the Lincoln Tunnel and pounding the pavements looking for an affordable, side-street hotel for Norm. When asked how many nights he wanted to reserve, Sergeant Singleton anxiously confessed that it could be "anywhere from two to four nights, maybe even a week," to which one desk clerk replied with a smile: "You must be getting ready to ship out, soldier."

"Yes, Sir," Bob answered.

The clerk understood the situation. He was used to accommodating GIs. Civilians always seemed to go out of their way to help military guys. But then, it wasn't bad for business, either.

Norm was on a train the next day. She arrived at Penn Station early Thursday afternoon and asked the cab driver to take her to the Roxy Hotel, as Bob had instructed her by pay phone. Bob told her that he couldn't make it to the city until around 6:30, but not to worry—he would be there. She was waiting in the lobby with a big smile on her face when he got there. Bob's pass was not for overnight, but they made the most of their short time together. They were thrilled that he had managed to finagle two overnight passes for that weekend. For some reason, troops generally did not ship out on weekends; perhaps the dock workers had something to do with that.

In their last days before his departure Bob did his best to relieve Norm's anxiety about his overseas assignment. He couldn't divulge his destination, even if he knew it. But he was at ease about his situation. He knew that his assignment would be involved in setting up a gunnery school, even though he didn't have a clue whether it would be in Italy, England, or elsewhere. He facetiously told Norm that, as a "project guy," he would have "first-class" travel accommodations and half-believed there was some truth to this claim. He had been led to believe that, as an NCO on a CIS project assignment, he would be treated better than average. The frustrating part was not knowing when they would be shipped out. He told Norm that he could leave on a moment's notice and would have no way to notify her from base. And information on all troop movements was censored from soldiers' correspondence. "Loose lips sink ships," they were told. He advised her that if he didn't show up at the hotel at the usual time, she should assume that he's departed and take a morning train home. She already had a train schedule and a return ticket to Lancaster.

On Monday evening he didn't show up at the regular time, but Norm received with mixed feelings a good-bye call from a pay phone outside the Camp Kilmer security gate. As planned, she checked out the next morning and took a train home. She would not hear from him until later that week. His letter showed a new return address, "Sqd. B-1 A.A.F., A.P.O. 1626-B, c/o Postmaster, New York, N.Y." and was stamped "Passed by U.S. Army Examiner 47105." Its contents and tone revealed his newly acquired sensitivity to the censorship process:

*Oct. 23rd*
*7 P.M.*

*Dear wife,*

*Don't have too much to write about, so will use this air mail form you gave me. It'll come in handy for such occasions, so I will be able to use them. Too bad I can't write the long letters I used to, but you know how it is? Under the circumstances I know you understand. Each time I write, I can at least make a little love to you anyhow, can't I...that'll make the letter a little longer anyway. Right? I'm still leading a rather easy life, and do have a lot of time to myself. Too bad army life couldn't always be this way...but then why an army at all, huh? I can dream though can't I? Ha! Ha! Our group is still all together, and as I said before, I think I am fortunate to be where I am...that is, if I had to make the move I am about to. We sure seem to get the best of everything, and I see it more each day. Later on I'll tell another of our "first class" priorities. This one I sure didn't expect.*

*Well Hon, what time did you arrive home? I was wondering about you all day. I'm sure glad I got the chance to call you last nite, cause I did so much want to give you "good bye," and at the same time, I know it put you more at ease to know just what was what. I hope you're feeling much better on arriving home this time than last, and that everything is now O.K. Please let me know when you write. Will close now honey, so till later, remember I'm thinking of you always, and please don't worry, as I'll be O.K. ...loving you more than any other person could ever hope to, Your Hubby, "Bob"*

He didn't know it yet, but her response would not come until after Thanksgiving, the next time he would receive mail. As millions of others before him, he would soon find out what it's like not to be in the state-side army. By early October the mailing of Christmas gifts to military personnel overseas had already reached a peak at the Lancaster city post office.[3]

As he had probably divulged to her on the phone outside the gate, his group would ship out the next morning. To where he didn't know. She should not expect to hear from him until after what he guessed would be a "nine- or ten-day trip." He would not hear from her until his first overseas mail call. But he carried her loving thoughts in a tiny pocket edition of the New Testament, enclosed in a silver case. It was a surprise gift that he discovered in his shaving kit on the night he checked into Camp Kilmer. Inside the front cover in her beautiful handwriting was the following inscription:

*Darling,*

*May God protect you and keep you safe from all harm.*
*Please bring him back to me dear God...my husband.*

*Your first love,*
*Your Wife*

# CHAPTER 7

# GREAT YOHO

EVERYTHING THEY OWNED, including newly issued woolen underwear, steel helmet, and equipment required for overseas combat duty, was either worn or packed into one of two bulky duffel bags that each soldier lugged with him. Like hundreds of thousands of GIs before them, they were hauled by trucks to the docks of New York harbor and delivered to what was called a liberty ship. A typical liberty ship was a converted passenger liner that was leased to an allied government, like the French, to transport troops and cargo. It was well known in advance by troops going overseas that living conditions on these previously luxury liners were nearly unbearable. More often than not, thousands of soldiers would be crammed together so tightly that officers had to sleep in rope hammocks hung four-high, enabling several dozen men to be squeezed into a stateroom designed for two; and enlisted troops had to compete for deck or hallway space when they weren't sleeping in shifts below decks or hanging over the ship's rails purging food that was unfit to eat. It was often impossible to make it to the rails in time, further contributing to the fetid atmosphere on liberty ships.

Bob's group was told that conditions would be different for them, but they had heard all the horror stories and were naturally quite skeptical. So, after a surprisingly civilized first day on the water, they began to believe that it just might be different. This was apparent in Bob's first shipboard letter to Norm. The header read "*October 25th, 5 P.M., Somewhere on the Atlantic?*" and the letter went on as follows:

> *Dear Normie,*
>
> *How long it'll be till you get this letter is hard to say, as you can readily see where I'm at just now, and we can mail no letters until we hit port. That will be for a while yet, too, so it may be quite a while before you get this…I only hope the delay didn't have you wondering or worrying about me. I told you to expect that though, so maybe that did help some,*

*huh? I sure do hope so! From now on, I think the delays shouldn't be so
long...wouldn't see why, anyway, but of course one never can predict that,
either? Let's hope not, anyhow! Before writing any further, Honey, how
are you? Please let me know each time you write, as that's what I'm most
interested in. I wonder about you all the time? Also, please don't worry,
and keep your chin up as everything is going to be O.K.*

*Incidentally, I'm still restricted as to what I can, and can not say,
about my trip, so don't wonder why I don't mention too much about it. If
I could, I know you wouldn't worry...in fact, if I were to tell you all I
could, maybe you wouldn't believe me anyway. I know I didn't when it
was first told to me, but since it's proven out right, how can I doubt it?
What I'm trying to say is, "we're still getting those 'first class' priorities,"
if you know what I mean? We hit the "gravy" again, Hon, and I'm not
kiddin! Our good fortune has sure been holding up...just so it continues.
I guess it can't be all peaches and cream though, but a guy can hope anyhow, can't he? I'm on the water now just about one day, and by this time
I feel like an "ole experienced voyager"...probably don't look it though,
by a long shot. From all indications I think I'll enjoy my trip quite a bit,
considering the seriousness behind it. I hope you and I might be able to
take one together sometime. How about it, Hon? O.K.? I'm not hangin'
out over the rail yet, anyway. Never can tell though?*

*Our gang is still all together, and, in fact "exclusive," if I may use
that word. I mean it to the fullest extent too, Hon, and no joking. I don't
mean it like some of the others may...remember? I'm actually serious
when I say that! The only detail we pull on this trip is one 6-hr. tour of
guard duty, which just means walking the deck every once in a while, to
see that our boys are in line as they should be...this only at nite. I think
I'm on tonite from 7 till 1. Between times you do whatever you want...
read, write, etc. We pull no K.P. at all, and by the way, we eat 3½
meals a day...the ½ meal is our "tea time" at 4 in the afternoon. Don't
laugh, Honey, 'cause really I mean just that...we couldn't believe it at
first either, but now just accept it as daily routine. What we, too, thought
just a joke, has back-fired...we see it, do it, now believe it! As we all
say...just the thing for "picked men" Remember? Ha! Ha! Our meals
and quarters are average. Had porridge for breakfast, and rather liked it
(the first time I've eaten it). For dinner we had fish, liver & potatoes, and
rhubarb for dessert. That big home-made bread and tea with all meals.
Didn't eat supper yet but will shortly. We're quartered in separate state-
rooms, 4 in each, with two wash stands in each room. Who said I*

*couldn't afford a pleasure cruise. Oh yeah! About all I've been doing so far is reading, playing cards, and roaming the deck with some of the gang…mainly Jack. For a while we were playing a game of darts. The Red Cross has furnished us quite a few things to make the trip enjoyable…books, magazines, games, candy, also necessities such as soap, writing material, razor blades, etc. Really swell, I think, don't you? Well Hon, it's about chow time, so will stop for today. I'll try and write a little each day, that way you will have a nice letter by the time I get there. At least a long one, anyhow.*

He added a romantic closing to this first section of his letter, which would extend to six pages as daily installments were added during what turned out to be a 15-day voyage. This was the first piece of mail in a sequence identified by a number written in the upper-left corner of the page—a simple code that he and Norm had devised to determine if any piece of their daily correspondence was missing. Norm wouldn't receive letter number one until weeks later.

While in many ways his sea cruise was in stark contrast to the typical liberty ship voyage, it shared some similarities. Outside the harbor they rendezvoused with a small convoy that became progressively larger as they joined with other cargo vessels and occasional warships that patrolled the formation's perimeter. To reduce vulnerability to enemy submarines they followed a zig-zag course and operated under strict blackout procedures after dark. Despite a couple of warm autumn afternoons basking in the sun and "first-class" dinners served by the French-speaking crew, Bob spent his first evening on guard duty trying to enjoy a stroll on a beautiful moonlit deck without Norma. He already missed her badly and spoke of it in the second installment of his ocean correspondence, written after the morning life boat drill. As he wrote, Stewart lay on the next bunk, nursing a chronic bout of sea sickness, which kept him near the rail during their first two days and would render him pale and bedridden for most of the voyage.

By the end of the first week, it turned gray, windy, and much colder, reminding Bob of *"pictures at sea, which you see in the movies at times."* He had completed his cover-to-cover reading of the *Reader's Digest* issue that he had brought with him and finished plowing through three mystery novels provided by the Red Cross. But it wasn't long before he became bored with the first-class routine. He also was tired of the various dishes prepared with a *"foreign touch,"* whose names he said *"it would take the Ott girls on Franklin Street to figure out."* He pined for a chunk of Norm's Pennsylvania Dutch ham loaf and chocolate cake. He was restless and frustrated that after a week they were only halfway to their destination, which he understood was *"somewhere in England."* He was also eager to get back on solid land, bring an end to the anxiety of not knowing exactly where he would be stationed, engage his mind in any worthwhile task, and reconnect to loved ones through precious mail that was probably piling up at some military outpost. Idle time only facilitated thinking about his current state—in the middle of an angry ocean filled with invisible enemies, heading for a strange country under a cloud of random bombardment. The daily life boat drills only highlighted his vulnerability. He reflected on this, but didn't dwell on it. His thoughts were mainly with Norm.

The boredom was interrupted with an out-of-the-ordinary occurrence on the eleventh day at sea. The ship's engines came to a dead stop just before midnight. Commotion erupted in the hallways as bleary-eyed troops swung open stateroom doors to find out what was going on. Restricted to quarters after hours, they decided to appoint a couple of representatives who, by process of elimination, understood enough French to investigate topside. They returned in short order with the scoop: one of the French crewmen had become sick and died, and the ship was dropping anchor until the morning, when an at-sea burial could be performed. The passengers should expect to receive official instructions after breakfast to report on deck in dress uniforms to *"pay tribute"* to the deceased seaman.

Despite the somber mood of the occasion, Bob found the burial service quite interesting. It was a cool, but clear morning. The troops stood at attention in their assigned area on deck as a wooden, coffin-shaped box, with French flags draped from above and below, was ceremoniously carried forward by six pall bearers. The solemn detail shuffled in echelon up makeshift steps to a temporary platform erected on the edge of the deck. They appeared to struggle with the dead weight of their comrade. A stubby chute projecting over the ship's rail betrayed the grim finality of what was to come. The Americans, not understanding a word of the foreign incantations, watched with the others in silence. The flags were ceremoniously removed then folded. Then, with an astonishingly impersonal shove by the skilled clergyman, the shrouded corpse plunged like a rock to meet its watery tomb in a violent splash. At that point the novelty of the experience changed to sadness for Bob. He wondered if the deceased seaman had a family and what kind of life he had left behind. There wasn't much of a story here; he simply died at sea.

In less than a half-hour they were underway again, running at full steam to catch up with the convoy. With no other ships nearby it felt especially lonely on the vast ocean. Another day went by before the crew told them they were about to join up with other ships. The sight of eight or nine vessels spread on the horizon was a pleasant one. Spirits were further lifted the following day when the crew prepared a sumptuous feast for dinner: *"two nice pieces of beef, peas, carrots, turnips, a real tasty dessert, and even a glass of wine."* The special occasion, which for security reasons couldn't be disclosed in Bob's increasingly lengthy letter, was reported to have been a celebration of DeGaulle's birthday, despite the fact that the heroic French leader wouldn't turn 54 until November 22nd, nearly three weeks later. However, Paris had been retaken two months earlier; and, of more immediate significance may have been the announcement by the Allies that Greece was liberated from the Nazis on that day. In any event, the French crew just may have been looking for an excuse to have a party on the last Saturday before reaching port in a country where the cuisine was nothing to look forward to. Uncomfortable about sampling the French wine, Bob felt compelled to explain his transgression during that evening's writing session: *"I can still walk straight though Honey, so don't worry."*

A few days later they would be within sight of land, but had no idea when or where they would dock. *"It is a good feeling, and that's for sure!"* he wrote in his first V-mail. *"Funny thing you know you're near land without having to see it, as the air smells much different."* A V-mail was a photographically-reduced copy of a single-page letter on a standard form, introduced by the government to minimize weight and expedite delivery of massive amounts of correspondence generated by servicemen and their families. They were encouraged to use this medium to help the war effort. Bob told Norm that, when he reached port, he would send his first V-Mail at the same time he air-mailed his regular letter—as an *"experiment"* to determine for later reference which mode arrived first. He was skeptical; since V-mails were *"free,"* he thought that they would take longer to get there. In the final closing of his long letter, he commented:

*The weather is just as I expected...rainy, cold and a bit foggy...the first*
*I've been in a cold climate for a long time. I'll finish this now darling, as*
*if I hold it up any longer, with censorship and all, it may be delayed too*
*long. I'll write again as soon as possible. In the meantime, please don't*
*worry, ...keep your chin up...and remember I'll be thinking of you al-*
*ways, and loving you even more.*

                                        *Your Hubby*
                                        *"Bob"* xxxxxx

*P.S. Quite a few land birds flying around the ship...starlings, I*
*believe. Seems funny to see them again.*


THEY ARRIVED AT THE PORT of Southampton, an immense, sheltered
harbor on the southern coast of England. The surface was blanketed,
as far as one could see through the fog, with boats of every imaginable
kind: coming, going, moored, and docked. Their ship had to anchor
for a day before dock space became available and the troops could
disembark. After long hours of anticipation, eager to stand on firm
ground but uncertain about what was next, the wobbly-legged travelers
lugged overloaded duffels in attentive silence, marching out-of-step in
a crooked line to a designated staging area. Surrounding them was a
collection of ancient buildings that would serve as a temporary station
until invisible logistics warriors could exercise their proprietary art of
sorting, picking, and channeling the arriving herds to hundreds of
outposts across England. Familiar voice commands from troop leaders
were now interspersed with clipped instructions delivered in a curious
version of the language that confirmed they were in a foreign land.

    Bob was shocked when he learned that one of his group's first
port assignments would be KP duty. So much for exclusive treatment.
It made him think of Sheppard Field and Bake, wherever he might be.
That seemed like years ago. Was *this* the *real* Army? His attitude about
mess duty improved slightly when they learned it was customary for
the latest arrivals to perform KP for the groups who preceded them.

    The following day Bob's group was fed in turn by the next group
of arrivals, then trucked to the train station, where they were loaded on
a train heading north. They still didn't know their final destinations.
Despite the secrecy, the trip was reasonably pleasant. They traveled in
old-fashioned hand-polished cars with cabins that were accessible by

narrow hallways along the side. It was comfortable. Bob felt that his string of luck had continued.

They got their first taste of local culture during a late-night stop at a station somewhere between Southampton and Birmingham. That's where Bob discovered his currency problem. Ever the optimist, he had *"crossed the ocean with a little over $2"* in his pocket, but, by the time he boarded the train, he had *"65 cents left."* He was running low on air mail stamps, and because the locals would not accept U.S. currency, he needed to convert his pocket change for some combination of *half-crowns, worth about 50 cents, florins (40 cents), shillings (20 cents) and three-pences (worth about a nickel).* In late 1944 the dollar-to-pound exchange rate was about four-to-one. Like the other GIs in his group, he had few opportunities to exchange his pocket money. They had been told that their first overseas pay would be issued in local currency; however, that wouldn't happen until they reached their assigned duty stations. It made their journey a bit more challenging, as Bob described to Norm in his next day's letter from Birmingham:

*Somewhere in England*
*Nov. 10, 1944*

*Hello Honey,*

*By this time I imagine you received my first letter...also the V-mail...so now that I'm somewhat settled (temporarily, anyhow), I'll write you another. I'll number the ones not V-mail. O.K? That way you can keep track of them. Don't forget to let me know which of the others you received first, as I may use the V-mail from time to time. At times it does come in handy. Right now...and in the near future...will be some of those times. Understand Honey, I would write every letter air mail from now on out, but I can't because I must now go easy on my stamps...till we get our money exchanged, anyway. American money isn't worth a damn over here. You may as well not have it (Of course I don't have much anyhow!)...*

*Golly did I laugh last night...at a train station where we stopped a short while, we went in to get something to eat. After talking a while, the cashier finally decided that she'd take American paper money, but no silver. (You paid before you ate.) There were 4 of us, but only one had a dollar bill, so he handed it to her, and asked her to take it out of there. She asked how many, so we said "How much apiece for a meal?" She said one and three (1/3), but that was Greek to us then. (It*

*means, one shilling and three pence...about 25¢). The fellow who owned
the bill said, "Take it as far as it'll go." Gosh, did we laugh! She said
she'd give us each a ticket, altho we still owe her a penny (English
money), but we could forget that. We thanked her and went on. It sure
was funny though!*

This was part of a long letter that Bob wrote at an RAF (Royal
Air Force) base outside Birmingham where his group had a layover of
a few days. In his first letter written there he talked about the beautiful
countryside, funny automobiles, bobbie sightings, strict rationing for
even the most insignificant items, and unexpectedly nice base accommodations. But he had nothing good to say about the English cooking.
A postscript requested that cookies be sent to his permanent APO
address as soon as possible.

His lifestyle at the British base got old, quickly. It was constantly
cold, rainy, and foggy, and his quarters were poorly heated. He went to
bed bundled in a heavy socks and sweater, and covered with four wool
blankets. In a note sent the next day by V-mail—due to lack of air mail
stamps—he uncharacteristically complained about the English weather
and their rationing policy. That morning his group had received their
first allotment of ration coupons for soap, razor blades, cigarettes, and
candy. He purchased three candy bars and returned allotted coupons
for items he didn't need. Hoarding unused coupons was prohibited,
and most of the guys didn't have enough cash to utilize them anyway.
Laredo was looking better all the time. He dreamed about his last
seven months on Zaraguzie Street.

Norm wouldn't receive this letter for 18 days, so he would be
lucky to have his cookie request filled by Christmas. The portion of his
letter which quantified his travel time from port would be carefully
sliced out by a military censor's sharp blade. The unknown examiner
would be less lenient with a letter that Bob had written to his parents.
That one was returned with editing instructions.

Like a bad joke often repeated, their group was assigned KP duty
the next day. The natural jokers in the group decided to transform it
into a hilarious event for everybody involved. It wasn't hard to find
good material. They had traveled in uncomfortably close quarters since
Laredo, therefore the smallest personality quirks were by now well
known to all. And there was no sport in letting anybody off the hook.
It was the last time that all the Project 25 guys would be together.

Later that day they were individually interviewed by *"the Lieutenant"* to ascertain aircraft preferences, which would influence their base assignments. The choice was either B-17 Flying Fortresses or B-24 Liberators. Bob went for the popular B-17s. So did Stew and Jack, although their choices made no difference to him. He confided in a letter to Norm that he was tired of Jack's constant griping and avoided getting too close to anybody in the old group. They were to be shipped out the next day in as yet unnamed groups of 10. By the time Norm received this letter, its date, sequence number, and postscript had been carefully excised by the censor's knife.

On November 13th, a day before departing, they were rewarded with a mail call. Bob scribbled a V-mail to Norm excitedly reporting that he had received her first letter, dated 11 days earlier. He said that most of the guys received a letter apiece and implied that they compared notes to see who got letters and which were the best, rated according to relationship of the sender. Bob was a definite winner, but Stew was *"gripin',"* because his only mail was from a distant aunt who wrote him twice a year. Bob wouldn't have to put up with any more griping, because the group would be split up that day.

The only familiar names in his new traveling contingent were *"Porter, Browne, and Fred Sanford."* The four of them, plus seven guys from a project group that joined them in Greensboro, were trucked to the railway station the next day. Birmingham station was a major hub in central England. Hoards of anonymous troops and civilians rushed about, sharing the experience of connecting to somewhere in England. Bob's group of 11 knew only that they would board the same train, head in the same direction, and get off at different stops along the way.

It was another pleasant ride through the English countryside, which Bob remarked about in a superficially upbeat letter to Norm. He mentioned the nice *"limey"* soldiers he had come into contact with. But he also highlighted the dwindling size of his group, expressed concerns about postal logistics, and, probably in response to concerns expressed in her letter, emphasized that she shouldn't worry, as he had *"not even seen a plane yet."* He would mail his letter at the next stop, where a brief layover was scheduled—a town called Bedford.

He perked up when he heard the conductor's announcement, because his sister-in-law Becky had told Bob that Butch was stationed somewhere near Bedford with the 379th Bomb Group. Butch couldn't be any more precise than that in his censored letters to her. Bob had decided that, in addition to mailing his letter at the station, he would make some inquiries. On the station platform he approached the first civilian he saw, an elderly English chap. He explained that he was a soldier in transit and asked if there was an American air base in the area. In a sharply accented dialect the spry old gentleman replied, "Oh yes, me lad! Yes, me lad. This is the place. The 379th is just down the road at Kimbolton!"

"That's just what I wanted to hear!" exclaimed Bob. "My brother-in-law's there!"

"It's just around the corner, me lad. Just around the corner!" Bob later learned that, according to the locals, everywhere in England is "just around the corner." He wouldn't have enough time to make a side trip in any event. But he was elated by his discovery. In a strange country so far away from home, it was exciting to know a relative was nearby and contemplate how a reunion could be arranged. It would also help to cure his increasing homesickness. Bob's travel companions were people he hardly knew, and that group had now shrunk to about a half dozen. During the layover Bob shared his discovery with his lieutenant, who was thoughtful enough to help place a telephone call to Kimbolton. They were successful in contacting the base but unable to connect with Butch, who was not in his barracks or at the mess hall, where they had him paged.

Another call was placed from the next station. This time they were informed that Captain Powl was "on pass," most likely in London. Bob left a message stating where he could be reached and suggesting they should try to get together. Craving familiar company, he desperately hoped that Butch would receive the message. There were now only three other guys in his travel contingent: Browne and Porter from Project 25, and a "Project 24 man." With one air mail stamp remaining and a station away from payday, Bob used a V-mail form to tell Norm about his call to Butch. He reported that he had actually gone so far as to request assignment to Butch's base, which was supposedly denied "because he was needed elsewhere." He and the three others had orders to get off at the next station, a place with a funny name: Great Yeldham.

ON NOVEMBER 16th, three-and-a-half weeks after departing Camp Kilmer, his train made a brief stop at a tiny rural station in what was barely a town. It could have just as easily passed for a country village in southern Lancaster County, like Liberty Square or Rawlinsville, except for the roofs of houses and barns, which were covered with dark slate, burnt-orange tile, or straw-thatch, as in childhood storybooks. The travelers were met by a soldier clutching copies of their orders. He was the driver of one of those now-all-too-familiar Army trucks—the kind that feature a shallow cargo bed with personnel benches along the sides, monstrous all-terrain tires, and sagging tarpaulin roof. The weary foursome hoisted their duffels over the tailgate and climbed in to set out on the last leg of their journey. With a hard clank and clatter of the transmission, their friendly driver jammed the olive-drab machine into gear and launched into what sounded like a Chamber of Commerce spiel: "Gentlemen, welcome to Great Yoho! I'm takin' you to the finest base in the Eighth Air Force—the home of the 381st Bomb Group! It ain't the Ritz, but it's the best in this man's army!" It would take less than 10 minutes to reach their destination, Ridgewell Aerodrome, Station 167. They rumbled down a secondary road past some old farm buildings and a quaint old tavern called the King's Head. If the driver hadn't mentioned it, they wouldn't have realized that they had arrived in Ridgewell, a hamlet in about the same league as Great Yoho.

The sign posted outside the guard shack identified the place as home of the 381st Bomb Group and 432nd Air Service Group. The driver displayed his paperwork for the guard. They were waved under the candy-cane gate and stopped at a cluster of corrugated metal huts that looked like huge steel drums cut lengthwise, placed hollow-side down. These classic structures were British Nissen huts, named after a Canadian engineer who invented the legendary pre-fab buildings. GIs frequently called them Quonset huts, named after the town in Rhode Island where the American version of the Nissen was originally manufactured. The driver instructed his four passengers to go inside and report to the group CQ for instructions. The CQ welcomed them and explained that they would report to First Lt. Wayne W. Hart, who was in charge of the gunnery school. Each was further assigned to one of the four operational squadrons in the 381st Bomb Group: the 532nd, 533rd, 534th, and 535th. Bob was assigned to the 535th.

The driver then delivered them to their respective squadron locations, reached by following the narrow perimeter road which encircled the base. They initially drove in a northerly direction, although it was hard to tell. The skies were still gray at midday. It was about a mile to the first cluster of metal huts, which were near what looked like streets of a homeless subdivision sprouting a crop of short driveways ending in cul-de-sacs. The latter were circular parking areas called hard stands, each of which was home to a Flying Fortress. The hard stands, for defensive reasons, were widely dispersed around the base and inter-connected by a network of tarmac and taxiways. The driver pointed out the markings VE painted on the side of a partially disassembled bomber on the nearest hard stand. He said it was the radio call sign of ships in the 532nd Squadron. Browne jumped off there and offered a little wave of "thanks and so long" as his duffel bags were heaved over to him. Without hesitation the truck rattled off in a clockwise direction around the perimeter road, by-passing an isolated cluster of bunkers in the distance, which was the bomb depot, according to the driver. Next they came to the 533rd Squadron, located on the northeast side of the base and unloaded another passenger. The layout of this area was similar to the one on the northwest corner of the base. Another plane under repair was parked here. No other planes were in sight. The driver confirmed what was now obvious: all the operational ships were out on a mission that day. The third passenger was dropped at the 534th on the southeast corner of the base.

Bob was now the lone passenger. His destination, the 535th Squadron, was the fourth and last stop. To get there they had driven about four miles in a complete circle, back to the southwest corner of the base near the main facilities. The driver pointed to the hut down over the embankment and instructed him to report inside to the squadron CQ. With a tentative wave he wished Bob good luck and drove off.

"Sergeant Singleton, reporting for duty," he croaked to the guy behind the desk. It sounded more like a question.

"You're one of the gunnery instructors," the CQ asserted without looking up. "We need those around here," he added facetiously.

"Yea, I imagine you do," Bob said with a nervous chuckle. To himself he was thinking: "These guys have been flying combat missions—and I'm gonna tell them how to shoot a gun?"

"Gotta keep 'em sharp," muttered the CQ as he shuffled through the stack of papers on his desk. Finally, he looked up and said, "I'm sorry, but I can't put you in with the flyboys." Apologetically, he explained how the air crew barracks were full, and that, until the next batch of crews finished their tours and went home, a bunk with the ground crew was all that was available. He said that the squadron Flight Surgeon who monitored the air crews, a Maj. Wistar L. Graham, would occasionally check in to keep him abreast of barracks vacancies. Then Bob was pointed in the direction of his new home away from home: Hut 18. It was a dingy-looking Nissen hut on the outside of the perimeter road with an auspicious-looking dirt-covered bunker behind it. He would find out later that a bomb shelter was buried under the mound of dirt.

Bob stepped out of the CQ's hut feeling disappointed, somewhat dejected, and very lonely. His old friends were nowhere to be found, and his travel buddies had been progressively split up into "groups of one." As the last one off the truck at the end of the line, he suddenly felt like he was on the outside looking in. The prospect of living with a bunch of grease monkeys didn't help. The subject came up early in his first letter to Norm from Ridgewell:

> I sure felt lost though, when I left the other boys, and I don't mean maybe. Felt like a lost sheep! When I walked into my barracks, it was like when I walked into Mr. Bell's room at Manheim Twp. [High School] the first time...alone, and not a familiar face in the crowd.

However, being the kind of person that he was, it didn't take him long to make some new acquaintances, one of which was a total surprise. The letter continued:

> I must say, however, I'm in with a very nice bunch of guys, and I feel quite at home already. There are two other gunnery instructors in the barracks, besides me, and all the others are ground crew men...mechanics, refuelers, and such. Get this now—the one gunnery instructor, of the other two in the barracks, is also a C.I.S. project man (project #9), ...but to top it off, he's from none other than Lancaster, Penna. How about that Honey! Isn't that swell? I met him tonite for the first, his name is John Rutherford. A really swell guy! I didn't talk to him too much yet, as he and another guy planned to go to a movie. He invited me along, but I told him that I had to write you, so I guess we'll talk it out later...

Meeting John was such a welcome coincidence that he would always treasure the memory. When John walked into the barracks that afternoon, as part of the normal introduction ritual he asked Bob where he was from and was surprised by the answer: "Pennsylvania."

Bob was equally surprised when Johnny retorted, "So am I."

"Where in Pennsylvania?" asked Bob, continuing with the drill performed thousands of times by GIs in search of familiar ground.

"It's a little town you've probably never heard of," John replied, "so I'll say 'Lancaster'."

Completely astonished, Bob exclaimed, "Come on, now! I'm from Lancaster too!"

When Johnny explained that he was actually from Millersville, a county village that Bob also knew quite well, the coincidence had all the makings of a new friendship. Bob couldn't believe how two guys who had lived within a few miles of one another would end up sharing a metal hut with a bunch of grease monkeys—six thousand miles from home—near a strange place called Great Yoho.

When John returned later that night they talked until midnight. That's when Bob got the full scoop on his new friend "Johnnie," life in Great Yoho, and what a gunnery instructor in the 381st Bomb Group should expect. Johnnie had grown up in Lancaster, first on East Ann Street then on East Clay Street not far from Ed and Bernie's gas station. He graduated from McCaskey with Bob's former class. Johnnie enlisted in the Army right after Pearl Harbor and went to MP school after basic training. Unfortunately, he couldn't get qualified on the big, .45 semi-automatic pistol due to an aggravated wrist fracture. An avid amateur photographer, he had injured it as a teenager on a picture-taking mission to Safe Harbor on the Susquehanna, where he fell off the chimney of some old blast furnace ruins. The Army gave him a disability discharge less than three months after he enlisted. When his injury subsequently interfered with his job as an apprentice typesetter, his employer referred him to a respected bone surgeon at Elizabethtown Hospital. Dr. Chambers, the surgeon, told John that he wouldn't be charged for the operation if it enabled him to be accepted back into the service. A bone graft was performed, his arm was placed in a cast for six months, and some nerve damage was repaired in a follow-up operation. By May of 1943 John successfully reenlisted, not having been asked to pay a cent by the good doctor.

On his second Army stint John attended aircraft armament school at Lowry Field in Colorado, following basic training in Atlantic City, New Jersey, of all places. They billeted at the Dennis Hotel when they weren't marching and singing on the Boardwalk. Then he went to gunnery school at Harlingen Field, Texas, completing a course similar to the one at Laredo. He had enlisted with a desire to see action, but due to high demand for instructors, was retained as an MOS 938. Frustrated, he was sent to the Laguna Madre sub base off South Padre Island, Texas, where he instructed firing at moving targets from ball turret guns mounted on truck beds.

After several boring weeks and 65,000 ear-shattering rounds of ammo, he finally discovered a way to escape this fate. He heard about the project teams that were being formed to set up overseas gunnery schools and without hesitation volunteered. Before being shipped out he first had to complete CIS training at Buckingham Field, where like many before him he learned to instruct the "Army Way: First you tell 'em what you're *gonna* tell 'em; then you *tell* 'em; next you tell 'em *what* you just told 'em; and, then you get 'em to tell it *back* to you." Of course, he and his counterparts were never told where they were going to be assigned. But when they were outfitted with cold weather gear, they figured they were going to England. John went through CIS with two guys from Bob's barracks in Laredo: Whitey Wegner, who ended up at Ridgewell in the 532nd; and Paul Sedlak, who traveled to England with John and Whitey, but was assigned to another base. Their travel group departed Camp Kilmer on July 1st and arrived at Great Yoho on the 31st. Their voyage on the SS *Columbia*, a converted French liner stuffed with thousands of GIs, was a typical liberty ship cruise.[1]

When Bob arrived in England three-and-a-half months later, he considered John a veteran. Not only had John flown on 10 combat missions, but on his third mission as tail gunner on a ship called the *Tomahawk Warrior*, he had survived a near miss with an 88 mm antiaircraft shell, which came through the tail about a foot from his position, creating a gaping hole before exploding in a blast of shrapnel above the aircraft. John was the first to explain the combat role of a gunnery instructor to the new kid from Lancaster. He said that instructors were required to fly at least three, but no more than six missions per month to get some combat experience. That way they would better understand aerial tactics and gain credibility with their combat-hardened students. And, like regular air crews, they would be eligible for release after completing 30 missions.[2]

In his letter to Norm that evening, after describing the surprise meeting with Johnnie, and mentioning the Lancaster people they knew in common, Bob shared the news about his flying prospects. He downplayed the potential risks, but was generally candid, as they had agreed:

> *Now for a little bit about my set-up: From what I hear I must run six (6) missions right off the bat...then one per month, thereafter. All of the rest of the time I'll be instructing. Rutherford tells me it's really a pretty good deal. I think I'll like it and get along O.K. He has 10 in since he arrived, which is not too many in comparison with a regular gunner. He claims that today you are pretty well escorted by fighters, and very few ships are being lost. "Flak" is the worst thing you have to contend with, and most of it is just over your target. Just don't worry Honey, please, as I'll stay on the ball and I think everything will be O.K. I'll let you know each time I fly. O.K? You know I'll do all I can so as to get back safely to you ...I love you too much to do otherwise...*

The remainder of his letter described his new barracks *("those 'round-roofed' kind...seen in the movies [that are] a little chilly though...especially in the morning")*; the food *("chow here is O.K.")*; his proximity to the PX (post exchange); and the prospect of a partial payday, which would facilitate his purchase of air mail stamps on the following day. He continued with suggestions on how to handle Christmas gifts for friends and relatives, then added what she might send to him:

> *...a cake or two of some soap, some brushless shaving cream, a comb, some shaving lotion, some tooth powder, some wool socks, then maybe some candy & homemade cookies. Truthfully, those things I need more than anything! (except you). Don't go to any extra trouble though, please. If you can get a roll or two of film, Hon, send it and the camera too, if you don't mind. No hurry though, so don't put yourself out. I will be able to get some nice pictures if I have it.*

It wouldn't be long before he could take pictures showing what aerial combat was all about. But his first few weeks would be learning about the 381st from the ground.

# CHAPTER 8

# TRIANGLE L

THE MEN AT RIDGEWELL were part of a gigantic war machine, the Eighth Air Force, which unleashed an intensity of destructive power that was previously unimaginable and ultimately brought the Germans to their knees. The Eighth was "the largest air striking force ever committed to battle and was America's first air force raised for offensive purposes."[1] It was a huge organization, consisting of operational commands, air divisions, wings, and groups. The 381st Bomb Group (Heavy) was one of three groups, in one of five combat wings, in the first of three air divisions of the Bomber Command. In addition to the Bomber Command, the Eighth had a Fighter, an Air Service, and a Ground Air Support Command.

When Bob arrived in England in late 1944 the commander of the Eighth was the legendary Maj. Gen. James A. Doolittle, who reported to Lt. Gen. Carl A. "Tooey" Spaatz, head of U.S. Strategic Air Forces Europe. These men followed in the tradition of Gen. Ira C. Eaker, the pioneering leader of VIII Bomber Command, organizational predecessor of the Eighth Air Force. General Eaker championed the risky, but ultimately effective strategy of precision daylight bombing, which had a major role in winning the war. At its peak the Eighth had more than 200,000 personnel and 4,000 aircraft, assigned to 40 bomber groups, 15 fighter groups, 2 reconnaissance groups, a special operations group, and 12 specialist and training units.

A fully staffed and equipped bomber group in 1944 was made up of four squadrons. Each group was stationed at one of 77 wartime air fields, most of which were situated on the vast, green plateau in east central England known as the Midlands and further concentrated in the eastern portion, sometimes referred to as East Anglia. You could deduce where an aircraft was stationed by its markings. The painted symbol on the vertical stabilizer indicated an aircraft's assigned group. Bombers in the 381st displayed the letter L in the center of a painted, solid triangle on their tail. The triangle signified that it was part of the

First Air Division. A circle or square was used for ships in the Second and Third Divisions, respectively. All Triangle L aircraft were B-17's stationed at Station 167, Ridgewell, Essex, England. Side markings on the planes further identified their assigned squadrons. These were the radio call sign letters VE, VP, GD, and MS, which identified planes as part of the 532nd, 533rd, 534th, or 535th, respectively.

To each man stationed at Ridgewell the 381st was his air force, Triangle L ships were the family jewels, a B-17 "Fort" was his best friend, and his group commander was king. Ground as well as air crews were loyal to their group and extremely proud of Triangle L bombers. Lt. Col. Joseph J. Nazzaro was their first group commander. A West Point football star, he was responsible for forming and leading the original group, which was activated in Pyote, Texas in January 1943. Colonel Nazzaro led the Triangle L ships to Antwerp, Belgium on their first combat mission in late June 1943, the month they arrived in Ridgewell. His men were impressed that he flew in the lead ship on their first five, anxiety-laden missions. That might not seem out of the ordinary, but in the early months of 1943 the odds were such that only one man in three completed his operational tour, which consisted of 25 missions.[2] Nazzaro's presence in the cockpit was viewed by the men as beyond the call of duty for a group leader, who usually directed operations from behind the lines. A demanding, but highly respected leader, "Colonel Joe" was in charge of the group until being promoted to Eighth Air Force headquarters in January 1944. During his watch the 381st established an impressive bombing record, despite the grim fact that only a few men from his original group survived their tours.

THE 381ST WAS ONE OF THE FIRST bomb groups to arrive in England. In June 1943 the German air and ground forces dominated Europe and North Africa. England already had been blitzed by the Luftwaffe, and parts of London were in rubble. The 381st flew their first bombing raids well before U.S. fighter planes arrived in England. Many of their early missions were flown unescorted, directly into the onslaught of enemy fighters and through a heavy barrage of ground-based anti-air-craft fire, especially around high-value targets. The first few months were the worst, with planes and crews lost on about half the missions flown. The group took its heaviest toll on the day of its 20th mission, August 17, 1943. Their target was a strategically critical, and heavily defended conclave of ball bearing plants in Schweinfurt, Germany. It was a brutal encounter. Sixty of 375 Eighth Air Force bombers launched from England failed to return that day in one of the most horrific air battles of the war. The 381st was hit especially hard. Only 15 of 26 Triangle L planes returned, one of the greatest losses sustained by any bomb group during the war. Ten planes, carrying 100 crew members, were shot down; the eleventh plane ditched in the English Channel. Half of the original group was gone by the end of this raid. The 381st was nearly broken. Two days later they were again ordered by headquarters to send up every ship they could, which then amounted to less than a squadron in size, and 10 more airmen ended up reported as missing in action. The situation was bleak. A week and two missions after Schweinfurt, only seven ships could be launched in response to another order for the 381st to put everything into the air. These were some of the darkest days in Ridgewell.[3]

Replacements of men and airplanes began to flow in after that, and the group slowly began to recover. After losing a ship in an early September raid, the 381st gradually increased to a full complement of flyable aircraft and was able to fly 10 missions in a row, mostly over targets in France, without losses. However, by October, the Eighth was once again sending planes over heavily defended targets in Germany, and their losses mounted. During a two-week period the Eighth lost 102 planes, climaxing with a second raid over Schweinfurt, when 60 of 320 planes didn't return. During this period the 381st lost 11 more planes and over 100 men, most of them in the missions to Bremen and Anklam. To some observers it appeared that "the Eighth was flying itself to extinction."[4] Most air crews of the original 381st were gone. Half were lost by the Schweinfurt raid of August, and the other half were lost in the Bremen and Anklam raids of October.[5] In the latter raids, many airmen had accumulated close to 20 missions and were approaching an end to their war. What some of these battle-weary young men might have seen as a glimmer of light at the end of a long dark tunnel was just an exploding shell of a faceless enemy that mercilessly blasted them out of existence.

Ridgewell air base became a different place after the fall of 1943.[6] Replacements arrived, not as complete air crews who had trained, traveled, worked, and played together, but mostly as individuals who would be assigned to mixed crews and different airplanes from mission to mission. Needless to say, the new air crews didn't see a lot of hope in the possibility of completing their tour and going home. But the new guys appeared to be seasoned. Unlike their predecessors, they understood the seriousness of the business they were getting into. The original crews had no idea what to expect, and their leaders were more "jittery," according to their Chaplain James Good Brown. Pilots on early missions had a greater tendency to abort the mission and return to base if something didn't sound right; and, they heard all sorts of noises in the engines, "like rats in the attic."[7] The original crews also had a tendency to huddle together before briefings and commiserate their fate. Since they had spent so much time together, they knew the names of each other's loved ones and freely discussed how bad news would be shared. And they painfully grieved their losses. This is not to say the newer guys were hard and unfeeling. On the contrary, they were in the company of men who took their first steps into the un-known—men whom they respected as veterans. Mission briefings became shorter, smoother, and more professional in tone. However, one thing never changed: base personnel who were not on a mission always "sweated out" the return of planes.[8] They grouped together in silence on the tarmac around the control tower, passively playing games to pass the time or just gazing into the sky, anxiously waiting to count their returning ships.

In January 1944 Col. Harry P. Leber Jr. took over as Group Commander. His second-in-command was the Air Executive, Lt. Col. Conway S. Hall, who had previously been group Operations Officer under Nazzaro. By this time three of the original squadron command-ers were either dead or in a POW camp. The commander of the 535th Squadron, Maj. William W. Inglehutt, had been taken prisoner after being shot down in the Bremen raid of October '43. His duties were turned over to Maj. Frank Chapman, one of two remaining original pilots in the 535th. On January 4th Chapman ended up being the last pilot of only a few in the original group who completed 25 missions.[9] He was the only pilot in the group whose plane was named after him. And his plane, *Chap's Flying Circus*, was the last of the original 381st bombers to go down; it ditched in the North Sea later that month. When Chapman left, Maj. Charles L. (Roy) Halsey was brought in from outside the group as the third commander of the 535th. An out-standing professional, it wasn't long before he was promoted to colonel and reassigned in April 1944 after completing 39 missions. Halsey was succeeded by Capt. William Cronin, who was commander of the 535th when Bob got there and until the end of the war.

Each leader had a unique personality. Some were liked; others were tolerated. But they were all highly respected for their experience. Rank and position weren't the real determinants of status at Ridgewell. The ground crews looked up to air crews, and the number of missions flown determined the pecking order among the flyboys. The more missions flown, the higher one ranked on the unofficial pyramid. It took months for Chaplain Brown to persuade the group commander to permit him to fly on a mission. The chaplain deemed flight experience essential to enhance his status and to better identify with his flock. He was one of the few Eighth Air Force chaplains who could make this claim. To him flying on a mission was in some ways less painful than sweating out the group's return or writing letters of condolence to families of boys killed in action.

At the pinnacle of the aviation hierarchy were the heroes and legends. Of course, most of them were dead, and they weren't talked about much. One of the 535th legends was Capt. Eddie Manchester. He was the very popular and likeable pilot of the bomber named *T.S.*, which in July 1943 collided head-on with an attacking FW-190 over France, limped back on three engines, and executed a belly landing on the English coast with chunks of the enemy fighter lodged in the place where his number three engine used to be. Miraculously, Eddie and crew walked away from that one, but Eddie was killed three months later on his 20th mission, the fateful Bremen raid of October 1943.

The winter, spring, and summer of 1944 brought more missions and persistent losses. The 381st lost planes on about two-thirds of their missions flown during the first three months of the year. This included the "Big Week" of late February, when the Eighth Air Force executed massive raids—forces of more than 1,000 bombers—on the German aircraft industry and flew its first mission to Berlin on March 6th.[10] These missions had a great impact. German fighter strength began to decline, exacerbated by a shortage of fuel and pilots. In June Allied ground forces landed on the beaches of Normandy and began pushing across Europe. On June 22nd, exactly one year after its first raid on Antwerp, the 381st had 140 missions to its credit as well as a list of Presidential Citations, Distinguished Service Crosses, Silver Stars, Distinguished Flying Crosses, Air Medals, and Purple Hearts. By that time—with the exception of Colonel Hall, Group CO, and Colonel Shackley, Air Exec—all the flyboys at Ridgewell were replacements.

Only about 10 percent of the original air crews had survived 25 missions.[11]

DESPITE THE PROGRESS that was being made, planes continued to be lost on about one of every four missions flown. Air crews could find no reason to celebrate as they flew to their targets through a seemingly endless barrage of exploding anti-aircraft shells, which was usually the most concentrated over critical target areas. Referred to as flak, these exploding bursts of shrapnel accompanied by black puffs of smoke were the air crews' nagging companions and most feared adversaries. Flying through flak was a bit like playing Russian roulette. The strain was constant, and air crews often cracked under the pressure.

It's interesting to note that from the very beginning flight duty was strictly voluntary. That always begged the question: why did these men continue to go up? According to Chaplain Brown, it really wasn't about patriotism. There was never a "rah-rah, let's go kill the Germans" kind of attitude. Nobody had aspirations of becoming a hero or sacrificing himself for his country. But it could be said that they did it out of a sense of duty. There always existed, and the leaders seemed to reinforce, a certain amount of peer pressure—in the form of loyalty to the group and fear of letting down your buddies or being seen as a coward. As Chaplain Brown points out, the men desperately wanted to avoid getting killed, because they loved life so much and had loved ones back home to live for.[12] They simply wanted it all to end, and many believed that would come about most quickly by persevering for 25 missions. It's not surprising that, of those who made it, very few volunteered for a second tour.

Since talk of heroics was an unpopular subject, conversational lore around base was deflected to the airplanes themselves, each of which took on its own persona. Cartoon-like "nose art" on a bomber frequently ascribed personality to the ship, but its true character was more likely acquired as a result of its unique combat history. When Bob arrived in Ridgewell some of the planes had reached celebrity status and were even considered "famous." He mentioned some of their names in his first Station 167 letter to Norm:

> *Our group is...the best squadron here. They're sure proud of it, as I suppose I will be too, after I get working with them. Such famous ships as the "Stage Door Canteen," "Hell's Angel," "Magnolia Blossom,"*

*"Mizpah," etc. are all ships of this squadron. Maybe you remember
reading of some of them. I know I do.*

The *Stage Door Canteen*, named after a New York City service club
that was one of the most popular in the United States, was christened
in June 1944 at Ridgewell by Mary Churchill, daughter of the British
Prime Minister. In attendance was a contingent of movie stars,
including Vivian Leigh and Lawrence Olivier. It was part of a promotion of a new Stage Door Canteen club, located in London and
modeled after the successful New York club.[13] The new ship was
christened on the hard stand once reserved for the famous *Tinker Toy.*
That ship, before going down over Bremen in a late 1943 raid, first
appeared in a movie showing a B-17 production facility and always
seemed to miraculously reappear after violent missions, despite dead
crew members, missing pieces of its structure, and innumerable holes.
Similarly, *Mizpah* was one of the Forts that kept making it back, eventually flying over 100 missions and surviving the war.[14] The *Hell's Angel*
was a new plane named after the famous one originally assigned to the
534th, which was shot down in the notorious Schweinfurt raid on its
third mission.[15]

Notwithstanding the famous ships, the Boeing B-17 Flying Fortress was a legend long before it entered the air war in Europe. Less
than two weeks after Pearl Harbor a small group of the early-model
bombers were deployed from the Philippines to attack a Japanese aircraft carrier. While they never found their prime target, one of the
bombers, which early in the mission had become separated from the
others, made it to the target area only to be welcomed by 18 waiting
Japanese fighters.[16] It was nothing less than a miracle that the crippled
plane made it back to base in the rain, despite a battered tail, an engine
out, broken control cables, a punctured fuel cell, destroyed belly gun,
smashed radio, failed oxygen system, two flat main tires, no tail wheel,
1,200 bullet holes, one dead, and two wounded crew members.[17] Many
similar, and some even more harrowing stories would be added to
Fortress lore when the Eighth began flying missions in Europe. The
legend only got larger with time as design changes were progressively
made to improve the aircraft's power, altitude, range, speed, armor,
armament, and instrumentation. Bigger, better, and more battered airplanes would continue to limp back with crew members, engines, and
critical parts missing.

The 381st was on its 214th mission on the day Bob arrived at Ridgewell in late 1944. Amongst all this Triangle L pride and fame, it would not have been surprising for a new arrival to find the atmosphere on base a little heady, if not intimidating—especially for a relatively untested gunnery instructor assigned to improve the shooting skills of veteran air crews. But this didn't seem to faze Bob. He had already made some acquaintances and was now focused on getting acclimated to his new surroundings and engaged in his job.

CHAPTER 9

# GREASE MONKEYS

HIS FIRST MORNING AT RIDGEWELL was cold and cloudy. After a breakfast of tasteless cereal, bland powdered eggs, and coffee, Bob reported for duty at the gunnery school office. The officer in charge was First Lt. Wayne Hart, who reported to the Squadron Executive Officer, Capt. Richard L. Tansey, one of the original members of the 381st. Tansey seemed somewhat aloof, but Hart was an affable guy who didn't take himself too seriously.

Hart was from a city in northeastern Ohio called Ashtabula. He liked to tell a worn-out joke to help people correctly pronounce the name of his hometown. It went something like this: "A traveling salesman got lost passing through town late one night and needed a place to sleep. He came upon a farmhouse, knocked on the door, and explained his situation. The accommodating farmer said that there was a place to sleep in the bed next to his daughter Beulah, but reminded the salesman that he had a shotgun in the house if any hanky panky went on. The weary salesman gratefully accepted the arrangement, slept soundly through the night, then left early the next morning. When neighbors spotted him leaving, gossip started going around the village. The embarrassed farmer was compelled to reassure folks that the visitor had slept all night with his 'ash to Beulah'."[1]

The gunnery instructors were a decent bunch of guys. Master Sgt. Bill Ingram was Chief Instructor at the school. A little bit older and more reserved, Bill was responsible for scheduling instructors' duty hours; he was an important guy to have as your friend. Bob was glad that Bill lived in Hut 18. In addition to Bob, Bill and John (nicknamed Shorty by the group) the other gunnery instructors were Boyle, Browne, Deaton, Henthorne, Porter, Roderick, Wallis, Wegner, and Young. Their official responsibilities included leading review sessions on the caliber-fifty, conducting aircraft identification classes, and teaching air-to-air firing techniques on an electric simulator called a Jam Handy. None of this training had been conducted on base before

the project teams arrived. As the war had progressed, the frequency of
air-to-air engagements had been declining, along with air crew firing
proficiency. Hence, Bomber Command headquarters insisted on the
gunnery school projects. The program had the intended side benefit of
keeping air crews busy when they weren't flying missions. Not surprisingly, combat-experienced students weren't particularly receptive
to the program; and, understandably, their self-conscious instructors
viewed it as a joke.

The strained atmosphere at gunnery school required some GI
ingenuity, so the instructors came up with a solution that would please
everybody, including their supervisors. They decided to set up a live
firing range, officially called a trainer, which in reality would be a
sportsman's skeet range, equipped with 20-gauge shotguns and clay
pigeons. Students could actually enjoy themselves while refining their
aiming techniques. It would improve the attitude of both students and
instructors.

The idea surfaced about the time Bob arrived at Ridgewell. He
was told on the morning he reported for duty that one of his initial
tasks would be helping to set up the trainer. On top of that he was
given permission to take most of his first day off. Perhaps life in the
real Army wouldn't be that bad after all. The reason he got the day off
was a complete surprise, conveyed in a V-mail to Norm:

*November 17<sup>th</sup>*

*Hello Darling,*

    *It's a bit late tonite, so I better just scratch off a V-mail. Don't
have any air mail stamps as yet anyway, so I guess it's just as well.
Right? Hope to get paid soon now so should have some shortly, so don't
get mad at me. O.K? Now for the big news: Who did I see and was
with today, but none other than my Capt. brother-in-law, J. F. "Butch"
Powl himself. Don't roll over and faint either, as it's as true as the fact
that nite follows day. Honest, Hon, I'm still sitting here thinking it's all
a dream and just can't get over it! Little would one ever have thought it,
huh? Yes, and it sure was a treat, I'll tell you. Sure a glorious feeling to
see some one who is so close to you! It happened that two officers
stationed with "Butch" had to come over here to attend a court martial
today, so he hitched a ride along. It's the first for a long time that
anybody from his field had to come over here, but today was one day.
What a break, huh? Golly but it sure was good to see him! I was given*

*the afternoon off…from 10 AM on…so that I could be with him. We
sat in the Aero Club and talked for 4 solid hours, and still we have lots
to talk about. He left about 4:30, but we made plans to get together in
Cambridge as soon as I get better adjusted here. Tell "Beck" he looks
fine, and now we can build up one another's morale. I still have lots to
tell you, but will continue in tomorrow's letter. Lots of love and kisses,
"Bob"*

He didn't mention it in his note, but the main subject of his conversation with Butch that day was baby Diane. Butch knew that Bob
had held his baby daughter and asked a hundred questions about what
she was like. Of course, Bob raved about her, which not only made the
new father proud, but probably made him more homesick.

He was down to *"an English penny and 8¢ in American money"* when
he resorted to the V-mails. This medium had its limitations but wasn't
such a bad deal. Butch claimed that V-mails made it to Lancaster more
quickly and reliably than air mail. Nevertheless, Bob always preferred
the unrestricted length and personal touch offered by an envelope and
a stamp. He would use V-mails to test relative delivery efficiencies, but
it was strictly due to his temporary lack of stamps and money that he
wrote only V-mails that first weekend.

IT WAS FRUSTRATING not having received any mail since leaving
Camp Kilmer a month earlier. He craved reading Norm's words,
which spelled out the goings-on at home and provided questions that
he could respond to in his letters. During this temporary information
void he had little new to report other than his daily experiences. From
the tone of his correspondence, the weather was damp and cold, and
he missed the luxury of hot water in his barracks. The only source of
heat in the hut was a small coke-burning stove. Warm water was
something they *"got only in the shower room…a day's hike from the barracks."*
The wash room outside the hut had only cold water—extremely cold,
according to his missive. How he longed for those warm days with
Norm on Zaraguzie Street.

On Sunday, after attending church in the base gymnasium, Bob
spent most of the day in the Red Cross Aero Club, which usually had a
*"log fire"* burning. It was warm, quiet, and comfortable there, and desks
were available, making it a nice place for relaxed socializing, reading,
and writing letters. To pass time, he played a card game called "500"

with Johnnie, Whitey, and Browne, then sat down to write a long letter which would be mailed in a pre-stamped envelope borrowed from Johnnie. He finished his letter on a salvaged scrap of paper and enclosed a mimeographed bulletin from Chaplain Brown's worship service. The letter reassured Norm that he hadn't yet been issued any flight gear and included a request for some critical items needed on the ground: a mirror with stand for shaving and a two-cell flashlight for getting around a blacked-out base at night. He suggested that the latter might be a good Christmas gift idea for his parents. Little did he know that his request would not be received until January 18th.

He spent most of the next day at the gunnery school and the quartermaster's office on a requisition mission to beg, borrow, and steal critical components for the trainers: shot guns, clay birds, and skeet traps. The highlight of his day was a partial pay allotment: six pounds and four shillings. He didn't have time to make it to the post office but scratched off a V-mail to Norm that night. It included a promise that he would send her $25 for a Christmas outfit when he got the remainder of his pay; news that Johnnie was promoted to staff sergeant as a result of the number of combat missions he had accumulated; and assurances that he wouldn't do any more flying than required by his *"gravy"* job. V-mails were also sent to Roy and Ivy, Sis and Harry, and Laredo friends Bill and Jean Butts.

The next day included a run to the post office for new stationery and stamps, but he had difficulty filling a two-page letter with new information. His latest request was for Norm to secretly check with her old friends at the newspaper office to get the scoop on a recently discharged Navy guy who worked there by the name of Andy Bolock. Andy had become engaged to Johnnie Rutherford's girlfriend, Nancy Eaby, who broke her news to Johnnie in a Dear John letter. Bob's connections to John seemed uncanny: brother Ed also used to date Nancy, although he was probably spared a letter. On the next day, still desperately missing words from home, Bob resorted to V-mail to send Thanksgiving wishes to his *"Dearest Wife."*

The Thanksgiving missive to Norm made his day *"complete."* In it he eloquently described how *"it's so much different being away from you now"* and struggled to express *"if only you knew how I felt."* He also described Thanksgiving Day at Ridgewell:

*...mine was very nice, considering. I was off all day, therefore took in a movie this afternoon. ("Abroad with two Yanks") Not much of a story to it, but really funny! I imagine it was an old picture as most of them we see over here are. As long as I didn't see them though, I don't mind. Then too, they are "free," so what can a guy want? Our dinner was really swell...a real Thanksgiving feed! The tables were all decorated with lit-up "punkin" faces, candles evenly spaced, also, even linen table cloths were used. It certainly passed my expectations, the fact that we are at an overseas camp. Pretty swell I think, don't you? We had turkey, mashed potatoes, filling, peas and corn, cranberry sauce, celery, pickles, parker house rolls, coffee, cake, fruit and candy. Besides, it was even served to us, and not the routine cafeteria way. It really was super, no kiddin! The guys appreciated it too, as you can guess. Of course it still wasn't like being at home, but that would be only natural. Just wait'll we sit down to our own little Thanksgiving feed, Honey...won't that be swell? Oh Boy!*

He concluded the letter reiterating instructions for Norm to buy a nice Christmas gift for $25, the first $10 of which would come in a money order filled out earlier that day, and the balance of which she was told to borrow from her regular monthly allotment from his pay if the remaining $15 money order didn't make it before Christmas. That outcome was likely considering that mail service seemed to take longer than a month. But that would get straightened out soon.

IN THE MEANTIME, Bob was gradually getting to know the characters in the barracks. Lucky for him, Bill Ingram happened to be assigned to the next bunk. Bill, a few years older and more seasoned than most of the enlisted guys, was a quiet man who minded his own business and would turn out to be a good friend and ally at the gunnery school. But except for Bill and John, most of Bob's barracks mates were ground crews who belonged to the 432nd Air Service Division. They were mainly mechanics, refuelers, electricians and oxygen men. Outside the barracks Bob would have had little reason to associate with them. They tended to hang around together and ate in a different mess hall than the air crews. Their food was supposedly better, but the flyboys didn't care. While airmen enjoyed all the supposed glamour—the lucky ones would arrive, complete their tours, then go home—the "ground pounders" stayed for the duration of the war. They seemed to live in world of their own. Payday would come, and an hour after pocketing their money, many blew it in a game of craps or poker. Bob referred to them as grease monkeys, which was as much a reflection of their sloppy appearance, coarse language, and outrageous behavior as their military specialties. Actually, they were a diverse collection of unique personalities, some very unique indeed.

Their ranks included guys referred to by surname or nickname, like PFC Alley, Hook Barret, Bentley, Brooks, Corky Clark, Huff Collins, Dick Crippen, King, Lane, Doc Neiss, Toby Tobias, and Webb. Corky and Huff were oxygen men. Corky owned a unicycle and entertained the guys on the hard stands during the anxious waits for returning bombers. Toby had another nickname: Boston Blackie; at least that's what Johnnie called him. [2] He was a short, dark curly-haired guy with a Boston accent who bunked between Johnnie and the wall of the hut. An amateur photographer, he liked to go to the Piccadilly district in London, find a lady of the evening, rent a room, take pictures of his subject, and display them on the barracks wall.

PFC Alley was another popular character who worked in the quartermaster unit. He came to Ridgewell originally as a gunner but quickly determined that ground duty was more suitable to his abilities and temperament, despite the cost of his demotion to PFC. He found his niche in the supply office. Resourceful and entrepreneurial, PFC Alley could procure almost anything anybody needed—as long as the requestor was discreet enough not to ask how it was done. Alley was the one who made sure Hut 18 had more than its regular ration of coke for the stove. Bob never admitted it, but Alley probably contributed to the rapid equipping of the skeet range. He was also known for running a dry cleaning business for the crews, although the unmistakable odor of 100-octane fuel betrayed the source of his cleaning fluids. On top of that he was the leader of an informal detail that would occasionally leave the hut at night, sneak into the bordering farm, and "borrow" a chicken or two, which weren't available at the mess hall. The ritual included beheading, plucking, and gutting, then boiling over a coke fire in a helmet filled with water. On more than one occasion Bob, a selectively finicky eater, was offered a sample of the delicacy, but refused to take it. He had to admit that it smelled good, however. Their polite English neighbors reported the missing chickens to the MPs, who regularly posted notices of the complaints and made direct inquiries at the grease monkeys' hut. Of course, everybody acted dumb about the chickens. It could have gotten more dicey with the billy goat, however. Thankfully, Alley hid that creature out back in the bomb shelter until they were ready to harvest it.

It's well known that the English people suffered during the war. Their condition wasn't just the result of the bombing or the menace of V-1 buzz-bombs, euphemistically nicknamed doodle bugs, which frequently droned overhead on trajectories to the major cities. Local citizens were deprived of the most basic comforts and conveniences, especially the people who lived in the tiny village of Great Yeldham. People there could still be seen carrying water from the town pump in buckets hung from yokes carried on their shoulders. Some of the poorest folks were said to have lived in barns with livestock. Food rationing only made the situation worse. The disparity in rations between the GIs and the townspeople was a little embarrassing. While understandable, it still seemed unfair. But the English people never complained. The Yanks were there to save them.

The Americans became friendly with the locals and with the English girls in particular. It was not uncommon for GIs to be invited for an off-duty dinner at a private home. Occasionally, the Ridgewell guest would take along a house gift of sugar or butter, borrowed from the commissary, to the innocent and appreciative host family. One of these ambassadors lived in Bob's hut. He was a character who looked like he belonged in the mafia and was known in the hut as "the wop." Not only did he keep his girlfriend's unwitting family well supplied with precious stolen commodities, but he also sold contraband to other families in the neighborhood. It was rumored that he had the nerve to steal items from the officers. John once bought a nice pair of shoes from the wop, but ended his association after hearing this gossip. Bob also kept his distance. Fortunately, the wop lived at the opposite end of the hut, "where all the stuff was going on."[3]

Despite these goings on, by and large the grease monkeys were a good-natured and fair-minded bunch of guys. On nights when John had to get up before dawn to fly on a mission, they set up a makeshift, folding screen around his bunk to block out the light and attempted to keep their raucous poker banter turned down to a civilized level. Bob would receive the same consideration when he began flight duty.

Bob expected that his first combat mission would be scheduled soon. Earlier that week he was issued his bulky flight gear, designed for use at high altitudes and cold temperatures, and was instructed on its proper use. He also received a standard issue 1911-A1 Remington .45 semi-automatic pistol, to be used in the event of capture by the enemy. Some air crews had inferred from briefings that, if shot down, they should avoid being captured at all costs; because, as retribution for bombing their homeland, angry Jerries were ignoring Geneva Convention rules and inflicting various forms of their own heinous justice.[4] Bob filtered out hearsay; he was more intent on focusing on the procedures to be followed on mission day; and, as instructed, he checked the bulletin board in the orderly room every day to see if his name was included on the list of assigned air crews for the following day's mission.

TWO DAYS AFTER THANKSGIVING Bob finally received his first batch of mail at his overseas address: two letters from Norm, one from his mom, and a card from Bill and Jean. It wasn't a month's worth, but the letters were much appreciated, as he wrote to Norm: *"They made me feel so much better after I read them. To see your handwriting again was a treat in itself! They mean everything in the world to me."* The letters from home were dated October 31st and November 4th. Bob wrote his reply between church and a movie on Sunday. In language that couldn't be censored he divulged the latest to Norm:

> *I thought I had something to do [today], however it was later cancelled. Seems as if a person here doesn't really know when he has a job to do, until he's almost doing it. Guess it's just as well though at that, huh? After all, does it make much difference?*

Perhaps it made more difference than he thought, or more than he was willing to say. One aircraft failed to make it back that day on a raid to Altenbaken, Germany, the group's 217th mission, and the mood on base changed from holiday gaiety to somber silence.[5] In the same letter he confessed that he was not smoking the pipe that Norm had given him as a gift, saying *"I always had such an awful taste in my mouth when I got up in the morning;"* he wrote more than usual about their future together, adding *"how I pray for that day soon to come;"* and, in a seemingly nonchalant aside, reminded her to keep the payments current on his Artisan's life insurance. In closing he wrote: *"Till tomorrow then darling, I'll have you in my heart always,…wherever I may go, you'll be right with me."*

Bob had promised Butch that he would be in touch after getting settled. The next day he inquired about the procedure for telephoning Capt. Powl of the 379th Bomb Group at Kimbolton. He was sent to the special services office next door to the gunnery school. Just as the officer in charge there was about to explain the procedure, he recalled that on the next day he would be making a trip to a base located near Kimbolton, and Sgt. Singleton could hitch a ride to that point. As luck would have it, Bob got permission to take a day off and returned to tell the officer that he should expect a passenger in the morning.

Despite an early start Bob never arrived at Kimbolton until about two in the afternoon, having hitched the final leg of the journey in a limey car. Butch was surprised and thrilled to see him; but, as he was on duty, they spent much of their time together at Butch's post in the armament office and on the flight line, meeting Kimbolton associates and comparing notes on Triangle K and L operations. But mostly they talked about their dear wives, updating each other on news from Lancaster. Following a short, but enjoyable afternoon they agreed to try to get two-day passes for a visit to Cambridge during the week before Christmas.

Bob left Kimbolton around five o'clock, knowing that he was on his own to negotiate the 60-plus miles back to Ridgewell. His plan was to take advantage of the loose but reliable system of Army trucks that shuttled between air bases and nearby towns, the so-called liberty runs. He caught his first ride on the run from Kimbolton to Cambridge, which was about the half-way point, but missed the truck from Cambridge to Ridgewell. After anxiously hitching a ride to a nearby town, he caught an alternate liberty run back to Ridgewell, managing to arrive in just enough time not to be declared AWOL.

What he would have given to have had the blue Chevy or tan Chrysler on that day. But that was like a fantasy from another life. Bob didn't even own a car anymore. In one of the weekly letters received from his dad, Roy mentioned that the Chevy wasn't getting much use. He suggested that, rather than paying for insurance to have the car sit idle, they might consider selling it. Automobiles had been rationed since February and were becoming scarce as the nation's factories shifted to full wartime production. An attractive price could be commanded. And Roy happened to have a buyer. Cousin Joe McMichael, Frank and Laura's son, was helping out as a salesman at the shoe store and needed a car. Joe had offered to purchase Bob's Chevy for

$1,000—almost $200 more than he had paid for it new. A thousand bucks was the equivalent of many months of Army pay. Bob felt that the deal made sense since Norm wasn't using the car anyway. In one of two letters and two V-mails waiting for Bob when he got back to Ridgewell—they were dated earlier than the last ones received—she reported the sale of the Chevy. In that night's letter Bob described his surprise visit to Butch and suggested how they should coordinate paying off their loan to Roy and putting the cash windfall toward a nest egg.

BOB WAS SCHEDULED TO FLY again a couple of times later that week, but the missions were cancelled due to poor weather. This was not an uncommon occurrence, but it contributed to anxiety about his up-coming combat experience. On two days earlier that week Johnnie had flown missions over Germany, both of which were completed with no Triangle L losses. The Eighth's bombing raids were wreaking havoc on the enemy, and newspapers reported that Allied ground forces were now approaching Germany.[6]  Thus, while Bob was a little tentative about flying, he felt that the odds were in his favor and quietly envied the number of missions Johnnie was accumulating toward completion of his tour.

    In the meantime he tried to focus on his work at the gunnery school and lived for letters from home. The day after the Kimbolton trip he received another batch of mail, including one from Smasher Smith, who was now back in Laredo waiting for a CIS slot that would probably never open—now that priority was being given to returning veteran gunners. One of Norm's letters included a photo of herself. He poured over her letters "*a half dozen times,*" savoring every word. In his December 2nd letter he replied to some of her concerns:

> ...*but really I'm not allowed to tell you very much...As yet I haven't done anything at all, that is any more dangerous than what I did back in the States...As far as doing the real thing as yet, I haven't. I've been scheduled to, however, several times, but circumstances prevented it.*

    He went on to tell her that he was asked to join a basketball team by one of the guys in the barracks who worked in the communications department. Their team played in an informal league at various towns in the area. "*To keep his mind occupied*" Bob agreed to play when he wasn't busy. Certainly, it would provide relief from hanging around the barracks in a frustrating waiting game.

On Sunday, December 3rd he was scheduled to fly again. For the third day in a row he was awakened by the CQ in the middle of a cold, damp English night and transported by truck to the mess hall and then to the flight line—only to experience a mission being scrubbed again due to poor weather. He returned to the hut and, no doubt weary, slept until he was *"too late for church."* When he spotted his name on the mission list for the next day, it was hard to get worked up about it. The routine was getting old. In addition to feeling cold, he now felt tired and irritable. After dinner he scratched off a short V-mail to Norm. He told her that he had been scheduled to *"work"* again, *"but found out that I didn't have to, later."* The grease monkeys also seemed to be getting a little testy lately; it could have been the lousy weather, but it was more likely because somebody had stolen the only radio in their hut. They all suspected that the culprit was the wop.

Nevertheless, that night the guys in Hut 18 did their best to control their behavior and keep the noise down. Both Bob and John were scheduled for another mission attempt on the next morning, and the privacy screen was set up. As Bob lay awake, his mind unsettled, he heard a loud, purposeful whisper from one of the grease monkeys, who were playing cards on the other side of the privacy screen. "Hush up, Alley!" a voice retorted. "Singleton and Rutherford are trying to sleep!" Instantly, the room became quiet. All things considered, the grease monkeys were a pretty decent bunch of guys.

Eventually, the wop would be caught in his black market scheme, picked up by the MPs, and reportedly taken away for three weeks of detention. But a few days after that, a couple of roughnecks would show up at the hut and rifle through his foot locker, salvaging anything of value. The wop allegedly owed them a couple hundred bucks, probably lost in craps. In a note left behind to justify their actions the scavengers would promise to surrender the wop's personal items when he returned. But the wop would never return. Nobody knew what ever happened to him. Such was life in the Army.

William and Rebecca, ca. 1850

Ambrose, ca. 1880

Emma, ca. 1880

Roy and Ivy at
Atlantic City, 1916
(old post card)

Bobby, ca. 1925

Ivy and Roy, ca. 1950

Wilbur, Eddie, and Bobby in Franklin Street back yard

Manheim Township High School
May Queen, 1940

Norma and Bob

With gifts from the VFW women's auxiliary in hand, 17 recruits on their way to basic training receive instructions from enlistment committee Chairman at the Lancaster post office. Bob is eighth from right in center foreground with a dazed look.

(*Above*) Shultzie and Bob demonstrate "pre-flight brace" at Mustang Field.

(*Below*) "H.P." Singleton in PT-19B

Bob and Norma, March 26, 1945

(*Left*) Walk leading from Hut 18 to 535th Orderly Room and (*Right*) Bob on skeet range

B-17 formation contrails seen from nose position

Trailing formation and flak seen from tail position

Bob and Johnnie
behind Hut 18

Bob, Sandy, Bobby, and Norma, 1951

Singleton's Shoes, 1960

Norma and Bob, 1964

Return to Great Yoho, 1995

381st Bomb Group Memorial, Station 167, Ridgewell, Essex, England

# Chapter 10

# Milk Run

Oddly enough, to air crews in East Anglia, one of the more unforgettable parts of flying a combat mission was what came before it. It was the cold, harsh, almost nightmarish routine of being awakened in the middle of the night, shivering in the dampness, stumbling about in the dark, eating breakfast on a uneasy stomach, waiting in suspense for disclosure of mission objectives, then mentally preparing for frequently on-again, off-again launches. Half-asleep, apprehensive, and generally reluctant air warriors silently executed their robotic procedures and personal rituals. They carefully adhered to checklists and hardly spoke to one another, except for first timers, who self-consciously eavesdropped or shamelessly asked for reassuring words from crewmates whom they usually perceived as more experienced, confident veterans.

Early in the pre-dawn hours of December 4th, Bob was once again startled out of a dreamy and incomplete sleep by a grasping hand firmly shaking his shoulder. "Time to get up" was all that was said by the night duty officer who made the rounds. Mechanically, Bob went into motion without thinking. It would serve no purpose to speculate on whether today would be the real thing or why he was doing this. Hurriedly, he pulled on fatigues, socks, and boots to cut the edge off the chill; hustled in blackness to the frigid latrine outside, where he hastily cleaned his teeth and combed his hair; and then returned to the dark hut to haphazardly make his bunk and collect basic necessities: a warm overcoat and his harnessed forty-five, which he slung over his shoulder. Somewhere in the darkness Johnnie was shuffling through a similar routine. On the way out the door a voice could he heard from a nearby bunk. "Good luck," said their friend.

They walked down to the end of the foggy path leading from the hut to wait for one of the trucks that rumbled around the perimeter road at regular intervals. Squealing brakes announced its arrival, and a hand reached out from under the canvas to assist boarding passengers, who would fumble for an empty seat on one of the side benches. With a hard clank of the transmission and growl of the engine they were off. The only sound was truck noise. The only sight was the intermittent, orange glow of a cigarette. The predominant smell was a mixture of musty dampness, gasoline fumes, tobacco smoke, worn leather, and body odor. Nobody spoke, officers or enlisted men. Bob wondered what everybody was thinking. The pick-up procedures were repeated at each stop until their arrival at the air crews' mess.

Except for the mess hall's relative warmth, smell of fresh coffee, and clinking of thick porcelain and kitchen utensils, the atmosphere wasn't much different. Muted social chatter that normally suffused a cafeteria was all but nonexistent. It was morose and eerie. Regular crews presumably sat together; but, as an unassigned crew member, Bob placed his tray on the nearest table. He didn't know with whom he would be flying or what their mission would be. He would find out soon enough. In the meantime mushy powdered eggs and watery powdered milk only served to remind him how far he was from home.

After breakfast the crews again boarded trucks, which delivered them to the briefing block. There, posted on a large board, was a list of names and assigned crew positions, with corresponding aircraft and hard stand numbers. Bob was assigned to WG (waist gunner) position on #538, which designated the last digits of the aircraft's tail number. Next they quietly walked next door to the equipment room to pick up their flight gear, which was stored in lockers. Since high altitude flight gear was bulky and constraining, crew members often put on only the critical items like thermal underwear, saving the heavy outer wear until closer to takeoff time. Depending on crew position, varying amounts of inner and outer wear were needed to deal with the extreme cold at high altitudes—temperatures that dropped to below minus 50 degrees centigrade. Items of clothing that weren't put on immediately, parachutes, and other paraphernalia were slung over their shoulders or toted to the waiting trucks in large duffel bags.

Dealing with flight gear was a small feat in itself. A complete set included: electrically-wired thermal underwear, nicknamed the "blue bunny suit;" fleece-lined leather pants and jacket; electrically-heated leather gloves with nylon inserts and cord that connected to the flight suit; fleece-lined boots; Mae West; flak vest; lined leather helmet with attached earphones and goggles; flak helmet; handgun and holster; oxygen mask with throat mike; and parachute harnass.[1] During flight, crew members in the warmer sections of the aircraft, like the area around the cockpit, usually didn't wear every item. Those in the coldest sections, like waist, tail, and ball turret, normally needed the works.

A B-17 BOMBER CREW consisted of ten positions: pilot, copilot, navigator, bombardier/nose (chin turret) gunner, radio operator, engineer/top turret gunner, ball turret gunner, right waist gunner, left waist gunner, and tail gunner. The first four positions were held by officers. When enemy fighter attacks lessened in the latter part of the war, missions were usually flown with one, rather than two waist gunners. In addition, the bombardier was replaced with a toggalier in many of the bombers. The toggalier had the same duties as a bombardier, except he was a non-commissioned officer who went through a crash course on bombing and would normally release bombs on a signal from the lead ship in the formation, which was always manned by a bombardier and equipped with a Norden bombsight.

Bob was relatively indifferent to having drawn waist position on his first flight. The waist was one of the coldest areas in the aircraft due to the large side windows, which had openings in the plexiglass for the machine guns. It was coldest in older-model B-17s, which had open side windows. As part of Bob's gunnery instructor orientation, he would be scheduled to fly a combat mission in each gun position except top turret, which was usually occupied by the flight engineer, and ball turret, a position for which he was three-quarter inches too tall to qualify. Ball turret gunners had to be less than five-feet-nine in order to fit into the tiny bubble located under the belly of the aircraft. Shorty Rutherford described to Bob what it was like in that position:

> You're in a cramped position, located outside of the airplane. Only with the guns pointed straight down is the turret's entrance hatch exposed to the inside of the airplane. Once you squeeze inside, latch the hinged door, and elevate the gun barrels, the hatch is on the outer side of the fuselage. You worry about the turret getting stuck and not being able to get out. The procedure is to place your parachute and shoes by the waist door, although I wear my chest pack with one clasp attached, one hanging, and keep my shoes with me. In the ball turret you have to make sure the guys up front warn you before they use the relief tube so that you can rotate the tur-

ret with the window facing the rear. Otherwise, urine will
freeze up on the window. This was a problem before they
made it a strict procedure.[2]

Gunner lore, unsubstantiated by statistics, often referred to the ball
turret as the most dangerous spot on the plane because of its exposure
to fighter attacks from below and the fear of getting trapped inside,
especially in the event of a gear-up crash landing with a jammed turret.

More than an hour before takeoff pilots, navigators, and bombardiers attended the all-important pre-flight briefing, where they learned
the particulars of the mission: primary target, route of flight, formation
and rendezvous procedures, initial point (IP) for the bombing run,
alternate targets, expected resistance, etc. Other crew members went
directly to the hard stands to execute their pre-flight duties. Some took
a short detour to one of the small chapels, located in the briefing
block, where airmen had the opportunity to settle up any outstanding
items with their Creator. Bob thought about making a stop, but, always
optimistic, buoyed by strong faith, and anxious to get on with it,
jumped on the back of the next truck heading for the hard stands.

As his truck came to a stop next to the shadow of a still sleeping,
but imposing flying machine, ordnance crews were already in action,
completing their tedious drill of loading 6,000 pounds of different
types of bombs into the bomber's belly, a process begun hours earlier
and one that was probably more dangerous than they made it look.
Simultaneously, crew chiefs silently went through their slow, methodical ritual of cycling the props of the big bird. In a two-man continuous
rotation, they leaned on the lower tips of the huge propellers and
heaved them in a sweeping arc as they walked along the leading edge
of the wing, following a ritual intended to gradually break down the
resistance of the glutinous engine oil that had settled and cooled overnight in the sumps of the giant radials. Even in the darkness Bob could
see that #538 was a relatively new-looking silver G-model, with few
telltale signs of pock marks, scratches, or major repairs. Either he was
too preoccupied to notice or the ground crew had not yet decorated
the nose of their ship with its name, *Wild Bill*.

One of the first duties of an air crew member was to retrieve the
"guts" of his machine guns, which after each mission were cleaned,
lubricated and stored in a heated armament shed to ensure proper
functioning of their precision firing mechanisms. The guts of a caliber-

fifty consisted of the barrels and all the moving parts—essentially everything but the gun mount. Each gun was marked to identify its location on the aircraft, and each air crew member was responsible for collecting his gun from the armament officer on duty and installing it at his crew position.

As a gunnery instructor, Bob had this part of the mission procedure down pat. He dropped his duffel outside the waist door, went to the shed to collect his first gun, and confidently strode back to the airplane with the gun hoisted over his shoulder—not that it was light duty carrying an killing machine having the weight of a filled, raw milk container. He repeated the procedure for both waist guns. The other guys followed a similar routine. Nobody talked much. They were strangers to him, and Bob assumed that they had all previously flown together. In the minimal talk that took place, one of the guys learned that Bob was a gunnery instructor and asked for help installing his gun. Bob didn't know whether to feel important or skeptical about his fellow crew member's lack of confidence. He wouldn't think of trusting somebody else to install his guns. Bob used the opportunity to confess to his new acquaintance that it was his first mission and asked what to expect. The other guy laughed nervously, admitting that it was only his second. As he helped with the guns, Bob kept his ears open to pick up any tidbits that might give a clue as to what might happen that day. Other than knowing how to fire a machine gun, he felt that he had little training for this role.

The hard stand was a beehive of motion, but much of it was nervous energy. Crews would climb into the hatches and crawl back outside. They installed, reinstalled, arranged, and rearranged the long, heavy belts of linked ammunition, which were stacked in serpentine loops inside wood and metal-banded ammunition boxes, one box per gun and 300-500 rounds per box, depending on gun location. Each ammunition belt was around 27 feet long, which led to the expression "the whole nine yards"—usually after it was fully spent. On missions where intense fighter activity was expected, particularly during the early raids, resourceful gunners smuggled extra belts aboard, contributing to a not uncommon tendency for Fortresses to take off with more than their 6,380 maximum allowable number of rounds and at gross weights dangerously in excess of specified limits.

Anxious crew members reappeared and clustered together when the truck carrying the pilot and remaining crew arrived. The pilot's name was Lt. David Sweetland. He shared essential mission details with the anxious crew and asked for questions. Nobody asked what was really on their mind. Their target was a concentration of rail yards in a German town called Soest. He said it would be a routine mission. There wasn't much else to be said. When the order was given to board, crew members pulled on the rest of their outer gear and climbed through the waist door or belly hatch. Their duffel bags would remain with them throughout the mission. After boarding the gunners hung their belts of ammo in their guns. It was now only a matter of getting the go signal, a green flare launched from the control tower. That signal, coordinated with others like it across dozens of bases in East Anglia, triggered a sequence of pre-briefed engine start times and taxi procedures for the Ridgewell bombers.

Bob couldn't see the arcing green flare from his seated position on the ammo box but knew the mission was on when #538's number-one engine rattled, fired, and belched a cloud of pungent smoke. His heart rate immediately picked up. The sound of a B-17's Cyclone engines is distinctive and unforgettable to anyone who has ever heard them. Each big radial, in sequence, transitions from a metallic rattle of initial rotation to a muffled boom of ignition, then gradually settles into a rumbling quartet of four engines. Multiply this by dozens of aircraft, and the resultant din that emanated from the darkness of Great Yoho could just as easily have passed for a surrealistic invasion of giant killer bees as the awakening of a fleet of friendly Fortresses.

As the bombers taxied in procession to the takeoff position, the rookie waist gunner squirmed to steady himself on his ammo box, which inclined downward to a bouncing and swaying tail section. A pattern of roaring engines in the distance announced the takeoff roll of aircraft at the front of the battle procession. At 30-second intervals each bomber gunned its engines and released brakes. After about 15 minutes in the taxi procession #538 maneuvered into takeoff position. Following a brief pause at idle power, Lieutenant Sweetland pushed four throttles firmly to maximum power, and the Cyclones quickly revved up to a loud, whining roar. Bob's heartbeat picked up, and the heavy bomber clawed its way forward. The rate of acceleration felt extremely slow compared to PT-19s, and the lumbering monster seemed to refuse to let go of the ground. A three-point liftoff was barely perceptible as thirty-plus tons of bombs, armament, men, and machines struggled into the air. When the clumsy landing gear groaned then bumped against the Fort's underside, her passengers were tempted to breathe more easily. But the moaning engines betrayed her struggle to gain altitude, and grim recollections of overloaded planes lost during the takeoff leg kept anxious crew members on edge.

For the next half-hour little seemed to change except the temperature and air pressure. Outside the two waist windows all that was visible was a combination of darkness, fog, and the shadowy blur of cloud interiors as they entered the dense overcast. The altitude change required intermittent contractions of throat muscles to release the throbbing pressure buildup in the airmen's inner ears. Each bomber climbed at 300 feet per minute on a pre-briefed, vertically spiraling course above the field, using for fixed reference a radio beacon called a buncher, which with luck guided them above the cloud deck within sight of the other squadron aircraft, where they followed coordinated procedures for assembling into squadron and group formations. Air crews implicitly trusted their pilot to accomplish these challenging, but well-rehearsed maneuvers in the lousy English weather. Nevertheless, the first sign of blue sky and the glint of sunlight off other ships was a welcome sight for everybody.

Through the framed view of the side windows Bob intently watched his squadron forming up. In wide, sweeping arcs a dozen planes organized themselves into four-plane elements stacked below the squadron leader. The other squadrons performed similar routines at thousand-foot intervals. The lead squadron flew between high and low squadrons in what was called a combat box stagger formation, which was designed for concentrated saturation bombing and effective defense against fighters. They would proceed in this arrangement to a rendezvous point over the English Channel, where they would join up with other Eighth Air Force bomber groups. The groups would then sequence themselves at about four mile intervals or fall into a combat wing formation organized for maximum, concentrated, defensive firepower.[3] Bob couldn't identify much beyond his own formation of Triangle L ships, but for as far as he could see through the glare of the sun, there were glistening, organized clusters of tiny-looking aircraft. The formations flying at higher altitudes were followed by spectacular, streaming white contrails created by a combination of engine exhaust, propeller wash, and certain atmospheric conditions. Despite anxiety about the mission, Bob was captivated by the fantastic beauty of the silver Fortresses gleaming in the morning sun, the bright blue expanse surrounding them, and the soft white carpet of cumulus below.

Earlier during the climb-out phase each crew member had been reminded by intercom to "go on oxygen," a signal that the aircraft was passing through 10,000 feet. The gunners were also given the signal that it was okay to test guns, and through the insulation of his ear phones and head gear Bob could hear muffled, but sharp bursts from other guns nearby. He moved off his ammo box, checked his ammunition belt, crouched behind his gun, and pointed the weapon down and away from the climbing formation before squeezing off a burst. Same thing on the other waist gun. They were trained to know that it was a good idea to cycle a few rounds, just to make sure that live ammo was in the chamber and ready to fire. It was strange; his trusty caliber-fifty felt and sounded different than it did on the range. He couldn't describe it. But the machine gun's harsh retort shocked him back to the strange reality of the moment.

It took over an hour for the armada to form up and get pointed toward the target, a three-hour flight away. When the whining engine noise finally abated and the Fort finally settled into straight and level flight, it became apparent how cold it was at 25,000 feet. Icy edges of goggles and oxygen masks etched sharp imprints on damp facial skin. Numbness in toes and fingers betrayed imperfections in the design of the insulated, heated flight gear. But relative to psychological stress, these were somewhat minor inconveniences. Like the others, Bob just wanted to get on with it and get it over with—whatever *it* would be. Due to the thick layer of clouds below them, there was little to see on the surface, which by the second hour of the mission would have changed from sea to land. What a way to visit Europe for the first time. An unfamiliar nasal voice chirped on the intercom, saying something about a "friendly bogey at eight o'clock, slightly above the horizon." Another voice confirmed that it was some aircraft from their fighter escort. Bob craned his neck, and after a lengthy search spotted miniature shapes in the distance. It was a lot easier to identify aircraft types on flash cards at gunnery school. These were probably P-51 Mustangs; they were said to be the best all-around fighters in the war. It sure was nice to know they were out there.

But the security net wouldn't be there the whole way. Fighters had shorter range capability than the big bombers and normally peeled off as the bombers approached the target. The bomb line had moved well across France by late 1944. Approaching three hours after takeoff the much anticipated moment arrived. Word came over the intercom: "We are now in enemy territory." At this point adrenaline started to kick in. Everybody was at their stations, wide-eyed and alert. Soon they could see in the distance tiny, black clouds of smoke—deceptively innocent-looking puffs, which from a distance didn't reveal the orange firestorm of exploding shrapnel that had instantaneously preceded their appearance. This was flak, the nemesis of bomber crews. Flak was an adversary feared as much as, if not more than, attacking enemy fighters. At least you had some advance warning of an approaching fighter. Flak would appear arbitrarily and virtually out of nowhere. Unfortunately, it wasn't always arbitrary. Firing 88 mm shells into giant swarms of attacking bombers was like firing shotguns into huge flocks of slow-moving geese. Unlike duck hunters, however, trained antiaircraft gunners set up box-like patterns of flak over the target area and had the advantage of time fuses on their shells, which could be set to explode at specific altitudes. Through trial and error the timing of the explosion could be adjusted to home-in on the center of the stable, structured bomber formations. The most deadly flak was that which exploded at the aircraft's altitude. Next was the flak set to explode above, because unexploded shells were known to frequently punch holes through bombers on the way to their pre-set target altitude. Bob recalled Johnnie's experience on the *Tomahawk Warrior* and his photos of the structural damage taken after the mission, which was disconcerting to say the least.

Contrary to popular belief, flak over target areas actually intensified as the enemy was pushed back across the continent. As the front line moved eastward, the Germans pulled back their antiaircraft batteries to consolidate defenses of the homeland and compensate for waning fighter aircraft capability, caused by dwindling supplies of fuel and pilots. Bomber crews knew this from intelligence briefings. Thus, no matter how much they had heard from veteran crews about how rough it was on the early raids, replacement crews were never complacent and never relaxed. Flak got everybody's attention, and the closer it got, the greater the chance of having to endure a terrorizing clamor of shrapnel hammering their thin aluminum shell, often piercing surfaces like hail penetrating tin foil.

Everybody tightened up at the sight of flak, and Bob was no exception. He wasn't paralyzed with fear or choked up to the point of being unable to function. But he was definitely "on his toes," in his words, keenly intent on what he was trained to do. Gunners constantly rotated their heads searching for fighters, while trying not to flinch at the red flash of exploding flak or the subsequent hailstorm. When the first barrage of flak peppered #538, Bob probably responded like others when they experienced it for the first time: he instinctively jerked his head down between his shoulders and crunched lower in his seat—as if the crouch would somehow provide a shield against the indiscriminate storm. On subsequent bursts the flinching moderated to an instantaneous tightening of body muscles and facial grimaces. Air crews never got used to it; just when they thought the worst was over, a random blast more nerve shattering than the last would follow. While the odds of taking a direct hit were statistically in their favor, with each burst that missed, natural instincts drove them to believe that the next one would be fatal. This phase of the mission could last for an hour, depending on the location and strategic importance of the target.

In the target area gloved hands rarely left gun handles, and few had to be reminded to minimize nervous intercom chatter. Air crews felt most vulnerable during the bombing run, which commenced at the pre-briefed IP. That's when the group leader locked in on a specific altitude, airspeed, and heading to the target—all the conditions that made it easier for antiaircraft gunners to zero-in on them. Add to this the fact that bomb bay doors were wide open during the final segment of the bomb run, which would last about a minute or until all ordnance was released. This could be complicated by the occasional tendency for bombs to hang up in the racks or for bomb bay doors to remain stuck in the open position, further exposing air crews to deadly shrapnel. In that situation seconds seemed like hours as bombardiers rushed back to physically kick loose bombs hung up in the racks or to manually crank the doors closed.

The waist gunner felt the most vulnerable during the bomb run, not to mention the coldest. Although the wind blast sounded worse than it actually was, it exacerbated his exposure to the frigid conditions. Bob's muscles were in a state of constriction as the aircraft lurched upward—the result of dumping its heavy load of bombs. Then after the all clear signal was given, the bomb bay doors were closed, and the aircraft banked away from the target area. Flak intensity began to subside after a while—about the time they were advised to increase vigilance for enemy fighters, which were usually deployed to intercept tired bombers on their way home and to shoot down crippled aircraft straggling behind the phalanx of the group formation.

Fortunately, they didn't see any fighters. But through the side windows and breaks in the clouds Bob could see far in the distance, below and behind them, what their mission was all about. Thick plumes of black smoke erupted from the surface of the earth. It appeared that the Jerries' rail system had been dealt a crippling blow. Bob's adrenaline-filled state of mind was not capable of considering whether innocent civilian lives might have been affected.

Alongside #538, the Triangle L formation appeared intact, albeit a little more stretched-out than on the way in. After about an hour-and-a-half into the return leg, soft music could be heard through the static of the intercom. Apparently, the cockpit had picked up the pleasant radio signals from a friendly broadcast. It was a subtle message that the crew could breathe easier. As they began letting down to a lower altitude Bob saw the flight engineer appear out of the top turret with portable oxygen bottle in hand, apparently in a rush. His purpose quickly became clear as he relieved his bladder in the empty bomb bay. He obviously had no patience for using the relief tube near his station. Bob, sympathetic for his fellow crewman's plight, envied his obvious relief and considered his own situation. He was surprised that he had held out as long as he did, regardless of the fact that he had not eaten or drunk anything since breakfast eight hours ago. As he raised up out of his crouched position, unplugged his heating wire, and grabbed a portable oxygen bottle, he was surprised by the extreme stiffness in his joints and muscles.

The English coast line was barely visible through the clouds, and the countryside farther inland was covered by the unrelenting overcast. The late afternoon sunlight changed to a murky tint as the formation split up and the bombers descended in trail. The rapid bleakness was offset by a moderation in temperature and the imminence of mission completion. The crew was advised that it was now safe to go off oxygen and time to prepare for landing. The rotten weather obscured anything worth seeing outside, and maneuvering through the soup seemed to take forever, especially from the increasingly unpleasant edge of the ammo box.

SEVEN-AND-A-HALF HOURS AFTER TAKEOFF, #538 met the earth with a squeak and a bounce, then settled into its vibrating, swaying, and inclined taxi mode. Conversation could be overheard in the cockpit, but Bob ignored the chatter when he spotted other crew members intent on getting a head start in the process of reorganizing their gear and dismounting machine guns. As the aircraft approached the hard stand, Bob could see the crew chiefs standing ready to welcome the flyboys, but just as importantly, to inspect their beloved Fort for flak damage.

When the big Cyclones finally rattled to a stop, the anticipated silence was replaced with a reverberating echo of engine vibration in their skulls and an underwater sensation in their ears—a nuisance that would disappear by morning. Other than quietly acknowledging the welcoming comments from ground crews, the exhausted airmen unconsciously went about their business of removing guns and placing them on the ground in a designated area where ground crews would clean them before stowing them in the armament shed. The flyboys were too tired to help, and the ground crews were more than happy to take over. The sweaty warriors gathered their duffels and boarded the waiting trucks.

With a familiar racket the personnel trucks delivered crews to the briefing block, where the mandatory post-flight interrogation took place. Waiting on a small counter outside the interrogation room were the traditional shots of whiskey for airmen returning from battle. Some said this was intended to loosen up the crews prior to interrogation. A clerk was posted there to check off the name as each shot was issued. Despite the quiet elation of having returned safely from his first combat mission, Bob had no interest in celebrating with whiskey. He had never acquired a taste for liquor, and such out-of-character drinking only would have diminished his sense of accomplishment. Roy would have been proud. The whiskey also made Bob wonder briefly about his old buddy Shultzie and where the war might have taken him. His hesitation may have been apparent. Before having a chance to decline his reward, a familiar face from Hut 18, standing among a small group outside, politely mentioned that he would be very pleased to accept Sergeant Singleton's allotment. Bob happily granted the request. He would learn that it was customary for ground crews to gather at the briefing block after a mission to welcome the air crews and, for some, to cheerfully scavenge a shot or two.

The interrogation process was conducted in a large, open room. Each crew was assigned a table, which was staffed with an intelligence officer and sometimes an officer from the operations staff. Bob didn't engage in the discussion. All returning airmen were required to be present, except for those who had been taken to the hospital. A list of standard questions were asked about such things as enemy aircraft sightings, when the IP was reached, when bomb cameras were turned on, and how much flak was observed. Bob determined that the consensus on flak was that it was "light" on this mission. It made him wonder what heavy flak was like. Fortunately, no Triangle L aircraft were lost that day, and they successfully destroyed their target. Perhaps this is what they called a milk run. But not exactly like Gottselig's. The officers stayed behind for more discussion after the gunners were dismissed.

As his stiff, worn-out body went through the labored motions of removing and storing his flight gear, he began to think about a hot shower, a cooked meal, a letter to Norm, but, most of all, a good night's sleep. His head still buzzed, and his mind raced. He had not fully absorbed the significance of what he had experienced that day, because his thoughts were scattered and his brain fatigued. His mood remained unsettled and contemplative, but he still managed to get off his daily letter before going to bed early:

*Monday nite*
*December 4th*
*7:30*

*Hello Darling,*
*I'm very tired tonite and would like to hit the sack a bit early, so this may not be such a long letter.[...]⁴ I can't tell you too much about what I'm doing, but I can tell you I did recently pay a visit to Hitler and his Nazis, and gave them a little bit of h--- in return for the heart-aches and suffering they have caused already. Even more, I done it for your [...] sake...if it wasn't for them, we'd probably be together right now. I'll have quite a bit to tell you someday, concerning the various blows dealt them. Please don't worry about me now, Hon, as I'm sure everything will be alright. If you are "on the ball," and wide awake, things usually work out O.K., and I'll assure you I am both, as much as possible. With a sweet, little wife like you to come back to [...] I'll*

*never be otherwise. Gosh Hon, you mean the world and all to me...I*
*sure do miss you! I hope and pray every day that we will be together*
*again soon. I certainly don't see how this thing can last too much longer,*
*do you? I certainly hope it doesn't anyhow! I suppose a couple million*
*others feel the same way, also.*

The letter went on to talk about hopes and plans for the future.
He remembered to ask if Norm had received her October War Bond
that was arranged for in his pay allotment. This would be the second
bond toward their nest egg. Before signing off to *"catch up on some sleep"*
he made a reaffirmation: *"so till later, remember I love you more and more each*
*day, if that's possible, and think you're the most wonderful wife a guy could ever*
*have."*

CHAPTER 11

# FEATHER MERCHANT

THE DAY AFTER THE SOEST RAID the atmosphere at Ridgewell was relatively subdued. While it wasn't time to celebrate, news reports were encouraging. Not only had the 381st completed another mission without losses, but they were part of a massive Allied initiative that struck a devastating blow to the Nazi rail centers in western Germany, contributing to the strategy of isolating Germans on the Western Front from their main industrial centers.[1] "Approximately 1,200 Fortresses and Liberators of the Eighth Air Force, escorted by about 1,000 Mustangs and Thunderbolts of the Eighth and Lightnings of the Ninth, yesterday hammered rail yards and industrial objectives in the Reich."[2] General Eaker was attributed to have been "predicting the success of new cloud-bombing techniques" when he claimed that "German targets are due for the greatest weight of bombardment they have ever received, and winter weather will not protect them."[3] It was comforting to be on the winning side.

Bob did not receive mail that day or have much to say in a V-mail to Norm, but he included a request that she send his overseas address to Shultzie, who might be located through the return address on his last correspondence from Laredo. Bob's first mission experience caused him to wonder how his old buddy was holding up under the pressure of combat flying, assuming that's how the Army was employing him.

The weather was miserable that week, giving weight to idle gossip that the fleet would be grounded until the latest frontal system moved through. The dreariness was broken by four letters from Norm delivered on the following day. They were written earlier than letters he had already received from her, but were more welcome than a ray of sun through the English gloom. In one letter she must have shared some difficulties she was having regarding petty family matters, because Bob went to great lengths in his next letter to provide elaborate context and consoling words on the matter. This would certainly be helpful for Norm, and the concentration devoted to his writing was therapeutic in

diverting his attention from the depressing reality of his own situation.
He finished his letter-writing earlier than usual that evening, because
the grease monkeys were *"sorta throwing a party"* in the barracks. The
menu would be interesting, as always.

The second week of December dragged on as ground forces in
Europe slugged it out near the German border and got bogged down
in bloody snow. During quiet moments GI's around the world and
anxious loved ones at home were already dreaming about holidays—
mostly past and future ones. Considering the horrible blows being
dealt at random to many families, the lucky ones were properly
conditioned to keep a stiff upper lip and stoically accept the present.
On December 8th, in view of the slow postal service and the fact that
his name was on the crew list for the following day's mission, Bob
decided it would be timely and prudent to send a Christmas wish in a
second V-mail to Norm. It was tediously penned in Gothic script:

## A MERRY XMAS
## TO MY
## DEAR WIFE!

During This Holiday Season
Though We May Be Far Apart...
My Love And God's Blessings Upon You
Grow Deeper Within My Heart.

From
Your Hubby
"Bob"

*P.S. Sorry I couldn't get a card Honey, but it's almost an im-
possibility. Hope this will convey the same meaning, just the same!
I just hope we may spend the next X-mas season together, and all
thereafter.*

He went to bed and fell asleep with this thought in mind. He never
heard the grease monkeys put up the privacy screen.

Around 4 A.M. he was startled out of a deep sleep. The realization
of having to fly on another combat mission caused his heart to flutter.
Was this a dream? The activities of the last three days had begun to

dull his recall of the first mission, and his subconscious had repressed those terrifying moments over the target area. But the frigid dampness of the barracks floor jarred him into action. This morning's routine was the same, but it seemed colder. He heard Johnnie also going through the motions in the dark. It was unusual that they were both flying. They had been told that gunnery instructors from the same hut would not normally be scheduled to fly on the same ship or on the same day. Perhaps this would be just another milk run.

The designated target was marshalling yards in Stuttgart, a large industrial center in southwestern Germany, which normally was a "hotbed of flak."[4] Bob was assigned to the tail gunner position on ship #590. As they arrived at the hard stand Bob could see that #590 had a name: *In Like Errol*. It was a G-model, but even in the darkness he could determine that this plane had seen action. He didn't recognize anybody. The pilot's name was Lt. Mead K. Robuck.[5]

The tail position was worse than the waist. It was cramped and isolated. The only way to access the position was by crawling on hands and knees through the narrow tail section. Doing this while lugging the guts of a caliber-fifty was a strenuous exercise. After mounting the guns he had to return for the ammo belts, which were normally loaded into the waist area by the armament crews. Once in position, the tail gunner sat facing to the rear on a bicycle-like seat with legs extended horizontally. There was barely enough room for him to bend his legs, which were crammed against padded knee-holds. A relief tube was located to one side and equipment hook-ups to the other. The machine gun sights were at eye level in front of the seat. Visibility was mostly up and to the sides between the aircraft's four and eight o'clock. Downward visibility was limited.

The tail was a critical defensive position on the bomber, because enemy fighters frequently approached from behind. Attacks to the rear had developed into a favorite tactic of the Luftwaffe after Me262 jet fighters were introduced in late 1944. The twin engine jets would hide above and behind the contrails of the formation, swoop down to quickly overtake the bombers, and often catch tail gunners off guard.[6] Bob wasn't yet aware of this tactic, but it had been made clear to him before the mission that it was the tail gunner's job to smartly call out any bogeys to their rear. Robuck reminded his crew to look sharp; Colonel Leber, the Group Commander, was flying in the lead ship on their mission to Stuttgart that day.

Triangle L bombers took off at 0800 and climbed through what now seemed like a permanent English overcast. Bob felt like he was trapped in a frozen meat locker, separated from the rest of the crew. The temperature dropped to minus 55 degrees by the time they leveled off at 30,000 feet. At this altitude crew members could quickly get into trouble if their equipment malfunctioned. That's apparently what happened to their waist gunner. Bob heard the agitated dialog on the intercom. The top turret gunner reported to the pilot that the waist gunner had passed out. The response from up front was to "get the hell back there and help him out!" It was several minutes before he reported back. The waist gunner had inadvertently disconnected his oxygen, but was now revived and reconnected. A weak acknowledgement confirmed that he was shaken, but conscious. While this was a serious matter, Bob had to chuckle to himself. Johnnie had recently told him about a similar incident where he had been instructed to leave his tail station and help out a waist gunner in similar trouble. Johnnie had the presence of mind to tote his portable oxygen bottle with him but forgot to attach his face mask. The pungent odor of crew flatus in the center cabin, induced by low cabin pressure, immediately tipped him off to his mistake. Johnnie enjoyed telling his buddies that "a fart saved his ass."[7]

At cruising altitude long white contrails were persistent on the way to the target, making the tail gunner's job particularly difficult.[8] Bob felt especially confined and vulnerable on the tail post as they entered the target area. And it didn't take long to figure out that Stuttgart was more heavily defended than Soest. Flak was more persistent and concentrated at the formation's altitude. Bursts were bigger, darker, and closer. Over the target it was horrible. Relentless flak sand-blasted the scarred and patched skin of old *In Like Errol*. It was like a nightmare. His muscles were tensed up, and time seemed to stand still during the bomb run. It didn't ease up until they were well out of the target area. No enemy fighters were spotted, but it didn't seem possible that all ships would return unscathed.

Numb from the experience, they safely touched down at 1530 and silently went through the process of deplaning and privately kissing the ground. Crew chiefs buzzed around their prized Fort, taking mental notes on anticipated skin repairs. The dazed air crews hustled off.

In the interrogation room there was scuttlebutt that a 535th ship was hit over the target and went down in France through an opening in the clouds. A day later that plane would be reported to have made an emergency landing—on two engines, with no hydraulics, and with five wounded crew members on board. Several other 381st planes also suffered damage but managed to make it back. It was matter-of-factly reported in the *Stars and Stripes* that, out of the 400 Eighth Air Force Fortresses sent to Stuttgart, four bombers were lost and a handful of airmen were killed in planes that made it back.[9] This would be received as encouraging news, unless you were the family of a crew member on the unlucky end of the statistic. In the same cold-hearted tone of military statistics, the flak over Stuttgart that day was observed to have been "moderate and accurate."[10] Bob sensed that the atmosphere in the interrogation room was more strained than after the last mission. The oxygen-deprived waist gunner was not present. He had been taken directly to the hospital to get checked out for anoxia but would be found to be in satisfactory condition. The medics would pay more attention to a gunner of a 532nd ship who had been severely wounded by flak—and would ultimately die after two days of blood transfusions and specialized treatment at a better hospital in nearby Braintree.[11]

This mission weighed more heavily on Bob than the first one. Others talked casually about completing 25 and going home, and with each mission more flyboys seemed to reach this coveted milestone. But, as far as Bob was concerned, there was nothing to be nonchalant about. It was ironic that he made no mention of his second mission to Norm. He wrote only a brief V-mail that evening. It opened with *"Gee Honey, I'm awful tired tonite, so please do forgive the V-mail!"* Then, it built up to what he was really feeling: *"I sure miss you more than ever Honey! Golly, I love you so much I can't describe it! You're EVERYTHING in the world to me Hon. I hope you know that."* Perhaps she would get the message.

THE FOLLOWING DAY started out like a leisurely Sunday but abruptly changed into an anxious day before a mission when Bob saw his name posted on the crew list for Monday, 11 December. Four new V-mails just received from Norm had a soothing effect, but he was frustrated that her letters and promised packages lagged behind in deliveries. That shouldn't have been a surprise to him. V-mail was said to be more efficient, and official communications, like base daily bulletins, encouraged personnel to use that medium rather than air mail to reduce the weight of non-essential military cargo going overseas.[12] So he resorted again to V-mail that afternoon, asserting without apology that he would use the victory medium until the holiday mail backlog had shrunk. He also reasoned that he wouldn't feel like writing a long letter on the next day, when he was scheduled for another mission.

He had hardly fallen into a deep sleep before the orderly's firm hand shook him awake. His thoughts were muddled as he sat in the cold darkness on the edge of his bunk. He was tempted to retreat back under the wool blanket. The only sound in the hut was heavy breathing. Even Johnnie was still; his buddy from Millersville wasn't scheduled to fly that day. Having already completed 14 missions, lucky Johnnie was half-way home.

Bob was assigned to the tail gunner position again, but this time on aircraft #553, piloted by a Lt. Valentino J. Malleus and crewed by another collection of strangers. The ship's name was also strange: *Feather Merchant II*. He wondered where those funny names came from. Perhaps one of the original crews on #553 descended from a family of pillow manufacturers or chicken farmers. What happened to Feather Merchant I? Who knows? This name certainly didn't offer any comfort or inspiration. It sounded more like the name of a weak bird. Then again, as the crew chief told him, this ship had been flying since May.

It took longer for the formation to join up that day, not only due to the weather conditions, but because of the sheer size of the armada that was being formed. It would later be reported that today's was "the largest force of heavy bombers ever dispatched in daylight on a single mission by the Eighth Air Force."[13] It was an impressive sight. From his tail position, Bob could see majestic planes everywhere. And he was only looking at a small portion of an organized mass of 1,600 Fortresses and Liberators, escorted by 800 Thunderbolts and Mustangs, which made up a column nearly 100 miles long. They were headed for rail yards and supply lines throughout western Germany from Onasbruck south to Mannheim. Triangle L bombers were near the front of the column and would make one of the deepest penetrations into enemy territory. The *Feather Merchant's* objective was to destroy a railroad bridge in Mannheim.

The mighty Eighth would have a successful day. Because German fuel supplies were now extremely scarce, the armada was unopposed by enemy fighters. They hit their targets through cloud cover, but not without a price. The flak barrage was intense. A dozen bombers and a couple fighters were lost due to *"heavy"* flak. In Bob's formation *"one ship blew up, due to a direct hit."*[14] He heard somebody on the intercom call out "ship off the right side hit!" after which he spotted the burning aircraft falling in a steep spin. Six chutes were counted leaving the plunging wreckage.[15] It really got the crew's attention and made Bob feel more alone in the tail. He feared that Johnnie was on that plane until remembering that his buddy wasn't scheduled to fly that day.

After eight-and-a-quarter excruciating hours they finally touched down at Ridgewell. Fatigued crews were uptight and agitated during the interrogation. The whiskey didn't seem to have a soothing effect on those who drank their allotment. It was the group's second mission in a row where planes had not come back. The 381st had suffered losses on 5 of the last 12 missions—after flying 11 without losses. As in the early days, young airmen were beginning to question what they were doing. It just didn't make any sense; they were supposed to be winning this war. Silly names like *Feather Merchant* no longer seemed to provide any redeeming humor. Bob was just thankful that the old bird got him home with only a few more scars added to her complexion.

Air crews subconsciously rationalized that their legendary Forts were invincible and would always manage to bring them home. Bob couldn't know it at the time, but three weeks later #553 would make an emergency landing in France and her crew would have to find a different way home. *Feather Merchant II* would soon be out of business.

Despite lack of nutrition since breakfast 12 hours earlier Bob was in no mood for supper or long letter writing. His V-mail started out similar to the last one:

> *Put in another pretty rough day today, so these V-mails come in pretty handy. That is, if you only feel like writing a little bit? My feeling is just like that now, too. I certainly don't feel like writing a lot, I assure you. Sure hope you don't mind, Hon! Say you do not, will you? I'll try and do better tomorrow nite.*

His last promise was wishful thinking in view of the fact that he was scheduled to fly on yet another mission the next day. Nevertheless, before signing off he managed to cheerfully respond to a few points in Norm's V-mails of the day before. As weary as he was, his daily "talk" with her, more than anything else, kept him going.

THE NEXT MORNING he saw himself going through the motions in what now seemed like an out-of-body experience, or the repeat of a bad dream. Even though he had three missions under his belt, he felt more uneasy. When he boarded the truck to the mess hall, he didn't bother to ask himself why the others weren't talking or what they were thinking. He knew the answer. He was just wondering if the missions would continue to get worse.

When he filed into the mess hall, it was apparent that something was different. He heard some quiet, but pleasant conversation in the chow line. Attractive ladies could be seen behind the counter assisting with serving. Their starched uniforms distinguished them as Red Cross girls, who usually showed up on special occasions. A nice touch to this miserable morning routine, Bob thought. As he filed through the chow line he helped himself to another unexpected treat: *fresh* eggs! What's the occasion? he wondered. He remarked about it as he sat down with a group of strangers. A voice from a couple of trays away facetiously grumbled something about today's being a special mission.

It was special all right. Their flight would take them deep into Germany to a town called Merseburg, located just outside of Leipzig. Their target was the Leuna synthetic oil refinery, one of the German's few, large refineries remaining. In area it covered a square mile. The plant was partly operating again after having been bombed 18 times.[16] By this time, the enemy was desperate for fuel. As a result, German antiaircraft artillery was especially concentrated around refineries, with "as many as 500 heavy flak guns at the most important sites such as Merseburg."[17] They were warned to expect a lot of flak on this raid.

Bob recognized the pilot, Lieutenant Malleus, with whom he had flown the day before on *Feather Merchant II*. And the crew also looked to be the same as the day before, which offered some comfort. But today they were flying in ship #018, the notorious *Los Angeles City Limits*. This Fort had seen more than its fair share of combat. A week before Bob had arrived in Ridgewell, this plane had aborted a mission to Cologne due to engine problems, which shouldn't have surprised anybody, considering what the plane had been through previously. An October write-up in the base daily bulletin told the story:

> Backed by superb teamwork, 1st Lt. John J. O'Connor, 535th Squadron, recently piloted the bomber "Los Angeles City Limits" home alone from inside Germany after flak and

fighters had left his ship with two engines dead and a propeller windmilling violently. Flak got the first engine on the way to the target and the bombardier salvoed his load in an attempt to help O'Connor keep up with the formation. Unable to do so, the pilot turned for home. A few minutes later "L.A." was hit by two Me163 jet-propelled fighters which O'Connor's gunners successfully fought off until a pair of P-51's showed up. However, cannon fire from one enemy plane had silenced a second engine and damaged its prop feathering control. Flying at only 4,000 feet the bomber ran into tracking flak shortly afterward. Necessary evasive action left it with even less altitude and a crash landing inside Germany seemed imminent. However, quick work on the part of the crewmen, who jettisoned everything movable, from guns and ammunition to the ball turret, allowed O'Connor to hold sufficient altitude and flying speed to get home to a safe landing. On-the-ball navigation brought the ship and crew over the Dutch coast less than 10 miles off course.[18]

Lt. O'Connor received a Distinguished Flying Cross for his exemplary performance on the mission; however, his tail gunner, S/Sgt. Marion O. Heilman, didn't return. Heilman must have bailed out over enemy territory, as he would be reported eventually as a prisoner of war.[19] Having expended his whole nine yards on the attacking jets, perhaps he wasn't in the mood to test his remaining luck in a crash landing.

Bob had the dubious honor of sitting in Heilman's seat on the mission to Merseburg. It would be a long mission, over eight hours. The armada was made up of 1,250 bombers and 900 fighter escorts.[20] They bombed through an overcast using instruments. Nevertheless, Bob recalls seeing heavy smoke through the cloud breaks. Surprisingly, there was no fighter opposition, and flak was reported as medium. The Eighth lost nine bombers and eleven fighters, but all Triangle L planes made it back. While Bob's group avoided the brunt of the flak, they were nonetheless tired and relieved.

With four missions now under his belt, Bob probably felt that he had sufficient experience and confidence to clarify his situation with Norm in that evening's V-mail:

*...I promised you a regular air mail tonite, but honest darling, I'm so tired I just got to go to bed! I put in another one of those hard days again...done the same thing as what I did yesterday...I hope you'll know what I mean??? Yes Hon, I have been putting in a few missions lately...please don't worry, however! The only reason I tell you I did, is that I promised you I'd tell you as soon as I did go on some. I promise I'll continue to tell you, too. Some of them have been rather "rough," but others, uninteresting. I'll have quite a lot to tell you someday. I just hope that day isn't too far off...it shouldn't be judging from the pounding we're giving those d____ Nazis, but then again, one never knows?...*

As no mission was scheduled for the 13th, after a routine day at the gunnery school, he wrote a long letter to Norm. It was his first air mail letter in a week. It read like a complete accounting of his current situation, which not only described his love, hopes, and dreams for the future, but also included an update on all mail sent and received, his November pay *("17£ (pounds), 3s (shilling) & 3d (pence)...about $68.65")*, a confirmation of latest pay allotments, and his forecast of earned flight pay and imminent promotion to staff sergeant. He also requested some basic necessities *("good wool socks...Readers Digest each month...some good Colgates' tooth powder")*. It felt good to be preoccupied again with mundane matters, and this state of mind would last for a few days. No mission was scheduled for the 14th, and his name wasn't listed on the mission roster for the 15th. A guy in the barracks who worked in the communications department invited him to play on their basketball team, the *535th Static Chasers*. A game with a group of officers had been set up to be played in a gymnasium at a nearby town. It would be a pleasant diversion. It also turned out to be a good physical workout. After returning from the game he actually developed a second wind and stayed up late to write to Norm, parents, and in-laws.

GROUND DUTY did not exempt gunnery instructors from early morning wake-up calls. On mission days when they were not sched-uled to fly, instructors took turns pulling support duty on the flight line. The job required circulating among hard stands before scheduled takeoff time and being available to assist air crews with machine gun installation problems. This duty, which they referred to as mission checks, required moving quickly between hard stands in a jeep issued by the motor pool. It was Bob's turn on the next morning.

Except for the unwelcome wake-up call, it was not an unpleasant assignment. On the contrary, zipping around the perimeter road in an open-top jeep could be quite exciting. Bob actually got a little carried away on his first time out. It seemed like forever since he had driven an automobile. He was still sleepy, but getting behind the wheel of the jeep almost felt as exhilarating as the first time he jumped into his tan Chrysler. As hard and obstinate as the jeep's stick shift was, it was a cinch compared to the late clutch. Bob dreamily relived the victory lap with Don as he gunned the engine and darted off for the hard stands. One critical difference, however, was the visibility, which—in the early morning, in December, in rural England, under blackout conditions— could easily transform fast driving into an accident waiting to happen.

Sure enough, Bob and the jeep ended up in a drainage ditch along the perimeter road in an isolated corner of the base. He found himself plastered on the dash board gazing into a blur of dark dampness, mud, and weeds before he figured out what had happened. No sooner had the shock worn off than the adrenaline kicked in, and his heart began to race in the accident's aftermath. It was a small miracle that he was not hurt, and, amazingly, the jeep was still in one piece. Thanks to the vehicle's four-wheel drive and rugged machinery—and Bob's intense motivation to get out of this embarrassing predicament—he somehow managed to maneuver the jeep to a horizontal attitude and up a nearby incline to the road surface. Cautiously and watchfully, he continued his rounds in the darkness, which ironically was now his ally, although it barely disguised his pallor and the clumps of English countryside on his bumper and bonnet. This scary and embarrassing little incident would never be discussed with his buddies or mentioned in his letters. It was much too close of a call. How would Norm receive such news? Like the family of the French sailor who got sick and died at sea? Just the thought of it made him cringe.

The nice thing about ground duty was that you could go back to bed after the planes took off. A few extra winks followed by breakfast and a hot cup of coffee helped to take the edge off. After that it would be an easy day on the skeet range. His day perked up when Butch called the gunnery school office to confirm hotel arrangements for their Christmas visit in Cambridge on the 21st. A V-mail from Norm made the day complete. She wrote it 42 days after he left port in New York; in the upper-left corner it was labeled "42."

Delivery of V-mail was now running about ten days, although not consistently. The next day was a mail *"blanker,"* according to his correspondence. Coming up empty-handed at mail call always put a damper on one's mood, especially around the holidays. In his next V-mail Bob mentioned that he was considering buying a used *"limey bike...no balloon tires & all front-hand brakes...and rather funny looking"* for £2½, about half the going rate. It would certainly make it easier to get around base, and a little gift to himself might help to fill the void created by the prospect of another Christmas away from home.

Sunday was spent the usual way. After breakfast he attended church; in the afternoon he and Johnnie went to an old movie at the base theater (*Kansas City Kitty*, starring Joan Davis); and that evening he wrote letters, his first long one to brother Ed, who was somewhere in the Pacific, and a V-mail to Norm, without which he *"couldn't sleep so well,"* especially with another mission scheduled in the morning.

HIS FIFTH MISSION was to Cologne in the tail of *The Columbus Miss*, with Capt. Raymond Beine and another group of strange faces. The weather was terrible, making the assembly process difficult. The 381st climbed to 31,500 feet, and with Colonel Leber in the lead ship, was the only group to make it to their target, railroad marshalling yards just outside the center of the ancient city. Bombing was executed according to the "pathfinder" method, also called PFF bombing, where the lead aircraft uses instruments to drop its bombs and the other planes drop on the leader's signal. Despite the increasing effectiveness of this method, this day's mission was trickier than usual due to a Headquarters-USAAFE policy that prohibited the bombing of Cologne's famous 700-year-old cathedral. Thankfully, there was no fighter opposition, and flak was light and inaccurate. They landed at Ridgewell 6¼ hours after takeoff with no bombers lost. They would be pleased to see intelligence photos published weeks later that showed the cathedral unharmed and its surrounding area in ruins, the successful result of multiple, precision Allied poundings during the past year.[21]

Bob didn't mention that he had worked that day in a noticeably upbeat letter to Norm, written earlier than usual in the evening due to the short mission duration. He should have been less fatigued than after an eight-hour mission, but perhaps he was also beginning to adapt to the combat routine and was becoming more confident about his survival prospects.

# CHAPTER 12

# CHANGE OF PLANS

BOB HAD BEEN AT RIDGEWELL for only about a month when he completed his fifth combat mission. He had managed to squeeze in his initial quota of missions during a two-week period of lousy weather. Just as he was about to return to a less mission-intensive schedule, he started thinking that perhaps he could survive 20 more and go home, where he most wanted to be.

A *"fist-full of mail"* received on Tuesday the 19th drew his thoughts to holidays and family. He looked forward to meeting Butch in Cambridge, but the prospect of not being home for Christmas—for the second year in a row—was wearing on him. While he was never one to feel sorry for himself, he couldn't help thinking how the war had interrupted his life and put his future plans on indefinite hold. He was frustrated and homesick. Roy needed him at the store, and Norm needed him at home. In his V-mail that evening, he softly chided her for banking the Christmas money that he had wired her, rather than buying a new outfit as he had requested, and he anxiously pleaded with her to share what she had learned from her physician, Dr. Kirk. Since having left for England, his letters implied that they were hoping for a pregnancy. They referred to their much-hoped-for baby as Sandy. Norm always liked that name, one that her cousin Esther had recently chosen for a baby daughter.

On Thursday Bob departed for Cambridge on a liberty run and a two-day pass. The weather was cold and rainy, but accommodations at the Garden House Hotel were excellent: soft beds, private baths, and hot water. Butch arrived later that evening. They spent their free time mostly enjoying each other's company and talking about their wives. They saw an American film *It Happened Tomorrow* at the "cinema," as the Brits called it, and went on a gift shopping mission, but came up empty-handed due to limited wartime stocks and shocking prices. Butch had to return in his borrowed jeep on Saturday, so they parted ways, vowing to keep in touch. Bob stayed in town for the remainder of the day doing more window shopping and writing letters at the Red Cross Club until it was time to catch the liberty run back to Ridgewell.

He reported back to base around eleven o'clock Saturday night, refreshed and cheerfully anticipating the next day's Christmas Eve festivities combined with a relaxed Sunday routine. Instead, he was greeted with an unexpected change of plans: a bombing mission was scheduled for the next day, and his name was on the crew list. It was like getting doused with ice water. Suddenly, he lost the urge to write his nightly V-mail to Norm. Quiet, forlorn, and suddenly ill at ease, he climbed into bed, not even bidding goodnight to the barracks gang, who had set up screens for both him and Johnnie.

With less than four hours sleep Bob felt groggy and lifeless when the orderly shook him awake. He sat on the edge of the bunk in the darkness still dreaming about Norm and thinking: *What am I doing here?...How my life has taken a turn!* It was hard to imagine that he was about to participate in a bombing raid on the day before Christmas. He didn't bother to notice what kind of eggs they served that morning since he had no appetite. As on most of his previous missions the other crew members were faceless, nameless strangers. Only the plane was familiar: #313, *The Columbus Miss*. This time he was assigned to the waist position, which, compared to the tail, was the only positive thing about his day so far.

Lt. Arthur Greenspan was the pilot. This young aviator hadn't flown many more combat missions than his waist gunner, but his briefing on the hard stand was delivered with apparent confidence. He reminded his crew that during the previous week Allied forces had been driven back into Belgium by a massive German counter-offensive, creating the notorious "bulge" in the enemy's front line. A few days earlier the Germans had demanded surrender of the American troops surrounded in Bastogne, to which Gen. Anthony C. McAuliffe responded with his famous retort: "Nuts!" Throughout the entire week the enemy had been shielded from Allied air poundings by a persistent cloud cover. But today skies were clear. The mission of the 381st was to *"support the ground troops fighting Rundstedt in the Ardennes break-through."*[1] The specific role of *The Columbus Miss* would be to bomb an enemy air field near Ettinghausen, a town located outside Frankfurt.

Triangle L bombers participated that day in the *"greatest air armada ever assembled."* Colonel Leber led the 381st, and they managed to get 51 planes in the air, one of the group's biggest launches to date.² They joined with a force of over 2,000 heavy bombers and 900 fighters; "the first bombers were entering Germany as the tail of the tremendous column was leaving England."³ Bombing was executed visually from around 20,000 feet. Due to better visibility and lower altitude, Bob witnessed the great event from a "box seat." In his mission notes he recorded his first sightings of *"jet propelled fighters... V-2's being launched ...[and] ground battles."* In his log book flak was classified as light and the mission *"highly successful,"* although there were later reports that some Allied bombs had accidentally fallen on friendly troops. In six hours they were back in Ridgewell and in time to join in the Christmas Eve festivities. It didn't turn out to be such a bad day after all.

Bob and John joined about 350 people at the seven o'clock Christmas Carol Festival, led by Chaplain Brown. The service was attended by base personnel of all religious faiths and by English people from nearby communities.⁴ Afterwards they returned to the barracks, tired from the emotional intensity of the day. But instead of going to bed right away, Bob poured over four unopened letters from Norm, which Johnnie had remembered to pick up while he was in Cambridge. One of her letters must have reported disappointment that her expected pregnancy was only a false alarm. He was too exhausted to formulate a comforting response, so before turning in he wrote a brief V-mail, apologizing for the previous day's gap in sequence, explaining that he *"unexpectedly had to work today,"* and promising to write a regular letter tomorrow. In closing he wrote: *"Well Darling, I do want you to know I'm thinking of you constantly this X-mas Eve, and miss you so much it's awful."*

RIDGEWELL WAS A BEEHIVE of activity on Christmas day 1944. The ramp was parked with many more planes than usual, because one of the trailing bomber groups on the previous day's mission had to land short of their destination base, which got socked-in with clouds late in the afternoon. The presence of stranded crews contributed to the loud merriment during a turkey feast in the mess hall. In the afternoon, a Christmas party was held for children from the local towns, and about 400 eager kids within earshot of the rumor showed up, overwhelming the Chaplain and Yanks who struggled to manage the pandemonium.⁵ Bob opted out of the party, electing instead to retire to his hut and spend a quiet afternoon alone, corresponding with loved ones whom he profoundly missed at this time of year. His letter to Norm reflected his frame of mind in its opening paragraphs:

> *Here it is X-mas Day, and I find myself way far away from the one I love more than anybody else in the world. Yes dear, it's awful, isn't it? If you only knew how I miss you? All I do is sit and think of our past days together...esp. at this time of year. Gee Hon, pray next year things will be different. If only we could depend on it, huh? I certainly think it should be though, if the coming year's progress equals the last year's. What do you think? We may be seeing a temporary setback in some places at present, but I know not for long. I think it's just the Germans' last push. The news may be making a big change right now, as I write this letter. I rather think it is (for the better, of course.) I wish I could tell you why I expect that, but of course you know I can't. Some day I can tell you lots [...]*
>
> *My X-mas as a whole hasn't been too festive, if you know what I mean [...] We have a few decorated trees at various places, and hear carols quite often on the P.A. system...that, along with a light frost this morning, does make it somewhat like X-mas. Just can't get into the swing of it though, without you...*

It was a long letter, responding to subjects both serious and trivial—armchair topics that would normally be discussed in intimate, face-to-face gatherings by the fireplace or around the dinner table. It wasn't the same as being there, but it was the best way to spend the holiday under the circumstances—circumstances that he would do almost anything to change.

Indeed, it was probably around this time that he decided to do just that. The prior week a notice had been posted on the bulletin board soliciting volunteers for the recently created air crew position of toggalier—a bombardier for all practical purposes, without officer credentials. The group was short on bombardiers and was seeking gunners who wanted to upgrade to the new position. Johnnie, always eager to see action, had already signed up and made a good case for the opportunity: full-time flight status, which guaranteed flight pay; the opportunity to accumulate missions faster and getting released before the war's end, which was still uncertain in view of the raging situation in the Pacific; plus the dubious benefit of flying in a more desirable seat in the airplane. On the other hand, there was a significant downside: more combat missions meant a higher probability of becoming a statistic. Moreover, it was possible that the war might end sooner than expected, as unlikely as that seemed. Then, there was the GI's sacred pledge: Never volunteer for anything in the Army. Bob, of course, was an independent thinker and always one to take control of his own destiny. Hence, on the morning after Christmas he submitted his name, and on the next day he received an affirmative response.

He would begin training immediately with the squadron bombardier, from whom he would learn basic procedures and get an overview of the top-secret Norden bombsight. Normally, this sophisticated bombing instrument was installed only in the lead ship, and when on the ground it was stored in a locked safe. In his next letter to Norm it's somewhat ironic that he wrote in more detail than usual about his regular job as a gunnery instructor, then, almost as an aside, mentioned his new position, downplaying its significance:

> *Say, by the way, I'll be flying some of my missions as the Bombardier from now on. Get that, will you? They were a bit short on them, so asked a few enlisted men to check out as same. We do everything but use the bomb-sight…we are so-called "Toggaliers"…we are instructed as to when we release our bombs, by a certain set procedure. We have quite a bit of responsibility on our hands, but I do believe it'll be interesting, and I'll like it. Two officers from my squadron (head Bombardiers) worked with me all yesterday afternoon, instructing me on how to do my job, and all connected with it. I'm sure I can handle it O.K! When I'll get my first chance at it, I don't know?*

His first chance would not come in the next couple of weeks, because he had already been scheduled to attend a required refresher course, "Sighting & Harmonization," for gunnery instructors. Since his letter went into more detail than usual about his job, he was concerned about censorship. Therefore, rather than sending it through normal channels, he hand-carried the letter to Lieutenant Hart, who could always be counted on to be a lenient censor. Hart was a reasonable and down-to-earth kind of guy, who stamped Bob's letter after a cursory scan.

On Saturday the 30th, Bob departed for an RAF base outside Blackpool, England, a popular seaside resort town where Yanks also frequently spent R&R time. Johnnie talked favorably about his recent trip to Blackpool, located in the borough of Lancashire, from which their hometown derived its name. When Johnnie was there he looked up the pen pal of an old friend who lived next door to him on Ann Street. Bob's plan was to spend a week in school, then take a few days leave to check out the resort, and perhaps visit Liverpool or London on the way back to Ridgewell.

He arrived on a Sunday night, and studies began Monday morning. The only thing memorable about this school was the food, which was prepared the English way: boiled, overcooked, mushy, and tasteless. It's probably where he decided to forever eliminate Brussels sprouts from his diet. Either for fear of retribution from RAF censors or because he felt empathy for the British people, Bob refrained from criticizing the cuisine in his letters. His comments were limited to:

> *Their theatre here is really nice...about the _only_ nice thing on the post, though.[...] I'll be sure glad to get back to my base though, for reasons which I can't tell you...I can tell you better when I get back.*

His return to more familiar cooking would be later than expected, because his refresher course was extended for an additional week. And the subject matter they covered actually turned out to be more challenging than he had anticipated, although he didn't spend much time studying. Blackpool, which reminded him of Atlantic City, offered too many attractions. While it was wintertime, during the first week he spent most evenings in town, frequently going to the cinema or ice skating rink, but mostly searching for decent food. Later in the second week he was assigned to CQ duty, which at least provided some quiet time in the orderly room to cram for examinations.

Before returning to Ridgewell, Bob decided to make a stopover in London and get a quick look at the eminent city. Not only was his time limited, but it was not what he expected:

> *...I did see some of the bombed buildings, etc. Gee, what a mess! One only realizes how much England really did feel this war. You sure gotta hand it to them, for holding out as they did. To see some of the people who were bombed out, sleeping down in the subways, alone was enough to convince me. Not a few either...hundreds of them!! Gee Hon, if I was ever to see you, or any of our Moms and Dads having to do something like that, I believe I couldn't stand it. I'd be mad enough to go*

*over and get Hitler myself, and give him the worst kind of torture I could think of, whatever it would be. Seeing things like that sure makes a guy's blood boil!! Isn't it awful, that people who supposedly are civilized, go on fighting wars like this? All because of one person, or just a few! I wonder what God thinks??*

By venting his anger in this way, perhaps he was mentally preparing himself for new responsibilities that awaited his return.

He was glad to get back to an *"American"* base; during his stint at the RAF base he was *"fed like a canary,"* losing nearly 10 pounds. It was not only the food that made his return a pleasure. Waiting at the post office were 40 envelopes and three boxes, including 22 letters from Norm, 10 from his parents, and the remainder, mostly Christmas cards, from friends, neighbors, and relatives.[6] The boxes included the camera he had requested and a collection of individually wrapped Christmas gifts. His next stop was the orderly room, where he would collect his monthly pay and "sign the payroll" to verify receipt of cash. He was disturbed to not find his name listed with the other sergeants, so he appealed for help. The officer on duty suggested that he look under "staff" and broke into a grin. Bob had officially been promoted to staff sergeant a month earlier, but a communications foul-up kept him in the dark. He also learned that during his absence he was awarded an Air Medal for having flown six combat missions. Having missed the awards ceremony, he was now simply handed the medal, plus accompanying ribbon, pins, and written citation. He decided to put the *"whole works"* in a box and mail it later to Norm.

It took him a couple of hours to read his mail and three nights to respond to all the correspondence. His first letter to Norm was mostly a report of his two weeks off base and the good news that awaited his return. It went on about how they should allocate their windfall raise of $30 a month—making his pay now $191.20. Priorities were paying off the loan to Roy and buying savings bonds for their future. The next letters responded mainly to specifics of Norm's letters. In one he offered consolation about the doctor's report, assuring her that *"everything will take place as we want it to, when I come back. We'll have the nicest little Sandy or Bobbie, anyone could ever have."* Then he went on to rave about the Christmas gifts he received and the little personal notes that Norm included with each one. Along with his camera, the packages contained a miniature Christmas tree, toy car, film, tooth powder, comb, chocolate, and caramels. Norm addressed the candy to both him and Johnnie. Candy was a luxury that couldn't be purchased in wartime England. Bob happily shared the caramels with Johnnie and also offered some to the grease monkeys, who always shared their treats with him.

Later that week Bob and Johnnie received a visit from Major Graham, whom they called Doc Graham, the Flight Surgeon. It was not unusual for him to stop by and check in with the displaced gunnery instructors—not just to keep them posted on barracks vacancies, but also to see how they were holding up under the stress of combat flying. He would often spend the evening with them. Johnnie skeptically viewed it as a visit from the psychiatrist, but Bob saw it as a social call and always welcomed the easygoing interchange. On this particular visit Doc Graham had news to deliver and was particularly chipper as he pranced into the hut. As they had been promised, some bunks were now available in an air crew barracks, so Bob and John could finally move into the more prestigious quarters.

The news was not unexpected, but the idea of moving in with the flyboys wasn't as enticing as it seemed a month ago. Bob and John had grown accustomed to their space, their hut's stove never lacked for fuel, and living with the grease monkeys hadn't actually been all that bad. Despite different backgrounds, lifestyle choices, and military status, they had always been treated with consideration and respect by their barracks mates. And they weren't put off by each other's company. Bob and John briefly looked at each other for concurrence, then politely declined the major's offer. Surprised by their decision, Doc Graham firmly challenged them to reconsider, but finally backed off when it was clear that the two toggaliers had made up their minds.

To Bob and John it didn't seem like an important change of plans or choice of major significance when they made it. But word of their decision quickly circulated among the grease monkeys, and from that moment on, their status in the barracks was elevated to a new level. No longer were they just transient flyboys waiting to move out, but they were kings of the hut. They could do no wrong. There was nothing that the grease monkeys wouldn't do for Singleton or Rutherford (a scary thought). Bob felt a bit uneasy about the mannerly and deferential way he was now treated by these rough characters. It seemed funny, but he would never laugh. A genuine bond had been forged.

It was now January 16th. Staff Sergeant Singleton was scheduled to fly his first mission as a toggalier on the following day. Captain Smeyer from Operations had stopped by the squadron gunnery office that afternoon and asked, "Singleton, think you're ready to fly in the front seat tomorrow?"

"Yes Sir!" was his honest answer. But he was still anxious about his new responsibility. He didn't want to make any mistakes. A good night's rest would definitely be needed. No problem; the privacy screen was already in place and the grease monkeys were especially well-behaved that evening.

# CHAPTER 13

# TOGGALIER

ON THE MORNING OF THE 17ᵀᴴ the wake up procedure was the same, but Bob's movements were more brisk and deliberate. During breakfast he nervously glanced at his watch, because he didn't want to be late for his first, formal pre-flight briefing. The top line on his list of toggalier's procedures stated "Get to the briefing on time."[1] As he entered the briefing room with the pilots, navigators, and bombardiers, he felt like he had joined the inner circle—like being with the team in the locker room before a game. Despite the fact that they were sitting on benches in a corrugated metal building it was all very professional and even a little dramatic as the room was called to attention and the curtains were pulled away from the big map on the stage, exposing that day's target and route of flight. The air was filled with anticipation as all eyes zeroed-in on the red line on the map, which stretched from England to their destination, and a green line, which indicated the route home.

Today they would strike marshalling yards at Paderborn in central Germany. He would fly in ship #102, the *Julie Linda*, with Lt. William Stevens at the controls. The plane would be loaded with ten 500-pound RDX bombs. These bombs were said to be of a more advanced design with a lethal dispersion pattern. Up until this mission Bob hadn't taken notice of what type of bombs were on board. But now it was his job to know.

On the hard stand, when he jumped off the truck with the officers, he felt a little self-conscious in the presence of the other crew members—all unfamiliar faces again. If they only knew how nervous he was and how badly he wanted not to "screw up" in his new role. It was uncanny how he spotted things he never noticed before—like how the bombs were loaded. The guys who delivered and loaded the bombs were "colored." Bob used to overhear gunners occasionally make crass jokes among themselves about how the loaders would turn white when they handled the bombs. On the contrary, their routine had become so familiar that, rather than conveying the bombs one-at-a-time from the trailer to bomb bay, some wise guy would occasionally "gun" the ordnance tractor, causing the bombs to cascade off the back of the trailer on to the tarmac, then chuckle as new, wide-eyed air crews gawked at the stunt.[2] Of course, the bombs were unarmed, therefore there was no danger. But today, the loaders treated the bombs like nitroglycerin on a truck with a flat tire. The RDX's had a different kind of fusing mechanism; therefore, each was being slowly, methodically, and cautiously conveyed by means of the bomb loading crane.

Bob monitored the procedure as he began his pre-flight duties. First, he retrieved the caliber-fifties marked for the chin turret. He laid them beneath the upward-angled snout of the proud Fortress before carefully hoisting each to its mounts. He briefly stood back to double-check his installation, admiring how the oiled gun barrels shimmered like polished bayonets in the hazy light of dawn. But new duties required his attention inside. Entering the B-17's nose section was trickier than through the waist door and executed the way only kids would imagine climbing into a war machine: through a belly hatch in front of the landing gear. Like the pilots and navigator, he would first heave in his duffel bag, then grab the overhead handles and pull himself up, feet first, through the hatch. This took some doing with the bulky personal equipment required for the nose position. In addition to high altitude gear, nose gunners were issued heavier flak vests, which offered extra protection behind the fragile plexiglass nose bubble; and due to the bulk of this vest, his parachute harness was rigged for a chest pack rather than the standard seat pack.

Once inside, Bob took a breath and pulled out his one-page list of toggalier's procedures, prepared by the Group Bombardier. He had already completed the first two items of the "After Briefing" items:

1.  Get flying equipment and go immediately to assigned airplane.
2.  Put your parachute, helmet and mask in nose compartment.
3.  Set in interval and ground speed. Put switch to "Train" position and counter on zero on the intervalometer.[3]

The intervalometer, on the electrical console next to his station, controlled the time interval between automatic bomb releases. He had been checked out on this equipment a few weeks ago, but was careful and deliberate about dialing in correct settings, which he had written down during the briefing. He rechecked the settings then stood up and side-stepped through the narrow passageway to the bomb-bay section. There he continued with his checklist items, one at a time:

4. Check bomb load thoroughly as follows:
   a) Put on lights in bomb-bays.
   b) See that shackles are on racks facing forward and that shackle arms are in A8 or A4 release arms.
   c) See that all bombs are hung properly and are not loose.
   d) See that all pins are in bombs and arming wires are in proper places with clips on them.
   e) See that the bomb-bay door retracting screws are clean of grease. Crank bomb-bay doors to open or closed position while on the ground. Do not open or close them electrically at any time while on the ground. Operate electrically in the air.
   f) Be sure there is a bomb-bay crank and an extension near the engineer's turret.
5. Check all stations for sufficient ammo supply.
6. Check chin turret belt feed, ammo and power unit.[4]

The last step brought him back to the nose section, where he completed his caliber-fifty checks before settling into his seat. The chair was small, armless, and lightly padded with a swivel base and backrest—very comfortable compared to the other gun positions, not to mention "the best seat in the house." The guy perched here could see almost everything that was going on outside. Situated in the center of a plexiglass hemisphere, he could see forward, up, down, and to both sides. From outside the airplane a nose gunner with all his equipment, including helmet and goggles, looked like a giant insect trapped inside a mason jar. Actually, the wide-angle visibility made Bob feel less confined and safer. Unlike in the tail position, he was not isolated from other crew members. The navigator sat at a compact desk directly behind his left shoulder, and the pilots' deck was located directly behind his head. It didn't matter that his closest neighbor was intensely hunched over aeronautical charts most of the time, working a circular navigation computer. Bob also had his job to do. Just having company made him feel better.

For the first time, Bob was able to see the arcing green flares that gave the go signal. When the aircraft began to taxi, he checked his console to make sure the bomb-bay rack switches were on. Then he sat back to enjoy the ride. As the Forts ahead gunned their Cyclones and slowly lifted into the skies, he was captivated by the wide-angle beauty of it all. In turn, *Julie Linda's* engines advanced to max power, and he realized that it was no time to relax. The take-off roll seemed scarier from his new position. As usual, the moaning Fort stubbornly held the ground for as long as it could, but Bob was now in the nerve-racking position of having to watch the trees at the end of the runway get progressively closer. After the gear came up and the ground started slowly moving away, Bob pulled out his checklist to review his duties during the climb-out and cruise phase:

1. Pull pins on bombs above 4000 feet.
2. Make sure bomb-bay rack switches are on.
3. Check tracing operation of chin turret and reticle lights.
4. At 10,000 feet notify the crew to go on oxygen.
5. Make oxygen checks frequently during mission.
6. Make all observations possible on bombing mission.
7. Warn all gunners at the first appearance of enemy fighters and their position. Also of friendly fighters and their position.[5]

After the navigator confirmed they had passed 4,000 feet, Bob detached his connections and worked his way to the bomb-bay area. Standing on a catwalk between the bomb racks, he carefully reached between the fins of each sleeping monster and disengaged its safety pin with a press and release motion of his thumb and forefingers. He counted 10 pins and stowed them in the designated container. Despite built-in safety mechanisms, this procedure always caused a stir in the pit of his stomach.

At a half-hour into the flight, back at his station and reconnected, he received word that they were passing 10,000 feet. He engaged his mike button and called for an oxygen check, attentively listening for acknowledgement from each crew position. Everybody checked in. So far, so good. Gun checks were performed next. Then he sat back and watched the glorious Triangle L formation completing their assembly ballet in the bright sunlight.

Today he didn't have to be told when they were approaching the target area, because puffs of flak could easily be seen in the distance. While he had memorized the procedures, he quickly reviewed the "Just before the I.P." section of his checklist :

1. Set all rack selector switches on panel to on, both internal and external.
2. Turn on master switch in all electric ships.
3. Turn up counter all the way to 50 just prior to opening bomb-bay doors.
4. Open the bomb-bay doors electrically when the leader opens his. If the doors don't open electrically have the engineer crank them open immediately. Release bombs immediately after the leader of the group releases his.
5. Have engineer check to see if bomb-bays are clear after bombs away. (Note: to salvo in all electric ships hold bomb-bay door switch to "open" position at same time you hit salvo switch).
6. Try to observe target damage.
7. When out of the target area make an oxygen and battle damage check.[6]

He also glanced at the comment at the bottom of the checklist:

A great part of the successful completion of a bombing mission and safe return of your crew depends upon you! If you carry out the above steps you will increase the efficiency of the group and your chances of returning home safely.[7]

Sergeant Singleton would get it right. That was his nature. Flak was generally light, similar to his first mission, but he was too focused on his new responsibilities to react to the intermittent hail. All switches were set up correctly when they reached the IP. Bombing was PFF. When he saw the doors open and bombs drop from the lead ship, he hit the salvo switch, which automatically opened the bomb bay doors and released the bombs at their pre-set intervals in salvo, and crisply announced "bombs away!" through the intercom. The familiar upward lurch of the aircraft indicated that bombs were indeed away, but before closing the doors he pressed down on the bomb indicator light switch to check that all bomb rack stations had released and waited for the top turret gunner's visual confirmation. It didn't require a prompt; everybody was anxious to get the doors closed as quickly as possible, especially the guys in the exposed mid-section. Due to the cloud cover, they would have to report BPO (Bombing Pattern Obscured) at the interrogation.

The trip home was relatively uneventful, except for a V-2 launch below the formation. It looked exactly like an American fighter pilot had recently described it: "a big 50-caliber bullet as long or longer than my Mustang, with flames spitting from it."[8]  This was Bob's second recorded sighting of a V-2, the Nazi's newest weapon. These guided missiles were being used with increasing frequency to deliver horror and destruction to the English people. Some believed that the enemy timed their launches to occur when Allied bombing formations were overhead—on the chance that their missile might also terrorize, or perhaps even strike, an attacking bomber and its unsuspecting crew.[9] Unlike V-1 buzz bombs, the new, supersonic ballistic missiles gave little warning of their arrival. They would have been more fascinating to observe had they been intended for peaceful purposes.

Safely out of the target area, the rookie toggalier called for an oxygen and battle damage check. Promptly and sharply, everybody checked in O.K. It made Bob feel like an important part of the crew. They were back on the ground in 6½ hours. One of the Hut 18 guys was waiting near the briefing block to scavenge Bob's shot of whiskey. Bob gave it to him with a warm smile. That night he wrote *"no trouble at all"* in his log, thinking that he actually might grow to like his new job. The only concern on base that day was the "heavy muffled, jarring" explosion of a V-2 warhead, which struck the village of Halstead, located about 10 miles away.[10]

THE TONE OF HIS LETTER to Norm that night reflected a rejuvenated spirit. It was his fourth air-mail letter in a row—not an abbreviated, post-combat V-mail. The letter was lengthy, upbeat, and effusive. He apologized for not picking up a money order that day as planned; he said that *"circumstances"* prevented it. He also expressed gratitude for

Norm's numerous favors and kind deeds, demonstrated by her nicely worded letters, thoughtful notes, meaningful little gifts, and attention to details on the home front, like keeping family members informed, drivers' licenses current, and Army friends posted on their whereabouts. But toward the end of the letter he couldn't resist sharing his feeling of accomplishment that day:

> *Well I really don't have much else to say, except that I did recently take a stab at Hitler, again. I flew the first time as Bombardier. (toggalier) Remember I told you they "checked me out" as one, here a few weeks back? I really feel now, as if I gave him, (Hitler), a sock in the belly. I always think to myself when I go on a mission, "This is one for Normie and Sandy...for keeping us apart." Right, Dear? I thought that especially, when flying as toggalier! Gee, it gives you quite a feeling, no kiddin! It's quite a bit of responsibility, but I done everything O.K. I was sorta afraid I may do something wrong, or else forget something. When I say "Bombs away", then's when I thought of you. I was thinking to myself, "There you are you dirty so and so,...that comes from my dear wife, whom you're responsible for taking away from me." (You gave him a pretty good sock, too, I'll tell you.)*

It was mid-January. The weather was cloudy and much colder than usual, even for this time of year. No mission was scheduled for the 19th, so Bob worked at the gunnery school. His name was on the mission list for the following day, but rather than hitting the sack early, he stayed up late with Johnnie, learning to develop photographic prints in a makeshift darkroom set up in an unused closet at the gunnery school. The opportunity to accumulate some once-in-a-lifetime photographs was not lost on him, and knowing how to develop pictures would be a useful skill after the war. Johnnie's interest in taking pictures hadn't waned since his childhood accident at Safe Harbor, but he had never learned to develop his own film. Toby, the grease monkey who practiced and displayed his craft, offered to share his expertise and loan the needed supplies for Johnnie's and Bob's maiden attempt. Johnnie didn't have to get up for a mission the next morning. Bob did, but he wasn't concerned about it. Things were going well for him. He even took the time to scratch off a V-mail to Norm before going to bed.

As they always say, if it seems too good to be true, it probably is. Bob's eighth mission on January 20th was not another walk in the park. The target was a rail and highway bridge in Mannheim-Ludwigshafen, a heavily defended industrial area in western Germany. His ship was #809, *PFC's Limited*, flown by Lt. William Clark. Due to poor weather the formation climbed 3,000 feet higher than planned, to 28,000 feet, where they would execute PFF bombing.[11] The temperature was minus 54 degrees, and the flak, reported as moderate, was especially nasty. In other words, it was like an average, cold day in hell. The plane took several hits. Lieutenant Clark was forced to feather their number-three engine, causing *PFC's Limited* to fall behind and eventually lose the group formation.

Through the intercom Bob could hear high-pitched chatter in the cockpit and nervous dialog between the pilots and navigator, who was frantically pouring over his charts. Because of the rotten weather and sub-standard performance of the remaining engines, it appeared that they might have to land somewhere in France. Bob instinctively patted his breast pocket to confirm the presence of his escape kit, which included a folded silk map of Europe, compass, language pamphlet containing common phrases in various languages, and his escape photo. The latter was a standard mug shot, which could be used by friendly resistance forces to forge identification papers. The lore among nervous air crews was that the enemy could always identify members of the 381st because their escape pictures were taken in the same French-style shirt and necktie provided by the base photo lab.[12] Bob had his picture taken in flight gear, but now wondered whether that was a good decision. Next, he reluctantly confirmed the presence of his Remington, secretly praying that he would have no need for it.

Bomber pilots were advised to make emergency landings in enemy territory or neutral countries only as a last resort. Toward the end of the war it was rumored that some crews would intentionally land in enemy territory with only minor engine problems—opting to sweat out the rest of the war detained on the ground rather than take more chances flying missions through flak-infested skies. Intelligence reports supposedly had revealed that the enemy was obtaining more than scant information from cooperative airmen. It's not clear if these reports were accurate, but it was certainly a sign that morale was low. At briefings it was made clear that, if emergency landings were deemed unjustified, there was some explaining to do. Commanders were now taking disciplinary action, including dishonorable discharges.[13]

As it turned out, the cockpit consensus in *PFC's Limited* was to press on to familiar territory. Hundreds of B-17 crews before them had lived through this situation and worse. But it was no less discomfiting for air crews experiencing it for the first time, Sergeant Singleton among them. Their plight was exacerbated by an incident that occurred over the English Channel. A dangerous oil pressure indication on one of the good engines prompted the co-pilot to initiate a shutdown procedure. With two engines feathered, the remaining ones were unable to produce enough power to maintain level flight.

As the bomber lost altitude, an argument in the cockpit erupted over whether shutting down the second engine had been the best course of action. Bob could not help overhearing all the cussing and commotion behind him. When aircraft altitude and cockpit protocol deteriorated to precarious levels, the pilot-in-command exercised his prerogative and ordered that the engine-in-question be restarted. To Bob's amazement, it started right up. *PFC's Limited* immediately leveled off, and the tone of the cockpit conversation became more collected, albeit sparse after that. Bob's anxiety didn't let up until they were safely back on the tarmac. In his mission notes he recorded: *"Weather, very bad! No instruments for landing 'blind'...really sweat it out!"* [14]

He had been afraid that they would not make it back that day, and he didn't like the feeling. Just when he thought that he had learned to cope with combat conditions, fear crept back into his psyche like an unwelcome intruder. It made him angry, and that must have been apparent to ground crews who welcomed them back to the hard stand. As he crawled out of the belly, within earshot of the welcoming mechanics he spit out something to the effect of "this damn plane isn't worth two cents!" Crew chiefs didn't accept insults to their planes lightly, but out of respect, they usually held their tongues with returning air crews. It so happened that Toby, the hut photographer, was one of the mechanics on duty that day and had his camera with him. He couldn't resist discreetly snapping a shot of his fuming barracks mate removing the chin turret guns. The expression in the photo said it all; it would appear on an enlarged print a couple of days later, displayed face-up on Bob's bunk without a note revealing its source.

Bob's attempt to put Norm at ease about his combat duty may have unintentionally exposed his own growing concerns after the close call on his last mission:

> ...*Well dear, today I really put in a hard days "work," if you know what I mean? Gee, if only I could tell you a few things? Darn it! Some day I'll really be able to tell you some real experiences. Some that I had, that really made me think, and I'm not just kiddin. Please don't worry though now, dear, as I don't mean it that way. I wouldn't want to worry you for the world. Please don't Honey. I'll assure you, you don't have to. Promise? It's just that I want you to know that I am helping a bit from time to time, to beat old Hitler...and also because I promised you when I left you, that I'd tell you all that I could. You promise me now, that you'll be good, and do as I say, and don't worry, O.K? After all, it's not as if I'm at it every day. You know very well the deal I came over here on...well that still holds. I'm classified as an instructor, and it cannot be changed. I know that as a fact, as fellows have tried to get out of it, and can't. Please Honey, if you ever believe me, do now! I'm not saying anything just so it may make you feel better, but it's the actual truth. Believe me now, and do promise me you won't worry, O.K.?*

He was scheduled for another mission the following day, and the wake-up routine was especially unwelcome. He hadn't had time to sort out his feelings from the previous day. A disquieting sleep pattern and freezing temperatures also didn't help. Their mission this day would be to strike a tank assembly plant in Aschaffenburg, a town near Frankfurt. He recognized some of the gunners from his mission on the 17th. But he didn't recognize any of the officers. The pilot was Lt. Vincent J. Peters. Peters happened to be one of the pilots of three 535th planes that failed to return on their New Year's Day mission, although his plane landed in friendly territory, and he and his crew eventually made it home.[15] Just as well that Bob didn't know. Today they would fly on ship #265, the *Hell's Angel*—a "famous" ship—another thing he didn't need. Fortunately, #265 was only a shiny replacement named after the legendary bomber that was shot down in the Schweinfurt raid. Bob just hoped that today's crew wouldn't try to remake history. He had already seen enough that week.

The most nightmarish thing about the mission to Aschaffenburg was the horrible weather and its consequences. The *Hell's Angel* carried

a maximum load of six 500 pound RDX's and six 500 pound incendiaries, making the takeoff run through the fog seem agonizingly long.
Due to a thick overcast the assembly process was also thornier than
usual. And at cruising altitude it turned out to be one of the coldest
missions yet—minus 60 degrees. It was hard to say which devil was
worse: the fog, the flak, or the threat of frost bite. In these conditions,
who needed an enemy?

The planes hit their target that day, but invariably, even after a
successful raid, air crews had to sweat out landing in severe conditions
at the end of a mission. Passing over the white cliffs of Dover often
symbolized a safe return to England, but to experienced aircrews it
was the sight of runway after a blind descent through the ever-present
overcast that provided the most relief. Before descending into the
clouds returning aircraft separated into a trailing formation behind the
leader. Each entered the cloud deck in sequence, according to pre-
briefed spacing. Ceilings often hung so low over the farm lands that
the first familiar sight coming out of the clouds could be the spire of
the old Ashen Church on the northwest perimeter of the base. Under
these conditions, which existed on January 21st, some planes would fail
to establish visual contact at their specified minimum descent altitude.
In such case, they would execute a missed approach procedure and
then attempt to safely renter the pattern, more often than not with
minimal fuel aboard. Air crews always worried about mistakes being
made during this blind choreography. While all the planes made it back
from enemy territory on the 21st, including the new *Hell's Angel*, two
bombers accidentally collided on final approach, just before landing,
resulting in the loss of both aircraft and all 18 crew members. One of
them was a 535th ship called *"Egg Haid."*

After this incident the mood was especially depressed around
base and in the surrounding neighborhood, which included many
Great Yeldham folks who had witnessed the horror:[16]

> The next day 17 bodies were removed from the crash site,
> with 16 identified by dog tags, dental records or wallet. All
> were badly mutilated, partially disintegrated, and all had en-
> tire third degree burns, with one body identified by exclu-
> sion. All were taken to the American Military Cemetery at
> Cambridge.[17]

On the morning that the bodies were being recovered, Bob found Toby's picture of the mad toggalier on his bunk. Always a good sport, he shared an abbreviated laugh about the *PFC's Limited* incident two days earlier. Laughter generally made things easier for him. But Toby could have chosen a better moment. Bob didn't think the incident was funny at the time or now. Especially after his latest mission. He was so physically and emotionally worn out that he wasn't capable of writing a letter that night. Not even a V-mail. It took a lot to break that ritual.

BOB HAD EARNED A TWO-DAY PASS for that week, but was indifferent about it. Nevertheless, he took advantage of the opportunity to go to Cambridge to seek out a haircut, a good movie, and some camera equipment that he and Johnnie needed. The trip would help to get his mind off the war. Shopping turned out to be more like a scavenger hunt. To find the photography supplies, he had to search in *"chemist stores (drug stores), book stores, department stores, 3d & 6d Stores (5 & 10's)... surgical supply stores...and even the ironmongers (hardware store)."* He found what he needed, except for some contact paper and film, which he would ask Norm to send from the states—a request that she would lovingly and quickly fulfill, as always.

Not surprisingly, the group didn't schedule missions for several days due to the miserable weather. Bob spent the extra time catching up with letter writing and procrastinated chores, like sewing staff sergeant's stripes on his uniforms. As he struggled with his needle and thread, he could hear Frank Sinatra crooning "What a Difference it Makes." The guys in the hut had recently chipped in 10 shillings apiece to buy a replacement for the radio stolen by the wop. Norm always referred to Sinatra as "The Voice." The music only reminded Bob of how much he missed her. He began his letter that evening by commenting on his new stripes:

> *...you used to put them on so nice. I'm sure helpless without you, and I'm not kiddin'! Johnnie tells me that all the time, he says you sure had me spoiled. I guess he's right, too, as you sure did wait on me hand and foot, darling. I certainly realize it more than ever, too!*

Next, he apologized for not writing the previous evening, explaining that he went to bed *"dead"* because of another change of plans—

*"There's a war to be fought, if you know what I mean???"* Then he went on to thank her profusely for two birthday cards, writing:

> *...If you only could realize how good it made me feel to read them? All I live for is you, darling. O why must this terrible war be anyway? I only hope Russia continues on, then maybe it'll be over soon? They sure made the whole picture look better, didn't they? I just hope they keep on!*

The next missions flown by the 381st were on three days in a row: January 28th and 29th, and February 1st. Bob was assigned to all three. On the 28th he would fly for the third time with the same pilot, Lieutenant Malleus, and most of Malleus's regular crew, not in *The Feather Merchant* or *Los Angeles City Limits*, but in the famous *Stage Door Canteen*. It was one of the few ships in the fleet that was still painted in the old, drab greenish-brown color scheme. For months now replacement planes were being delivered with a shiny silver finish. Today the *Stage Door Canteen* was flying to Cologne. And coincidentally, like the last Cologne mission, part of the group would never make it there. This time it was due to difficulties forming up over the target. Bob's ship ended up bombing a *"last resort target"* due to a malfunction in their lead ship, which was equipped with the radar for bombing through cloud formations. Planes of that type were referred to as "mickey" ships. According to his log, the *"...'mickey' ship went out...even had bomb bay doors open...."*

His logbook also reported flak as *"very heavy,"* which no doubt contributed to making this mission spine-chilling, if not mind-numbing. When flak intensity reached the "heavy" category, there was probably a tendency for an airman's subconscious to block out the horror in a protective shock-like response. Perhaps that's why Bob was unaware of a direct strike by flak that he "sensed was nearby," but never realized how close it actually was.

When they returned to base and parked on the hard stand, the ground crews congregated under the nose of their beloved *Stage Door Canteen*, gawking up and frowning in disbelief. Bob didn't realize what it was all about until he lowered his stiff body from the belly hatch and creaked forward. The crowd was inspecting a hole "as large as a soccer ball" in the fuselage, directly under the nose gunner's seat—his seat. A few guys shot a glance at the oblivious toggalier, as if he were a ghost returning from the dead.

It wasn't until Bob got to the equipment room that he discovered the heavy chunks of shrapnel in his duffel bag—jagged, angry pieces of metal that had careened through the aircraft structure before being brought to rest by the soles of the shoes in his duffel bag. Johnnie may have bragged that 'a fart saved his ass,' but Bob could now claim that shoes were his salvation. Sadly, there would be little humor or irony in it, and it was not until he lay in bed later that evening that his heart pounded at the mere thought of it. He made no mention of "working" in his nightly letter to Norm.[18]

Perhaps he made up his mind to just continue going through the motions, trying not to think about it, and hoping for the best. His next missions were to Coblenz and twin cities Mannheim-Ludwigshaven, both times in a ship called *Pair O' Queens, Bee & Gee*, with pilots he didn't recognize and a mix of new and familiar crew faces. Both missions were routine and successful. On the latter the 381st was the first group over the target, encountering *"medium"* flak. He had his *"best view yet of a rocket being launched."* All 381st ships made it back, except one that was forced to land in France before returning the next day. It was reported that the patched-up *Stage Door Canteen* returned from that mission with a propeller windmilling out of control, threatening to add the distinction of "hangar queen" to her resume.[19] Another ship called *Male Call* lost an engine on the way to the target, a second engine on the way back over the Channel, and a third on final approach. Some vacant buildings were knocked over during the precarious landing, completely wrecking the plane, but incredibly, all crew members walked away unharmed.[20]

Bob made no references to "working" or "circumstances" in his letters after these three missions. Instead his letters included extreme detail about his hopes and dreams for a home and family, suggesting savings and budgeting plans, housing options, and even names of suburban subdivisions where they might choose to live. He was now referring to his future children by name, as if their delivery would simply be a matter of submitting mail orders in proper sequence when he got home. February had just arrived, and he had accumulated 12 combat missions, enough to earn an Oak Leaf Cluster for his Air Medal, but, more importantly, nearly half what he needed to get his life back.

# CHAPTER 14

# FRESH EGGS

HAVING FLOWN ON THE PREVIOUS SIX missions, Bob earned the luxury of not being scheduled for the next one. His timing was fortuitous since the February 3rd mission was to Berlin, or "Big B" to the flyboys. It was the biggest raid ever on the German capital, where the group would suffer losses for the second time in a week and in two dozen missions flown since early December. One 381st plane was spotted going down in flames over the target and another ended up missing with no reports on its demise. Rather than making him feel lucky for not having flown on the Berlin mission, the reported losses may have fueled some doubts about the progress of the war and his chances of survival in this terrible game. Nevertheless, he managed to keep his mind occupied with his newly acquired hobby of printing pictures in their gunnery school darkroom—often until late after midnight. But that didn't cure his desperate wish to go home, which he expressed in another of his letters to Norm:

> *I miss you so much it's awful!! Oh WHY, can't we be together soon? Give me that one wish, and I won't ask another thing. With you and Sandy, a nice little home, and an average means of living, and I'll be the happiest man on earth. It'll be wonderful, won't it dear? A dream in reality...*

Unfortunately, the current reality was anything but a dream. He was assigned to fly again on the next bombing mission.

It was on February 6th. The fresh eggs at breakfast were a dead giveaway, but the stir accompanying the drawing of the curtains from the briefing room map confirmed it: they were flying into the heart of the enemy again today. Colonel Hall, who had recently been promoted to Group Commander, led the proceedings. Bob's heart sank as he stared at the long green line on the map, wondering if this would be the one. The primary target was in a town in central Germany called

Lutzendorf, near the heavily defended city of Merseberg. For good measure, in a show of boldness, their secondary target was Berlin, located a little farther to the north. Some planes, including Bob's, would go to Ohrdruf, a village enroute to the primary, where Hitler had built an elaborate underground military installation designed to house the High Command after it was bombed out of Berlin.[1] Bob remembered his mission to Merseburg with Lt. Malleus in the famous *Los Angeles City Limits*. Today he was flying with Malleus and his crew for the fourth time—but this time on the battered, "new" *Hell's Angel*. It should have seemed like familiar surroundings. He felt like he almost knew the crew: O'Neil, copilot; Lyons, navigator; Hall, engineer/top turret gunner; McCorny, radio operator/gunner; Lauter, ball turret gunner; Stubblefield, waist gunner; and Dunham, tail gunner. But he still didn't feel like he belonged there.

Something always seemed to go wrong. Four hours into the mission, the formation got broken up, and the *Hell's Angel* crew would have to find and bomb a target of last resort without the benefit of a lead ship. The rookie toggalier would finally have a chance to prove what he had learned—without the guidance of a bombardier or a bombsight. Through the static of the intercom Malleus explained that they would drop below the clouds, set up a low-level run, drop their bombs in "train" mode on "targets of opportunity," and then get the heck out of there.

Bob's adrenaline started to kick in. During a steep descent, he checked the switches on his control panel. Master switch-ON, check; rack selector switches-ON, check; arming switch-ON, etc. Everything was set, including four live M47 incendiaries and ten 500 pound RDX's on their racks. He could hear the other guys making bets over the intercom on whether the rookie toggalier would hit anything.

They leveled off several thousand feet above the ground. From his mason jar he could see farms, country roads, and wooded clusters slipping beneath the plexiglass at a couple hundred knots. To drop bombs in train he would first have to push up on the spring-loaded bomb-bay door switch on his panel and hold it there until the light went on. At that point all he needed to do was put his finger on the toggle switch and a bomb would be released with each squeeze of his trigger finger. He stood up and bent over in a hunched position with knees bent, leaned forward with head pressed against the plexiglass, and waited for the signal with his finger on the trigger. Nothing below them looked threatening. No enemy guns or flak. But once the bomb bay doors opened he would have little time to be discerning. His job would be to choose targets, estimate lead times, and "toggle" each bomb, virtually by gut feel. The pilot set up a bomb run along a long stretch of road. Bob was thinking that it reminded him of the highway from Lancaster to Neffsville when the signal came.

His heart was pounding. He reached down and pushed up on the bomb bay door switch until the indicator light came on, which seemed to take forever. His focus on the task was so intense that the next few minutes passed in freeze-frame. He hunched over, peered down through the plexiglass, and toggled his first RDX on a roadside building as it approached. Seconds later there would be a dull puff of smoke and cloud of dirt, which quickly dispersed behind them. As the next group of buildings came into his line of sight, he adjusted his lead point, but missed again. The next drops were more accurate, revealing some direct hits, but little in the way of lasting flames or skyrocketing debris. Intent on his task, he ignored the unsolicited groans and other reactions from his fellow crew members. A little more than half way through the bomb load, a distinct secondary explosion in a cluster of large buildings was called out by the tail gunner, and cheers erupted from unidentified crew positions. For a moment Bob felt like he was back in Laredo shooting clay pigeons from the back of a bouncing truck, trying to eke out a near perfect score with direct hits on the final rounds. Select, aim, toggle, bingo! Just as he methodically settled into his new game, the "all bombs clear" call rang through the intercom. He reflexively reached for the bomb bay door switch, and in the time it took for the doors to wind shut, the mental impression formed during the preceding minutes faded from his consciousness like a nightmare dissolving at sunrise. The rest of the flight went by in a daze.

The other crew members of *Hell's Angel* remembered the details of the bombing exhibition that day better than he did. Bob never knew and didn't care who won or lost the bets on his performance, but he'd never forget the cheerful jibes, pats on the back, and overblown reports given to the interrogator. Four Triangle L planes were forced to land in other bases in England that day due to poor weather, but his group had suffered no losses. Bob felt that he had done his job well and contributed to the team. Outside the interrogation room, the now familiar recipient of his post-mission whiskey allotment offered a toast to Sergeant Singleton after overhearing the remarks of returning crews. By the time Bob got back to the hut, the story had already circulated about the sharp-shooting toggalier, who was now being referred to as "No Sight Singleton." Bob modestly shrugged off his feat, but privately basked in the recognition. It had been a while since he experienced this sensation.

That evening, before writing Norm, he recorded his thoughts in the Remarks section of his mission log:

> *Primary target was Lutzendorf, near Merseburg. Our formation got "screwed up," so we bombed a target of opportunity; I bombed by instinct, and luckily hit a German town, somewhere nearby; Some fun! (What a bombardier I am?) The crew was betting on me...what a time we had! Flak- light; Got first good view of Zuider Zee; The "Jerries" even threw "flak" up at us there.[2]*

He also made reference to the incident in his nightly letter to Norm; however, his joy seemed more reserved and tentative:

> *...I'm very tired tonite, and expect to hit the "sack" shortly after I finish this, so I'll do my best to make it readable [...] the reason I'm so tired, I'll let you figure out. Probably you can guess why? [...]*
>
> *Well, darling, I'll now try and answer some of the questions you've been asking me in recent letters. First of all, about my flying [...] Honey I told you before, I believe, that when I fly still, I now fly mostly as Bombardier. Everyone mans a gun position, in case you wonder. (All except the pilot and co-pilot). We've been rather lucky so far, and don't have to use them too much, however. We just "sweat" that part out, and hope our luck continues. It's the "flak" that we worry about...pretty intense at times, I'll tell you. I'm sorry I can't say too much else, but I'll say once more, "Some day I will have lots to tell you." We'll spend some evenings still, just "reminiscing," O.K.? (You, Sandy & I) O-Boy! I might mention one interesting thing I seen already...I seen some V-2's being launched a few times already. I'll describe it all to you when I see you. Quite some experience! I guess I also had an experience, something which Ed would say, was "funny, but a serious thing, at the same time." It happened while I was flying as a Bombardier. Remind me to tell you some day. (Something to do with dropping the bombs.)*

Why he didn't elaborate on his first real trial as a "bombardier" may reflect sensitivity to the censors, but also may relate to his private concerns about the consequences of their actions that day. As he lay in bed that night, still highly strung from earlier events, mental images of innocent civilians in harm's way invaded his thoughts: old folks at a nursing home?...children at school?...distant relatives of Pennsylvania Dutch friends and ancestors? It made little difference that he couldn't see faces of the enemy. That was true on every mission. But this time they were flying close to the ground, the targets were undefended, and he alone controlled the trigger.

BOB DIDN'T WAKE UP until 11 o'clock the next morning, later than he had ever slept, thanks to Bill Ingram, who empathetically kept him off the gunnery school schedule that day. Bill knew that Bob would have an opportunity to make up for missed work at the school. Since the toggalier had accumulated more than his regular instructor's quota of combat flights, the gunnery school would now demand a greater share of his time. This, of course, would please Norm. She clearly had concerns about her new husband's combat flying. In one of her letters she reported that she had managed to track down their Laredo buddy, Dick Stewart, and was passing along his station number. She also didn't hesitate to point out that, unlike Bob, Stewart hadn't flown on any combat missions. Bob tried to put her mind at ease by emphasizing in his next letter that *"eventually he will though, you can rest assured."* He said that Stewart's report didn't surprise him, because, from what he knew, the *"majority of the guys he came over with"* also weren't flying combat missions. But he went on to make an admission of sorts:

> Truthfully, I think I have the jump on him, but maybe he doesn't think so? Our group is a bit more "on the ball," and got us started, instead of making us "sweat 'em out." The sooner he gets that initial quota in, the sooner he can make a little more money too. Why put 'em off, if you eventually have to put them in, anyway? (One may as well try and get all coming to him, I think. Right?) I can tell you now, truthfully, dear, from now on I'll just be working on that monthly quota, if you remember what I told you? I believe that will make you feel better now, huh? Anyway, I should think it would? In other words, the initial quota is in

*(even plus a few more), so things are under control just fine. Please don't worry now. Promise?? ...*

Bob and Norm both wanted the same thing—his return; they simply had different points of view on the best way for him to achieve it.

Due to the shortage of bombardiers, Bob was needed as a regular crew fill-in, but he was also needed at the gunnery school. Lieutenent Hart called Captain Smeyer in Operations to request that Bob's flying be cut back to the minimum. They were so busy at the school that Bob had to skip church services on Sunday so that he could help check out a large group of arriving crews. As more flyboys completed their tours, the replacement pipeline had to flow faster to keep up. As a result, Bob found himself conducting two lectures and several training modules on one day. On another day, when it was his turn to get up at 0330 for mission checks, he was scheduled to give a gunnery lecture in the afternoon to 70 officers and enlisted men.

He quickly earned another two-day pass, but, as before, was indifferent about it, as he told Norm:

*Some guys may think I'm crazy, but to them a pass means something different. (if you know what I mean?) To me, I just get even the more homesick to see you, whereas if I am kept a little busy, the time seems to go by a little faster.*

On Monday evenings he and Johnnie usually went to the Aero Club to hear the *"latest news summary"* given by the *"S-2 [intelligence] officer,"* who continued to report favorable progress by the Allies. Nevertheless, Bob tried to keep his mind off the uncertainty of the war by keeping busy writing, going to movies, and printing pictures until late at night—or until he and Johnnie ran out of contact paper, whichever came first.

He continued to live for Norm's mailings, and was never disappointed. He had just received birthday and Valentine cards plus a surprise birthday package from her, containing individually wrapped socks, nail file, mirror, latest issue of *Reader's Digest*, shoe store calendar, and flashlight from his parents. His response:

*...I don't know how to thank you for it...honest it made me so happy, I didn't know whether to laugh or cry! Thanks a hundred million times,*

*dear...you're WONDERFUL to me!! Gosh, that'll keep up my morale for another long stretch now...*

He also received from Uncle Elwood late delivery of a Christmas card—the popular kind with a built-in framed family photo—and longed for the day when he could send his own family greeting cards, using prints developed in his own darkroom. He went on:

*Oh dear, won't that be living though? If only God would make those dreams come true, soon, ain't? Oh well, maybe he will? Only he knows that! [...] Oh Honey, we have everything to look forward to, don't we? We'll be the happiest people in the whole world, won't we?*

As winter thawed and the weather improved, raids were launched nearly every day, ruthlessly assaulting the Reich's transportation infrastructure. Because his squadron was still short on bombardiers Bob was pulled back to combat duty within a couple weeks. He flew missions to Nuremberg on February 20th, Kobbelitz on the 22nd, and Hamburg on the 24th. Now deep into Germany, the sorties were all over eight hours long, and the formations were huge. On the 22nd the group was part of an Allied air armada of 6,000 planes. The visibility was good, and, according to Bob's mission log on the 20th, you could see *"Planes everywhere!!"* They dropped down to 9,700 feet and executed *"pinpoint bombing."* Fortunately, the 381st didn't lose any planes, but the sheer numbers involved made losses inevitable for the Eighth. The Germans were now concentrating their depleted resources on defense of their shrinking occupied territory, and they were managing to put more fighters into the skies. Bob saw one shot down over severely burning towns and villages around Kobbelitz and witnessed a B-17 get shot down over the North Sea. Sturdy old *Hell's Angel* managed to bring him back safely again on the 22nd, only to be forced down in Brussels with an engine out three days later, but eventually making it back to serve out the war.[3]

Combat seems like a game of chance. Bob flew on *In Like Errol* on the 20th, as he did on December 9th and would again on March 1st, when it returned in operating condition except for a flak hole in the ship. But on the next day, March 2nd, it was forced to turn back to base due to mechanical failure. It's also ironic that, on the day *In Like Errol* aborted, Bob was assigned to the even more worn-out *Stage Door Can-*

*teen*, which returned intact this time, albeit with only minutes of fuel remaining. His mission notes recorded the following remarks:

> *Took off in darkness 6 A.M; Briefing 3:15 A.M; No "flak"; Group ahead of us was hit by fighters; Came back with about 20 gal. of gas... thought we were going to land in Brussels; Had a little trouble with my oxygen mask.*

His comments sound blasé, but, it's amazing how small differences in schedule or circumstance, like a ship's assigned position in formation, could affect one's fate. Later that month *Stage Door Canteen* lost engines on missions of both March 10th and 14th. But that was how bomber crews lived—from day to day, and minute to minute. They simply played the odds. It's probably why airmen developed their own little rituals and superstitious habits, like carrying talismans or wearing only "lucky" socks on combat missions. It's also why their moods could instantly swing due to insignificant changes in the weather, aircraft assignments, or the breakfast menu.

BOB HAD ACCUMULATED 18 MISSIONS by March 2nd and was eligible for his second Oak Leaf Cluster. By that time his old buddies Porter and Browne had just earned their Air Medals. With only seven more missions, Bob's combat tour would be over. But Lieutenant Hart called Operations again, insisting that Sergeant Singleton not be assigned to fly *"unless absolutely necessary."* Doc Graham also stopped by that evening to ask for help printing pictures, but may have been checking to see where the scheduling conflict was coming from. For whatever reason, Bob was grounded for nearly three weeks, during which time the group flew 12 missions and recorded only one ship lost. He might have completed his tour during this period had he been allowed to fly. It's possible that Hart may have conjectured this eventuality and was serving in the school's best interests by delaying the departure of one of his experienced gunnery instructors.

The workload was indeed heavy at the school. Both new and old air crews had to be trained. The new replacements were younger, and they had not been trained over as long a period of time as the original crews. But their bombing results were good, and their attitudes were brighter, most likely a reflection of the progress of the war.[4] The only off-duty time Bob got was when Bill Ingram kept him off the schedule so that he could build barracks closets for the two of them out of old bomb crates. Bob never found it difficult to keep himself immersed in any kind of work, his new hobby, or letter writing. But he also made time to socialize, occasionally going off base for entertainment like snooker contests at the crowded King's Head pub in Great Yoho. In mid-March he got a pass to meet Butch again in Cambridge. With his flight pay, he was now earning more as a staff sergeant than Captain Powl, who had recently been promoted to head of Group Bombsight in the 379th. Most of Bob's earnings continued to go home as pay allotments or money orders. He and Norm had paid off Roy's loan, and they were now accumulating a nest egg.

MEANWHILE, THE GERMANS were taking a severe pounding, and their resources were being depleted. In early March the first American troops crossed the Rhine. Since mid-February the 381st had flown 26 missions with only one loss, recorded on the March 9th raid to Kassel. Norm told Bob in a letter that a fortune teller predicted that her hubby would be home in a few months. If only it were a matter of wishing. Unfortunately, the enemy just wouldn't quit.

Bob was finally assigned to fly his 19th mission on March 21st. Their target was an airfield in Rheine where Me262 jet fighters were based. The Eighth Air Force targeted 11 enemy air bases in northwest Germany that day, because during recent weeks it appeared that the Luftwaffe was preparing for a comeback.[5] The Eighth also began to employ a new tactic: first they concentrated on fighter bases; then, to hamper movement of enemy supplies and troops, the formation divided into squadrons, dropped to 10,000 feet, and hit every railroad bridge, highway bridge, and trestle inside a ten mile swath along the flight path.[6] On raids like this they needed bombardiers like "No Sight" Singleton. Flak was medium in the Rheine target area, but visual bombing results were good. Bob could see *"many fires burning."* All in all, it was a routine mission for the veteran toggalier, who was flying with a relatively inexperienced crew. They were back on base in six hours. Their new, unnamed plane, #693, looked as bright and shiny as the day she was delivered.

The enemy's last ditch effort to defend itself was taking a toll on bomber crews, however. On March 22nd a 381st plane went down with 10 men aboard, including 7 officers. "It was probably the first and only time that seven officers ever flew in one ship in combat."[7] This could have been a result of complacency or over-confidence on the part of men desperate to get home. A pilot's body was found in the tail gunner's position; he was probably trying to get another mission under his belt. Perhaps it was the same for the others. The plane was also flying with a full crew of ten, even though the group had been flying missions with nine-man crews for months now. No doubt officers had priority in the competition to accumulate missions. Regardless, the tragic loss of these well-liked and respected men impacted everybody on base. In addition, the accounts of aircrews on that mission sounded dreadfully like those of earlier days. According to Chaplain Brown:

> I saw men come into the interrogation room with wild eyes, strained eyes, frightened eyes. They looked worn and weary and tired....To many it was the worst they had ever flown. The flak was intense and accurate. The sky was black; the bursts were close; and the strikes were hitting our ships. Flak bursts were right and left, center and back, below and above, and ahead.
>
> Several men who finished their missions today said that this mission was the worst they had ever flown. Others said that they were scared worse than they ever were before....A bombardier said to me that he was alive only because the flak hit the bombsight and knocked it to pieces. He was hurled to the floor.[8]

Patton's army was crossing the Rhine, but the enemy still wasn't ready to surrender. They seemed more determined to take the invaders down with them. At night their guided bombs could be heard continually, zooming over Ridgewell on their way to English cities. In a close encounter on March 23rd base loudspeakers had to summon the men to their shelters.[9] On March 24th over an enemy airfield in Vechtel, flak brought down one Triangle L bomber and killed a waist gunner on another. These losses so late in the war weighed heavily on the minds of the air crews. At this point it would have been easy to understand why the flyboys might want to reconsider how they should finish out the war.

Just after the Germans had initiated their desperate last push, Bob was assigned to go up again. It was March 28th. He generally took things in stride, but after comfortably sitting out the war for the past week, the morning wake up call was as distressing as ever. It seemed like a grim repeat of earlier missions: *What am I doing here?*

Breakfast that morning was no consolation—fresh eggs. Groans in the briefing room were barely contained as the curtains were drawn from the big map showing a green line stretched to Berlin. Their target was an arms factory, which was expected to be heavily defended. Bob was assigned to *PFC's Limited,* of "twin engine" fame, piloted by Lt. Jeremiah F. O'Neil. O'Neil must have been promoted; he used to serve as copilot for Malleus, who was probably on his way back to the states by now. The rest of the crew were mostly new faces. Bob hoped the repaired power plants on this bird were in good enough condition to haul today's payload: four, 1000-pound Navy bombs and two M17 incendiaries. These weapons would certainly make a big bang in the Big B if they managed to get there.

Fortunately, the Eighth Air Force overpowered the enemy, and the mission was successful; however, it was anything but routine. At the conclusion of this 8½ hour sortie, Bob recorded the following in his log:

*Only had 45 minutes from briefing until takeoff...took off at 6:15; Tail gunner put in my guns; We assembled over France; Weather worst yet!! Flew by instruments most of time; Flak-heavy, but inaccurate; H2X bombing; One of our ships was badly damaged; We flew home alone, from France to base, due to bad weather...flew at 500' most of time; What fun!!*

Considering the conditions they flew in, these sounded like the words of a hardened, 23-year-old combat veteran. Perhaps it was the sight of Belgian schoolboys playfully throwing rocks up at their tree-skimming bomber on its return trip that made it fun. Or perhaps it was just newfound self confidence—unavoidably acquired after defying all the odds, flying repeatedly into hazardous conditions, and returning each time to write about it.

AS A RESULT OF THE ENEMY'S BIG PUSH, during the last week of March and the first week of April, the 381st lost planes on 5 of the 12 missions flown. It was a harsh, but necessary, cost of winning the war. On the other hand, March was a record month for the Eighth Air Force:

The 8th unloaded 73,000 tons of bombs on the Reich, sur-
passing by 15,000 tons its previous heaviest month.... The
heavies flew more than 28,500 sorties, bettering by 2,600 the
number flown during D-Day month, until now the record
month.... The record tonnage represents nearly two tons of
bombs dropped every minute during the month.... The 8th
lost 138 bombers and 99 fighters during March, or one plane
lost for every 200 sent out. At the same time, 410 enemy
fighters were destroyed, 250 shot down and 129 destroyed
on the ground by fighters and 31 shot down by bomber gunners.[10]

It was obvious that something big was happening that spring.
Raids were flown from dawn to dusk. Sometimes two missions were
flown on the same day. The sky was "polluted" with planes; B-17s and
B-24s were everywhere. One couldn't help believing that the war had
to end soon as a result of the air power directed at the enemy. As new
and old crews competed for mission slots, the gunnery instructors
would be scheduled to fly less often during this period.

Bob used his extra free time enjoying friends and seeing more of
England. He and the other project guys—Porter, Browne, and Rutherford—arranged passes to visit Cambridge, where they met up with
Dick Stewart, whom Bob had contacted at the station number for-
warded by Norm. They took in historic sites, went horseback riding in
the park, punted on the river Cam, and checked out the local pubs. It
was good to see Stew alive, well, and his old self. He hadn't changed
too much, although the last five months seemed to have put a harder
edge on his laid-back personality.

A funny episode occurred on the train platform. While they were
waiting for their train a gust of wind removed Stewart's hat and blew it
down between the railroad tracks. He whined about losing it, but they
were both afraid to climb between the rails to fetch it. A tall, young
English fellow overheard the conversation and offered to help. The
stranger lay down on his stomach and reached with his umbrella to
successfully retrieve Stew's hat. But in the process of doing so, his own
hat fell to a more precarious location. And in contrast to the Yank's
government issue bonnet, the Englishman's was a fine specimen. But
Stew, intent on the return of his own hat and the arriving train on the

other side of the platform, either didn't notice or didn't appreciate the Englishman's predicament. So, as the good Samaritan began to appeal for help, Stew brushed him off, saying he had to run. As they hustled away, Bob reminded Stewart that this wasn't polite, but Stew seemed dumbfounded. Bob couldn't help laughing at his friend's blank expression, and the image of this ridiculous scene kept them both laughing for a long time after that.

In mid-April Bob got a pass and spent a couple of pleasant spring days in London with Johnnie. They visited all the popular spots: Big Ben, Trafalgar Square, Buckingham Palace, and the sites around Hyde Park. As they were ending their day in a crowded pub, an English chap approached Bob and said, "Sorry to hear about your old man!" Caught by surprise, Johnnie and Bob both turned with a questioning look, as if to say, What do you mean?

"Your old man dying!" the fellow insisted. For a moment Bob thought of his father, who, according to recent letters, was not in the best health. His shocked expression must have revealed his misunderstanding, so the stranger clarified himself: "Roosevelt!" he exclaimed; "your president's dead!" That's how Bob learned of FDR's death on April 13, 1945. And he wasn't alone:

> At London's Rainbow Corner, hundreds of soldiers stood for several minutes in stunned silence when they heard the news. Some paled and others made no effort to hide wet eyes. Military police along Shaftesbury Avenue and around Piccadilly Circus reported the gloom swept over British and American alike. "Within a few minutes after the news the Piccadilly area was as quiet as a small back street," Cpl. Carlyle Everman, MP of Winchester Ky., said. Two British bobbies couldn't recall such midnight gloom, even during the blitz.[11]

It's sad that Roosevelt couldn't have experienced the final victory. A few days later, General Spaatz was reported to have remarked that, for all practical purposes, the strategic war in Europe was over. But incredibly, the Germans kept putting planes in the air and the 381st would end up flying 15 missions in April, sustaining losses on the raid of the 8th. Bob flew on three of them. They were all over eight hours long to strategic targets in Fassberg (near Hannover), Dresden, and

Munich. The formations were massive. Enemy fighter activity was astonishingly strong, but Bob's group was spared. This was fortunate since the 381st led the entire Eighth Air Force on the Dresden mission. Flak was milder than usual. That was another stroke of luck for Bob, who was forced to leave his nose station over the Dresden railway center to frantically kick out a 500 pound bomb that was hung up in the racks. He flew one more after that—to Munich.[12] That was his last combat mission. He had accumulated 23.

In a single month the Luftwaffe's fighter strength had diminished from an estimated 4,000 to roughly half that amount. But few of the planes remaining could fly, because the Germans had simply run out of gas, thanks to the relentless bombing of oil refineries that began in the early months of the air war. The Nazis thought jet aircraft would be the answer to the massive raids on their industrial centers, but "only too late did they realize the jets used twice as much fuel."[13] Clearly the enemy had been dealt a major blow.

THE END WAS NEAR. On April 23rd a celebratory R&R flight to Belfast, Ireland was scheduled. One of the 381st Forts was stripped down to accommodate the maximum number of passengers—30 men. Since it was a reward of sorts, each unit on base was asked to choose who could go from their group. Captain Tansey, 535th Executive Officer, was one of the lucky ones to get a seat on the flight. However, at the very last minute he had to cancel his plans, and Lieutenant Hart got the surprise chance to take his boss's place. He literally had to run to catch the plane before it took off. Had Hart not been in the gunnery school office when Tansey backed out, Bob might have had a chance to claim the slot. But Hart made it in the nick of time. Bob and Johnnie witnessed their friend from Ashtabula actually sprinting to the hard stand and jumping through the open waist door while the big bird's props were already turning.

As fate would have it, the happy bunch never made it to their destination. The aircraft and bodies of all 31 men aboard were found 200 feet from the peak of a 2,000 foot mountain on the Isle of Man, located between England and Ireland. The peak was known to have been frequently concealed by clouds and the doom of many previous aircraft flying low over the beautiful island. The men back at Ridgewell were stunned when they received the news. A large contingent, including Bob, attended the funeral on April 27th officiated by Chaplain

Brown at the American Military Cemetery in Cambridge. As long as he would live, Bob would never forget the sight of 31 flag-draped coffins and the memory of his good friend from Ashtabula rushing to get a coveted seat on that airplane.

THE 381ST FLEW THEIR 297TH and final mission on April 25, 1945. The end was now clearly in sight, but nobody knew exactly what to expect. Everybody was anxious, waiting for word on not only how it would end but, more importantly, when they could go home. Bob passed his time developing pictures, going to movies, enjoying the company of friends he probably wouldn't see after the war, and writing letters. It was now the height of springtime, and he could write letters outdoors, perched atop the bomb shelter behind his hut. At this northern latitude on daylight savings time it stayed wonderfully light until after well after 10 o'clock at night. His letters were about detailed plans for the future. He told Norm that he would send a drawing of the little house that he envisioned for them and mentioned that they could *"buy one on the GI Bill of Rights that Congress recently adopted."*

With every day that went by the news was more encouraging. Mussolini was executed on April 30th, and on May 3rd Hitler was reported to have been found dead. Then the desperately awaited news was announced over base loudspeakers at 2 A.M. on May 7th: the Germans had surrendered unconditionally. The war in Europe was finally over. At 8 A.M. Colonel Hall led a ceremony in front of the control tower, where, among other things, he summarized the 381st Bomb Group's battle record during the previous two years:

> During their twenty-two months in England they completed 9,035 sorties, destroyed 223 enemy fighters, and dropped over 22,000 tons of bombs. The group lost 165 ships and 1,290 personnel.[14]

Their group was a small, but important part of the mighty Eighth Air Force, which flew three-quarters of a million sorties during the course of the war, dropping nearly 700,000 pounds of bombs, and shooting down 11,481 enemy aircraft. The total cost to the Eighth was 47,000 casualties, including 26,000 men killed. A total of 6,656 aircraft never returned, and another 2,401 crashed in Great Britain or were written off for excessive damage.[15]

As part of Colonel Hall's announcement, everybody on base was excused from duty. Passes and furloughs for all military personnel in the U.K. were extended two days. He sternly reminded his boys that after tomorrow, officially declared V-E Day, it would be "business as usual." Each person would receive orders stating when and how they would return to the states and where they would be reassigned after that. All were invited to help themselves at the mess hall. But most of the hoards ran to the PX, where "mild and bitters" were sold. Beer flowed. Fireworks were set off on the flight line. The security gates were opened, and Great Yoho neighbors were welcomed to join in the celebration. The place literally went wild.

Indeed, it was a much deserved free-for-all. "At the end of a tumultuous day some twenty officers and men spent the night in the station calaboose!"[16] But, Bob wasn't a drinker or the partying type. He celebrated quietly by writing to Norm after a visit to the mess hall. It was the first in a long while that he would enjoy fresh eggs—sunny side up.

# CHAPTER 15

# GOING HOME

JOHNNIE LEFT RIDGEWELL ahead of Bob. He had earned his release after completing his 30th mission on April 7th and had received orders to ship out on May 10th with a contingent traveling by sea.[1] Bob was envious that his buddy would reach Lancaster first, but good-naturedly kidded Johnnie that he might return by air and get there first. Bob's hunch was confirmed by orders received on the 15th, which indicated that he would leave around June 1st with a group returning on B-17s. While he was excited by the news and desperate to get home, he had second thoughts about his itinerary. His letter to Norm explained the situation:

*Thursday evening*
*May 17th*
*6:45*

*Dear Honey,*

*In my letter that I wrote you last night (V-mail), I told you I had some news to tell you, so brace yourself, as here it is: I'm coming home!!! Yes, dear, it's true, and to show you that I do mean just that, I'll say it again: "I'm coming home to you" (Do you understand me, or are still a bit hazy on the thought of it?) I can't blame you if you don't believe it, as it was hard for me to believe at first too. Honest Hon, I was so happy I could have cried! I felt like yelling so that the whole world could hear me. I didn't know whether I was going to tell you or not, as I thought maybe I'd just surprise you, but I just couldn't hold it. [...] I know I won't sleep now, 'til I see you! I just can't do a thing now, since I know it...I'm all beside myself!! Why wouldn't a guy be that way with a sweet, little wife like you to come home to? Oh, Hon, I love you so much, I'll squeeze you to death when I see you, so be prepared. Now for the particulars: I found this news out on Tuesday...two days ago. You see what I mean when I said I didn't know whether to tell you or not? When we heard the news...about 2 P.M. in the after-*

*noon...everybody went wild. You can imagine?? All we know is that we'll be leaving here around June 1ˢᵗ, so I should see you around the end of June. [...] Now get this: Some of us are going by boat, some are flying. Yesterday I found out I was scheduled to fly, and would leave here the end of this week, which meant that I'd be in your arms, probably before you'd have even received this letter. However...get this...those flying...it is pretty certain...are scheduled for a short furlough at home, then right away would be off for somewhere else. Those going by boat... mostly ground personnel...after their furlough home, will probably be reorganized, before being assigned to other duties, which means, "in the States" a little while, at least. Anyway, that's what we all figure on! As a result, I had my gunnery officer call headquarters, and have me taken off the list of those who are flying home. As far as I know, he slung the deal O.K. Here's hopin', anyway! It means I won't see you until 2 or 3 weeks later, but I'm sure I done the right thing. At least I hope so? I think you'll agree, won't you dear? After all, the longer we can be together later, is the main thing, isn't it? I'm sure going with the group is the best thing then. If it works, that's one thing I can really thank the gunnery school for then, I guess? I would more or less have liked to have been able to say that "I flew the Atlantic," but the other does mean so much more to me. As of today, all training at the school has stopped, and everyone is busy crating their department's equipment for shipping. You can imagine the rushing around? If you see Johnnie, tell him I could have beat him home at that. I'll bet he'll really be surprised? I may see him at home there, at that? I got your V-mail today darling, and [...] what I want when I come home [...]*

Bob may have surprised his peers and pressed his luck by requesting a slow boat home. But understandably, he was concerned about getting sent immediately to the Pacific with the other air crews. It was public information that the greatest aerial bombardment of Japan was just beginning and the bulk of the Army's strength would be shifted to the Pacific theater. But he may also have been influenced by the gossip and misinformation circulating among the men on base, who were frantically jockeying for slots on the fastest itineraries home. The official Army policy stated that releases were governed by a point system based on length of service, overseas time, combat credits, and number of dependents. Bob's strong standing in this regard earned him a seat on an airplane. While the Army refused Sergeant Singleton's request to travel by ship, in the end it was all for the best.

Johnnie embarked from Liverpool on the liberty ship *SS Joseph Hollister* on the same day that Bob received his orders. The boat wouldn't arrive in Boston until 18 days later. Not only was it a typical liberty ship cruise, but the voyage was additionally complicated by the sheer numbers of oceangoing vessels headed to the States. Approaching the coast of Newfoundland in a huge convoy, the *Hollister* was involved in the "greatest mass collision of ships in history," according to the *Saturday Evening Post*. The report further stated:

> A westbound convoy of 76 Allied vessels was steaming slowly through a dense fog when one of them struck an iceberg. It discovered eight others near them and gave the alarm. Instantly the entire convoy swerved sharply with the result that 22 of the ships collided with one another in the following ten minutes. Yet none sank and no lives were lost. Incidentally it happened on the last day the vessels were required to remain on the Atlantic in the convoy.[2]

The lucky tail gunner of the *Tomahawk Warrior* later remarked about the incident: "We had a watertight compartment pierced. There was a hole in the bow big enough to drive a jeep through!"[3]

But the chaos on the high seas couldn't compare to the furlough frenzy back at Ridgewell. Crews scheduled to return by air were scrambling to ready their planes for the long trip. Several of the battle-stricken bombers were not in the best shape for transporting 20 men plus their gear across the Atlantic. Therefore, to ensure the planes would be in airworthy condition, each crew chief was assigned to a passenger slot on his own airplane. Combined with the interesting fact that some of the ground crews were afraid to fly, this "fly-on-your-own" requirement was a potent motivator. Some of the mechanics feigned sickness to avoid having to fly, but most scrambled to get their aircraft ready. If necessary, they would "borrow" parts to get it in flying condition. The competition for spares was so intense that many slept on their airplane on the nights prior to departure. The crew chief of Bob's plane, M/Sgt George Their, lived with his ship around the clock. His aircraft, the *Salvoin' Sachem*, was a relatively new B-17G, having just entered service in February—and he wanted to keep it that way. If George needed to leave the plane for any reason, he asked a buddy to cover for him. His dedication helped to put the other passengers, including Bob, at ease.

*Salvoin' Sachem* departed on June 3rd with a group of 16 other planes. They were with the first wave of a contingent of 2,000 bombers and 40,000 men who returned to the U.S. over a period of two months. Another 20,000 Eighth Air Force personnel returned by ship. Included among the returning bombers would be good old *Hell's Angel*, *Los Angeles City Limits*, which survived over 72 missions; and *Stage Door Canteen*, whose 100th mission was recognized in a ceremony hosted by movie star E. G. Marshall during his April visit to Ridgewell. Among aircraft left behind were *The Columbus Miss* and *Feather Merchant II*, both of which went down in January; and old, faithful *In Like Errol*, which survived until its 91st mission on March 30th, when, after having completed its bomb run with an engine out, it was shot down by an Me262 fighter over Hamburg—including four crew members with whom Bob had previously flown, two of whom were killed.[4] Like the wreckage of bombers scattered across the European continent, within a matter of months Ridgewell would become only remnants of a base, and within a few years it would be completely returned to farmland, the tarmac having been torn up and recycled into material for a new English highway network and abandoned Nissen huts having been converted to grain warehouses or tractor barns.

As the Yanks departed, they didn't look back. Bob's travel contingent assembled in northwest Wales, where they departed for Bradley Field in Hartford, Connecticut, by way of refueling stops in Iceland and Labrador. The first day of the flight was uneventful. Bob sat in his favorite seat in the nose. Most passengers sat in makeshift benches along the sides of the aircraft in the waist area. Bob spotted only one guy that he recognized, a waist gunner named Smith who flew with Lieutenant Malleus's crew in December. The plane's first stop was near Reykjavik, Iceland, where they were replenished with fuel, food, and a night's rest. On the second day they headed to a refueling point at Goose Bay, Labrador. Just before reaching Goose Bay they encountered storms, and one of the planes was struck by lightning, setting an engine ablaze. A steep dive initiated by the combat-trained pilot squelched the flames and led to a successful landing at their destination. Other than that incident, Bob would not remember much about his once-in-a-lifetime visits to Iceland and

Labrador, because, at the time all he could think about was getting home.

By the time they crossed the North American coast line, Bradley Field was socked-in with weather, so the formation diverted to another base south of Boston, where the crews were met by trucks and taken to Camp Miles Standish in Taunton, Massachusetts, an Army staging facility. Thousands of returning GIs, including Johnnie, had also processed through Standish after disembarking in Boston. But the facility wasn't prepared for this unexpected group of B-17s. Although Bob was safely back in his own country, he was now caught in an indefinite "snafu."

Norm was shocked to hear Bob's voice when she answered the telephone; she had not yet received his last letter. While their long awaited reunion should have been imminent, they were now separated by a tangled bureaucracy that would take a couple of weeks to unravel. It was frustrating for both of them. She reported that Johnnie, after all, had arrived a few days earlier and was now in Lancaster. One of his first stops was a visit to McGrann Boulevard to meet Bob's family. He had enjoyed a delightful dinner with Norm, her parents, and in-laws. The hosts couldn't refrain from quizzing him about Bob's activities; however, he was made to feel very comfortable and no doubt indulged in one of Vi's memorable home-cooked meals.

Bob, meanwhile, was checking in regularly by telephone, getting more disgruntled by the day with his predicament. He could do little more than hang around the barracks waiting for orders. It turned out to be a longer wait than expected; but, when he eventually got his paperwork, he boarded the first train headed toward Lancaster.

HOME NEVER LOOKED SO GOOD and never felt so temporary. He had only a one-month furlough before having to return to service, but at least he wouldn't have to face the prospect of leaving home the next time without Norm. They stayed at the Diffenbachs' except for a week-long second honeymoon in Atlantic City. After returning from the shore, rather than basking in the glory of a returning soldier, the flyboy immediately resumed his civilian role as a shoe salesman. Roy felt bad having to ask his son to work, but summer sales were beginning and they were short on help.

Bob wore his Army uniform to work. In 1945 men in uniform easily blended into the home-front landscape. They wore government-issue fashions with pride. Another change since Bob's last day at the store was the predominant influence of rationing on sales transactions. Shoe rationing had been tightened at the end of 1944, when the annual per-person shoe allotment was reduced from two to only one pair. Retailers maintained rationing accounts with each of their suppliers, and coupons were managed like accounts receivable in order to pass government scrutiny.

The 1945 shoe ration coupon was not issued until mid-year, an act which stimulated pent-up summer demand and created additional tension with consumers. Bob got a taste of it on his first day back. He had just "rung-up" his first sale to a quiet, elderly lady, but forgot to ask for her coupon. Savvy Charlie Adams caught Bob's mistake shortly after she left and ordered Bob to fetch it: "You gotta get that coupon, or we won't be able to replace those shoes!" On the double, Bob dashed out and located his prey ambling down the sidewalk. He was out-of-breath when he caught up with her at the street corner, where he gushed out an apology and polite insistence that she turn over her coupon. Feeling conspicuous in the midday flow of rubbernecking passersby, she sweetly made some excuse about thinking that this was one of the occasional "free coupon days" downtown, but Bob sensed her surprise and guilt at having been caught in a dirty little act. Regardless of fault, it was embarrassing for both of them. It saddened Bob to witness how a foreign war could tarnish the integrity of decent folks in such indirect and unexpected ways.

HIS FURLOUGH ENDED like an unfinished dream, but he was ready to get on with wrapping up his military obligation. With Norm along it would be a lot more tolerable. His orders were to report to an Army base in Sioux Falls, South Dakota, where he would await reassignment. And Norm would travel with him—whether the Army had an opinion on that or not. They traveled by train, arriving in mid-July, and checked in with the family services office to obtain base housing information. There they were given the name of a Mrs. Stewart, an Army wife who lived in town and rented out her basement to military transients during her husband's absence.

Mrs. Stewart's house was located in a leafy, suburban neighborhood with large lots. The accommodations were Spartan, but adequate. Carpeting covered most of the concrete basement floor, and a partition separated the sleeping area from the living area, which was equipped with a few pieces of furniture and a radio. Unlike Zaraguzie Street, these underground quarters had a private bathroom; however, cooking facilities were more limited. As a result they ate out a lot, and Mrs. Stewart occasionally invited them upstairs for dinner. Norm became friends with her landlady. The women went shopping together when Bob was on base. Norm also enjoyed taking walks around the neighborhood or to a nearby park where, as in Laredo, she spent warm afternoons writing letters.

At transition facilities across the country Eighth Air Force personnel were offered a menu of sports and education programs.[5] At Sioux Falls Bob was required to report only to regular PT sessions and scheduled reassignment interviews, where his personnel history and combat experience were reviewed and career options discussed. Aviation cadet training made him a candidate for OCS, and he was encouraged to apply. Officer Candidate School had been mentioned several times before, at both gunnery and instructor schools. Norm thought he should consider it, because it would require him to remain in the States for a period of time, improving his chances of missing the war in the Pacific.

But from the start, Bob was never a military guy. He liked his flying experience, but titles, ratings, and medals meant nothing to him. So it wasn't surprising that he decided not to sign up for OCS, taking his chances that the war might end soon. At the time, he was indeed taking a chance; in July 1945 massive bombing raids on Japan had only just begun. But as it turned out, he made a good bet—although he never could have imagined that the war would have ended so abruptly—with atomic bombs dropped on Hiroshima and Nagasaki on August 8th and 9th and the unconditional surrender of the Japanese on the 14th, which was officially proclaimed VJ Day.

The town of Sioux Falls went crazy on VJ Day. Since it was mainly a military town, the streets were thronged with rowdy, reveling servicemen. On this otherwise joyous occasion Bob and Norm actually felt sorry for the local civilians, who were made up of business people and families like their own. They witnessed, among other careless acts, an inebriated GI driving a jeep through the revolving door of a nicely maintained hotel in town, causing excessive and pointless damage. "Isn't that awful," remarked Norm. As far as they were concerned, the military life couldn't end soon enough.

BOB NEVER GOT REASSIGNED to an operational unit. He and Norm spent the next couple of months blissfully living off an Army paycheck, with no immediate responsibilities other than planning for a future filled with hope. It wasn't long until he received orders to report to Camp Deming, New Mexico, where he would await instructions for out-processing. As on prior occasions, servicemen were advised not to bring their wives to remote desert outposts. Deming had only one hotel in town; and, per usual, wives' stays were limited to three nights. As before, Bob would leave first and then have Norm join him after he had a couple of days to find off-base housing.

In Laredo it was a major challenge to find adequate housing. In Deming it was even worse. According to the rumor mill, many soldiers put up their wives at a place called Kern's Motor Court. So, when Bob arrived in Deming, he immediately went to check out the place. Kern's turned out to be an overrated "dump"—a row of seedy, dilapidated cabins. The price was right, but Bob wouldn't consider putting Norm there—even if there had been a vacancy. Instead, he proceeded to make a three-day reservation at the hotel in town and continued to pound the streets in search of a decent room. He hunted alone to avoid complications.

His persistence and resourcefulness paid off. He eventually came upon a tiny roadside motel with eight separate units organized in a horseshoe. It was called the Deming Motor Court. A manicured grassy island featuring a patio and water fountain was neatly situated inside the horseshoe. At one end of the open courtyard Bob spotted a young Army officer and luggage next to a Chevy with the trunk lid open— ostensibly in the process of coming or going. "Are you checking out?" Bob asked, praying for the desired response.

"Checking out," the fellow answered.

"Who can I see about getting a room?" Bob asked excitedly.

"The gentleman right there," he responded without looking up, tilting his head toward a towering figure in a big Stetson.

Bob immediately spotted the big fellow—all six-and-a-half feet of him—dressed in cowboy hat and pointed boots. Looking up at the giant he blurted out, "Sir, may I have this room?"

The response was almost too good to be true: "Yea, soldier," he replied.

The deal was closed almost too quickly, and Bob felt a need to explain: "Great! My wife's coming into town, I've just been out to

Kern's, the place is awful, and..." The big guy just listened and smiled, while Bob anxiously waited to be invited into the office to submit a deposit. To the cowboy this young sergeant must have looked like an obedient young beagle, waiting for the next command.

"Something else I can do for you, soldier?" asked the giant.

As Bob started to ask about a deposit to hold the room until he returned with his wife, he was cut off in mid sentence. The big guy, in a deep, resonant, and increasingly stern drawl, said, "Soldier, mah word is mah bawnd, and yers better be too!"

"Yes, Sir!" Bob barked back. "Thank you sir!" And he was off.

Bob would never forget the moment, the message, and the man. His name was Mr. Holbrook. He owned the place. It's how they did business down there in those days. He couldn't wait to tell Norm.

Norm traveled to Deming by train with Mary Deaton, wife of Bob's fellow gunnery instructor "Deat," who had served with him at Ridgewell and also made his way back to Camp Deming by way of Sioux Falls. Bob and Deat were on the station platform when Norm and Mary arrived. Rumors had already filtered back to new arrivals that married couples were competing for rooms at Kern's, so the first thing the girls wanted to know was if they were part of the lucky group who got rooms there. Norm looked disappointed when Bob explained that he had made other arrangements. Mary appeared likewise when all Deat could produce was a three-night confirmation slip from the hotel. Bob offered to take the girls out to Kern's to make them feel better, but they were resigned to their respective alternatives.

After Deat and Mary headed off for the hotel, Bob filled in the details for Norm, explaining how fortunate they were, while secretly praying that the big Texan would keep his word and save their room. He still felt vulnerable without a deposit and didn't relax until they parked inside the horseshoe, found the big cowboy in his office, and confirmed that their room was secure.

Bob sincerely expressed his gratitude to Mr. Holbrook: "You know, Sir, you sure taught me a lesson; more people should learn to do business your way."

"That's the way we do bid'ness down here, soldier," he replied. "Enjaw yer stay." Before heading to their cabin Bob mentioned his friends the Deatons, asked whether a room might be available in a few days, and whether Mr. Holbrook could save it. There was, and indeed he would. That afternoon Bob contacted Deat with the good news.

Mary would no longer have to settle for a shabby room at Kern's or worry about having to take a train back home. Four people could sleep well that night—all because a cowboy's word was his bond.

They were in Deming a couple of months. Bob didn't have any work to do on base. They mostly lounged around the motor court with Mary and Deat. Sometimes they brought groceries to the motel and had picnic lunches on the patio. Occasionally the foursome went to a football game at the big high school behind the motel. One day Bob took Norm on an expedition to Kern's to point out what she was missing and gloat about their good fortune. "You'd never put me in there! ...I'd have gone home first," she huffed. Of course.

Had they not been luxuriating in each other's company, their stint at Deming would have been less enjoyable. But they were in no great hurry to rush home, despite the fact that Bob knew his dad needed him at the store. In his weekly letters from Roy, Bob could sense the strain on his dad. Although shoe supplies were limited and rationing was still in effect, customers were inclined to stock up using their own ration allotment and sometimes coupons sold on the black market. Roy never admitted that his health was deteriorating, but it was clear he wanted his sons back at the store. Bob was delayed in Deming, and Ed was still in the Pacific, where he was working as a teletype operator. In desperation Roy finally wrote to the Adjutant General of the Army in September requesting accelerated releases of his two sons on the basis of their being "badly needed in the business." Bob made fun of his dad's weak rationale for their releases, but Roy could claim receiving a reply from the Acting Adjutant General, Maj. Gen. Edward F. Witsell, who said that "the soldier should be advised to submit his application to his immediate commanding officer for consideration by the appropriate discharge authority."[6] Bob never bothered to take the next step. He assumed that his discharge was imminent.

He checked in at the base every day, but usually left with no new information on his release. Camp Deming wasn't set up for out-processing personnel; they could only issue orders stating where one should report for discharge. Finally, in early November, Bob was told that he would be given a choice of two facilities for out-processing and discharge: Indiantown Gap, Pennsylvania or Albuquerque, New Mexico. After discussing it with Norm, they selected Albuquerque over their home state, opting to out-process first, then take a relaxed trip to

Pennsylvania as civilians on vacation. They figured his job would wait, and they could afford the extravagance.

Norm stayed in Deming while Bob traveled to Albuquerque on an Army bus with a contingent of GIs lugging duffels overstuffed with government-issue equipment. It took about a day to get there and would take another to get back. A day in between was needed for out-processing—a tedious drill of hurry-up-and-wait at an endless series of form-filling, question-answering, equipment-surrendering, and money-receiving stations crowded with hoards of restless short-timers on one side and staffed with an officialdom of hard-ass lifers on the other.

The equipment check-in operation was set up on long, low plat-forms that resembled baggage handling counters, positioned along towering storage shelves arranged in warehouse configuration. Various categories of equipment—uniforms, boots, fatigues, helmets, guns, etc.—were collected at each station. Bob had already turned in his flight gear at Camp Miles Standish. The only items he was allowed to keep were his leather bomber jacket, adorned with 535th squadron, Triangle L, and Eighth Air Force insignias, plus his military raincoat and a few other items. Everything else had to be returned and ac-counted for.

As Bob waited in the queue at one station, he happened to glance down the line, several stations ahead, and spotted a familiar face from the past in Army uniform: Joe Glacken, Wil's old buddy from the five points. The street gang always called Joe by his nickname Beans, a la-bel conjured up based on one of his regrettably distinctive adolescent behaviors. Just as Joe looked up in recognition, Bob blurted out the familiar greeting: "Hey, Beans!" Poor Joe instantly and reflexively grimaced, drawing an index finger to his lips and pleading through body language for Bob to keep quiet. Bob was initially shocked, but quietly complied, rapidly deducing that Beans likely hadn't disclosed the old nickname to his new associates in the professional Army. Joe briefly left his work station to approach Bob, confirm his little secret, and exchange some friendly words. Bob stopped back later in the day to bid his old buddy farewell. He learned that Beans had never served overseas but had done well for himself as an enlisted man—and, like many others, had happily forged a new identity in the process. That was the last that Bob saw of Beans.

It was a GI's presumed rite of passage to exploit the Army's inefficiency by sharing a little piece of Uncle Sam's excessive bounty.

Bob was no exception. He managed to salvage a valuable war souvenir through a technique practiced, shared, and often gotten away with by many of the homebound servicemen. The prize: his Remington forty-five, which he confiscated by hiding under his raincoat during the check-out process. Thanks to boredom-induced oversight on the part of one of the supply clerks, at least one sidearm slipped through the cracks that day. Bob never had an interest in guns, but that only added to the mystique and novelty of his war souvenir. It's good that Norm didn't know of his impulsive little scheme in advance.

Bob returned to Deming the following day as a civilian transported by Army bus. Then he and Norm packed their belongings before spending a final, cozy night at the motor court. In the morning they said their goodbyes to Mr. Holbrook, who by this time had become a good friend, especially after getting to know Norm. A taxi delivered them to the train station, and they boarded the first train headed east by way of El Paso, where they would make a two-day stopover. Bob found a "high-grade" men's store in town, where he purchased some needed civvies, including a handsome, double-striped gray suit. The other stop on the way home was St. Louis, memorable for the fermented orange juice that Bob guzzled at the train station. He should have taken Norm's advice and let it sit. She said that the returning warrior was a sad looking sight as he stepped out of the men's room in his new suit and with his face "as white as a sheet."

Although she had good reason, Norm didn't laugh. She sincerely felt bad for him. Having recently been suffering from nagging nausea in the mornings, she indeed knew how it felt. But she never complained, directing all her attention to Bob's temporary bout. That's the way she was—always looking out for the other person. Bob realized shortly after they got home that he was the one who should have been sympathetic. Dr. Kirk confirmed that Norm was pregnant.

# CHAPTER 16

# BOOMERS

IN LATE 1945, like thousands of others WWII couples, Bob and Norm set about starting a new life for themselves. Children of the Depression, they didn't bemoan the war years stolen from their youth, but made the best of circumstances, full of confidence that the future could only get better. Many veterans had put off their education and marriages. Most of them simply picked up where they had left off. Numerous careers and lives would be enriched as a result of specialized training and educational benefits provided by the government.

Roy, still not in good health, was relieved to have his son back at the store. With Norm expecting, Bob's first priority was to get back to work so they could afford a nice little place of their own. At a salary of $35 a week, the boundaries were clear. Through the classified ads he found an affordable apartment for rent and took Norm to see it. It was on the first floor of a three-story row house at 211 North Mulberry Street, a block north and block-and-a-half west of the shoe store. The owners, Mr. and Mrs. Renk, had recently purchased a house around the corner and decided to rent out the first floor of their old place. The second floor was already rented to another young couple, Gordon and Dolly Remly, and the third to Ray Keim, an elderly man who was treasurer and caretaker of the Elks Club on Duke Street. The first floor was being offered at a discounted rental of $40 a month; however, the deal required Bob to tend the furnace in the cellar, which provided heat for the building. Bob and Norm liked the place, and both sets of parents inspected it before their kids signed the rental agreement.

From front to back the apartment had a living room, bed room, bathroom, kitchen, and heated closed-in porch, which they identified as the perfect place for a crib. They invested in wooden Venetian blinds for each room. On their own and with help from parents, items of furniture were added one at a time. In no time Norm turned it into the little nest of their dreams. Compared to the apartment on

Zaragoza Street, she had plenty to work with, and she could earn some extra money by doing laundry for Mr. Keim. The five dollars she earned each month was saved for Christmas gifts.

Mr. Renk was very specific about how Bob should take care of the coal furnace. Proper maintenance began first thing in the morning after getting out of bed. He was instructed to first "riddle" the coals by turning an iron crank which extended from the hearth. This action involved carefully dragging the burnt coals over a sieve, allowing the ashes to fall through to an ash pit, but saving enough hot coals to ignite the new supply. Ashes were then disposed of in a metal container, being careful not to create dust. Next he would fully stoke the furnace and adjust the vents for a strong draft. About three quarters of an hour later, he was supposed to "bank" it, by adjusting the vents to cut back the draft. That would usually take care of it for the day. However, on exceptionally cold days, a little coal would have to be added in the evening, opening the draft for a short time to get it glowing; but riddling was not required until the next morning. The toggalier had no trouble remembering or executing these simple procedures.

Bob and Norm got to know their second floor neighbors, Gordon and Dolly, quite well. The played cards and often had dinners together. Bob once mentioned to their new friends how reasonably they were being treated by their landlord, but all the Remlys had to say was how Mr. Renk "watched every nickel." Apparently, one cold evening before Norm and Bob had moved in, Gordon called down asking to have the heat turned up, and Mr. Renk replied, "Just put your sweaters on, keep moving, and you'll be fine." Gordon implied that Bob better not carry out his furnace duties according to that policy.

Bob immersed himself in his work at the shoe store and put his war experience behind him, like most returning veterans. If it weren't for the occasional news features about returning heroes, he would have completely relegated his Army experience to ancient history. One of the few reminders was a notice published in the newspaper stating that any discharged GI with firearms in his possession should register with the local police within a specified period of time. It was well known that Nazi flags, German Luger pistols, and other wartime memorabilia were carried back by returning soldiers. He would have ignored the notice except for Roy's urging to do the right thing. Bob acquiesced and marched down to the police station to turn in his souvenir Remington.

At the police station two officers were handling the paperwork as veterans waited in line with their guns. Bob finally reached the front of the line and laid down his prize in front of Al Farkas, Chief of Police and a regular lunchtime crony at Bob Johnson's Buchanan Luncheonette on North Queen Street. When Al saw the stunning pistol, he looked up at Bob with a frown. "Where did you get this?" he asked.

"Brought it home, Al" was all that Bob had to say.

Al looked his friend in the eye and quietly, but firmly ordered: "You take that home, put it in your attic, and forget that you ever had it!" Al probably saved his buddy some headaches. The forty-five was considered stolen government property. Bob initially followed the Chief's instructions, but a few years later gave the gun to Clayt for his impressive gun collection.

In addition to working at the shoe store Bob considered picking up where he had left off in the Penn State extension program. His education plans became moot, however, when Roy suffered a heart attack in February at age 55. It was a shock. Roy survived the attack but couldn't return to work until later that year. In those days it was generally believed that a person who suffered a heart attack shouldn't expect to live five more years. As Ed would not get released from the Army for several more months, the burden of minding the store fell squarely on Bob. Hence, with new business responsibilities and a baby on the way, attending college was no longer an option. Fortunately, he would have no regrets. He truly liked his work and always felt that his career would be in the shoe business.

During Roy's recuperation Bob called him regularly to report sales figures. Despite a shaky economy in 1946—tight supplies, high unemployment, and labor unrest—the shoe business was doing well. Bob was fortunate to have Charlie Adams as his right hand man and unofficial mentor at the store. Charlie taught him a little about buying, which was a critical success factor in retailing. Once Charlie divulged that he thought they were "doing better" than Roy. Bob's youth and excellent taste may have had a favorable impact on style selections. Roy must have sensed this, because Ivy disclosed to Bob that his dad was beginning to feel that the business could get along without him.

THE HIGHLIGHT OF THAT YEAR was the birth of a baby on May 19th. As expected, it was a girl, her given name was Sandra Louise, and she would be referred to as Sandy. She arrived on schedule, but a Saturday night dinner with Mart and Vi in their Mulberry Street kitchen had to be interrupted by a four-block trip to the delivery room. Mother and baby came home in good condition, but Norm now worried that the back porch would not be warm enough, so they moved the crib to the bedroom. So as not to disturb the baby, Bob would now have to come and go through their back door via the narrow alleyway alongside the apartment.

The new parents were soon sleep-deprived, but in heaven nonetheless. It's what they had always dreamed about. Norm's life now centered around caring for the baby. After months of doting on babies of friends and relatives, she finally had a little girl of her own. The young couple proudly strolled through the neighborhood wheeling a baby carriage and making Sunday visits to one or both sets of parents in Grandview Heights—often promenading the entire distance with baby-on-wheels. Holidays were happier than ever with Sandy's arrival. The job was going well, and their future was filled with hope. They were totally caught up in it. No inconvenience could bother them. Other people's concerns didn't phase them.

Thanksgiving was always spent at one of their parents' homes. They alternated each year; this year the family gathered at Roy and Ivy's gorgeous, new stone house on Louise Avenue. Ivy put out one of her famous spreads: roast turkey, oyster filling, fresh cranberry relish, candied sweet potatoes, buttered and shredded carrots, corn pudding, mashed potatoes, and giblet gravy. It was always followed by freshly baked pumpkin pie with gobs of home-made whipped cream. The gathering featured two grandchildren: Marian and Harry's two-year-old daughter Linda and baby Sandy. Roy was on cloud nine. He loved kids. It was much colder than usual for that time of year, but nobody thought much about it. Festivities extended into the evening hours, when, with bellies full, everybody went back to "pick at" irresistible leftovers from the afternoon feast. As on their regular Sunday visits, Roy would drive them back to Mulberry Street early in the evening, but on Thanksgiving they lingered.

Just as it occurred to Bob that he should be getting back to check on the furnace, the phone rang. It was Gordon Remly, asking for him.

Uh-oh. "It's cold!" his neighbor moaned. "When the hell are you get-ting back here?"

Bob immediately felt guilty about his oversight, but tried to ease the tension with a little humor and chipper response: "Sorry, Gordon. Just put on your sweaters and try to keep moving 'til I get there." Gordon went ballistic. When Bob put down the receiver, Norm didn't have to be told that it was time to go home. It would be years later until Gordon finally admitted that he was a little hard on Bob over that incident.

Perhaps it was time to think about finding more suitable living accommodations. The Mulberry Street apartment was getting a little cramped, and they were already thinking about having a second child. Moreover, home prices had inflated about 40 percent since 1940.[1] Bob decided they would look into the housing market after their hectic winter shoe sales were over. In addition to that year's normal seasonal clearance sales, Lancaster Sales Day would be held on January 22nd, for the first time since July 1942, "when the war made holding of such sales impractical."[2]

Thank goodness Ed was now back. After more than a year with the occupation forces in the Pacific, he was released from the Army, unscathed except for a scary and unpleasant accident in the jungle one night when he fell into a garbage pit. He happily joined his dad and brother at the shoe store. According to Roy's advice, his sons split responsibilities according to their individual strengths. When not waiting on customers, Bob took responsibility for merchandising and buying, while Ed kept the books and managed payables. This worked out well for both of them.

Roy came back to work, but not full-time. Initially he put in only half-days. Then, on busy days he worked longer. After winter sales were over, he and Ivy started taking vacations—something they had rarely done before his heart attack. In February they went to Florida. Mr. and Mrs. Sweigart joined them the following year. Their vacations extended to three weeks or so. Roy soon discovered that the business could run without him and gave his sons a generous incentive: a 10 percent share each of their annual profits.

That spring there was an advertisement in the newspaper for a new subdivision in Lampeter Township developed by Ed Sheetz of Ephrata. It was located on a hilly farm tract, purchased from a farmer named Hostetter, just off the Lincoln Highway east of Witmer's bridge, which crossed over the Conestoga at Bridgeport. Sheetz named the development Eastland Hills and built two model homes that were being presented in an "Open House." Bob and Norm decided to take a look. They borrowed Roy's new Cadillac and invited Ed and Mollie to join them. Ed and Mollie were living in a tiny apartment on East King Street, and she was pregnant at the time.

The builder's models were located side-by-side on South Eastland Drive. Built from the same set of plans, the houses were two-story cracker boxes with about 1,800 square feet of heated living space, plus tiny attic, detached garage, and cellar large enough to accommodate a darkroom. The first floor had a living room with brick fireplace on one side, and a dining room and kitchen on the other. The second floor consisted of two bedrooms and a bathroom. It was consistent with the specifications Bob had laid out in his wartime letters. Norm loved it; so did Mollie and Ed. They returned for a second visit with Roy and Ivy. Roy offered to loan his sons $5,000 each for their down payments, and they cut a better deal by offering to purchase both models. Bob chose number 169, the one with white asbestos shingle siding; Ed took the yellow stucco one, which was said to be worth $500 more. Everybody was happy.

They moved in that spring. Despite the fact that good deals were also available on Fords and Chryslers that year, Bob and Ed were too strapped to afford a car, so they commuted to town by bus. By the end of the previous year the Conestoga Transportation Company had eliminated all trolley lines from Penn Square and replaced them with 26 new buses.[3] The bus dropped them off at Penn Square, a block-and-a-half from the shoe store. It was convenient, although they often had to juggle customers late in the afternoon so that they could catch the return bus, which usually departed from the square overcrowded, mainly with employees and customers of the big department stores—Watt & Shand, Garvins' and Hagers'—and the busy five-and-tens—Woolworth's, McCrory's and Green's.

Sometimes on warm days Norm and Molly would meet their men at the bus stop on the Lincoln Highway. That summer both wives were toting babies; Mollie and Ed's first child William Martin—named after both grandfathers and nicknamed Billy—was born in late June. A few months later Norm found out that she was expecting again, and her maternal glow simply intensified.

BY 1948 THE BABY BOOM was in full swing. Maternity wards of Lancaster hospitals overflowed with record numbers of expectant mothers and newborn babies.[4] Demand for food, homes, automobiles, and consumer goods put increasing pressure on industry to accelerate production of peacetime goods. Workers demanded higher wages and benefits. Inflation was emerging as a postwar phenomenon. That spring the U.S. government began airlifting goods to Allied forces in West Berlin, whose ground supply routes were cut off by the Russians. The Soviets were developing the bomb, and a "cold war" was on the horizon. But most Americans simply repressed the thought of another war. They had too much living to catch up on. The old Woolworth Building in Lancaster was torn down to make way for a modern five-and-ten. By the end of the year RCA announced introduction of a 16-inch television for $500, and WGAL TV was set to begin broadcasting in Lancaster. It was into this new world that Bob and Norm's second child, Robert L. Singleton Jr., was born on May 12, 1948.

That was just how they had planned it. Bob was now living the "dream in reality" he had written about in his wartime letters to Norm. He had the "sweetest wife in the world;" a daughter and son—in the desired sequence; a nice little house, which now had a darkroom in the basement; and an average standard of living, which only improved with the booming postwar economy. After Bobby's birth, they purchased an automobile, a gray Ford convertible. Bob and Ed got a deal on identical models. In October 1949 Mollie gave birth to her second: Edgar Robert Singleton, known as Eddie. The Singleton homes on South Eastland Drive became beehives for visiting grandparents, relatives, and other neighborhood boomers, especially on birthdays and holidays. Norm would find any excuse for a party, and swarming kids were always at the center of it. It was marvelously perfect, and most was recorded on film. Of course, pictures of the family or just the kids were always featured in an annual Christmas card photo.

Most young, growing, middle-class American families were living in a world that seemed comfortably insulated from an imperfect world around them. Communism was spreading in the Far East. The U.S. was secretly testing bombs and building a nuclear stockpile while promoting the potential benefits of atomic energy. Scientists from Franklin & Marshall College were actually prospecting for uranium in Lancaster County.[5] In 1950 Senator Joe McCarthy began his witch hunt for Communists, President Truman pushed to accelerate development of the H-bomb, and the conflict in Korea broke out. Another "peacetime" draft soon beefed up the ranks of depleted armed forces. But the majority of Americans reacted to these events like Bob and Norm. Thanks to a strong economy, civilian jobs were plentiful, the future seemed bright, and current events were at best items of interest, and at worst simply ignored.

THE SINGLETON'S HALCYON WORLD remained undisturbed until 1952. That was the year Roy suffered a fatal heart attack. He returned from the hospital, but never recovered. His last days were spent under an oxygen tent in the quiet bedroom of their Louise Avenue home. Norm and the children were there when he died on November 3rd. Grandson Bobby was the last to see him. Roy beckoned him into the room. With tears in his eyes, he extended his hand out from under the clear plastic tent. Bobby grasped it, not fully understanding; he was only 4 years old, the same age as his father when Ambrose died a generation earlier. Unlike Ambrose, however, Roy was an integral part of all his grandchildren's young lives. Known as Pappy Sing, Roy showered the kids with gifts and love, and they absolutely adored him. His death was a heartfelt loss for the entire family. He was only 61.

Bob was at the shoe store when he got the call from Norm. He asked Charlie to close the store, then departed. It was a devastating blow for him. Bob was very close to his dad. In addition to being a good father Roy was his best friend, benevolent mentor, and shining example of what a kind, caring, and giving human being should be. They were a lot alike.

Roy was a principled man who lived the values he believed in. He remained a resolute teetotaler until after his first heart attack, when his personal physician, Dr. Blankenship, prescribed a shot of whiskey as part of his daily regimen. Roy reluctantly complied by having Ivy mix a shot of I. W. Harper's whiskey with a small glass of milk each night before bed. Concerned about what people might think, he made Ivy keep his daily dose of "I.W.'s" a secret. Charlie Adams was the only other one to know about it, because he was the one who purchased the prescription. Roy wouldn't be caught dead in a State Store.

That was one of Roy's humorous eccentricities. Another was his affinity for soap operas. When his work schedule wound down to half-days, he always managed to get home by one o'clock so that he could keep up to date with the latest episode of his favorite soap opera. Ivy disclosed this little secret, and the kids made merciless jokes about it. However, after Roy died, they were glad knowing that he was one of the first Americans to own a television set and had the opportunity to enjoy it for a few years. They were more disappointed that he couldn't have held on for just one more day to see Eisenhower elected President in a landslide victory. Not only did Roy like Ike, the kindly general who led his son's Army to victory in Europe, but he was eager to see the 20-year reign of Democrats come to an end. Interestingly, Roy never cared much for FDR, because he didn't believe in government hand-outs. He didn't like the idea of having to match Social Security taxes that were withheld from employees' pay. He felt that it hurt the business and wasn't appreciated. But in the end he grudgingly acknowledged that Roosevelt helped people save for their retirement.

On the front page of the November 4th issue of the *Intelligencer Journal*, news of Roy's death was overshadowed only by huge headlines that reported a national voter turnout of "55 million people."[6] Roy was well-known in Lancaster. Bob, his eldest living son at 30 years old, took responsibility for making appropriate funeral arrangements. After consulting with Reverend Kettels, minister at First Church, the decision was made to honor their father by closing the shoe store on the day of the funeral. A notice was published in the local newspapers on November 5th.

The funeral and viewing on the evening before were both held at Snyder's Funeral Home on Orange Street. Hundreds of people were lined up for nearly a block to pay their respects. Friends, relatives, customers, and acquaintances, including several prominent people in town attended. Roy was known, liked, and respected. It was a comfort and a compliment to the family, all of whom were present except for the grandchildren, left at home under the care of Nanny Diff. Roy was buried in Mellinger's Mennonite Cemetery in one of his purchased family plots next to Ivy's folks and Wilbur. The week was physically and emotionally draining, especially for Bob.

The intensity didn't let up for a while. They were entering the busiest time of the year, and estate matters had to be worked out. The business was bequeathed to the three children, but they all agreed that Bob and Ed would immediately buy out Marian, according to their father's wishes, which he had expressed after his first heart attack. It was never in writing, but Sis acknowledged her father's intentions after the will was read in the office of Roy's attorney, Bob Appel. The lawyers asked for an independent third-party opinion on the value of the business, based on a current inventory count performed by Bob, Ed, and Charlie Adams. The brothers recommended their friend and competitor Symond Kantor, proprietor of Arrow Shoe Store. Sy was pleased to help and signed-off on their count after a cursory review. The valuation was set at $39,000.

They were told it would be about a year before the estate could be settled. In the meantime Bob and Ed had to work through their busiest season, which included spring buying, Christmas sales, and inventory taking on the last day of the year. At the time they still had to drive to Harrisburg or Philadelphia to meet with manufacturers' salesmen, because some of their buying accounts were not yet large enough to justify a salesman traveling to Lancaster. They often had to work late nights to manage the load.

Bob worked extra hard to make it an enjoyable Christmas for his family and to compensate for the loss of his father, who always made it a special time of year for the grandchildren. The days leading up to Christmas were absolutely hectic for retail businesses; but despite long, grueling hours with demanding last-minute customers, he managed to follow the Singleton tradition of hanging outdoor pine rope with strings of colored lights by the second week of December and setting up a lighted tree and train yard into the wee hours of Christmas Eve. Norm was a willing and enthusiastic ally. She went out of her way to make every day special by attending to the smallest details. The kids would never know anything but thoroughly magical Christmases.

It was amazing how Bob managed to enjoy the holiday and not complain; because, without fail, the day after Christmas was probably the most frenzied of the year, with customers lined up before the doors were opened to make exchanges or take advantage of sale prices. This pace kept up through the last day of the year, culminating in the grueling, late-night ritual of taking inventory while most people were out ringing in the New Year.

1952 would be the last year that they ran the business on a calendar-year basis—which required a December 31st inventory count—because that season's pace had extracted its toll. By January Bob was physically and mentally run down. He kept going until he couldn't any longer. A severe chest cold confined him to bed one morning in mid-January. Norm applied a drug-store chest plaster to help his difficulty with breathing. It provided some relief, but only a few hours went by before Norm had to call an ambulance. Bob was diagnosed with a case of double pneumonia and kept in the hospital—on oxygen—for a week.

The experience of the previous three months caused Bob to step back and reassess their situation. He had lived through too much, and had too much to live for, to risk compromising his health. At his doctor's suggestion he decided to take a little time off for rest and recuperation in a warm climate. Of course, he would not go without his family. Norm worried about the expense, but Bob figured: You only live once. He arranged a trip by air to Miami. Through a friend of his parents who lived there, he made reservations at the Lindsay Hopkins Hotel, a training school for hotel workers and managers, where you could get a nice room for five dollars a night. He told Norm that, if they couldn't do it for five-bucks-a-night, they probably never would.

The kids didn't fully understand the circumstances which motivated the trip, which was fairly extravagant for a young family in those days. They were too young to absorb the significance of their grandfather's death and were completely unaware of the seriousness of their father's illness. All they knew was that Santa had been very good to them and that Christmas was being followed by an airplane ride to a warm place. It was a magnificent vacation, even better than the shore. Riding on the silver, National Airlines DC-3 and big Eastern DC-4 was pure adventure. Pretty stewardesses handed out free chewing gum to help their ears adjust to every altitude change. And stepping off the plane into balmy evening air during the wintertime was a wonderful surprise. On top of all that were the tropical curiosities, like coconuts, pelicans, parrots, and alligators—all of which could be brought home in the form of a colorfully painted, carved, or stuffed souvenir of some sort. The vacation was recorded on 8 mm film with a home movie camera purchased for Christmas, allowing the experience to be relived for many years. It would be a snapshot of a wonderful life to come.

# CHAPTER 17

# SHOE PILOT

THE SINGLETON BROTHERS worked especially hard after Roy's death, conscientiously following the methods learned from their father. They tediously took "mark-downs" at the end of every selling season to recognize the depreciated value of out-of-style items. They never missed taking purchase discounts and borrowing money at four percent to profit from discounts of five percent. And they quickly established credibility with the banks. Before their father's estate was settled they used powers of attorney to sign checks from the business. Initially that was an inconvenience, but after a few months Homer Crist from the bank's Trust Department didn't even bother to review the expenditures. He just co-signed the checks. According to Bob: "It was easy. People trusted one another in those days." Upon settlement of the estate they would loan the money to buy out their sister. Fortunately, Bob Appel was on the bank board and would facilitate transactions. Everything was settled in nine months.

Bob and Ed had had the advantage of a generous inheritance. But like their father two decades earlier, they took on a hefty amount of debt and operated in an increasingly competitive retail environment. After making interest and principal payments, a great portion of the profits were reinvested in the growing business. The partners each drew $60 a week, which wasn't much different than the average weekly wages of a factory worker in the early 1950s. If either partner had a major household expense that required additional cash, they would draw against their equity accounts using profit estimates based on the prior year's experience. Since Christmas sales—a key determinant of annual results—were greatly influenced by general economic and weather conditions, profit estimates were rough until inventory was taken at the end of the fiscal year, which was changed to January 31st after 1952.

Managing cash flow was the greatest challenge. Because they wanted to take advantage of purchase discounts, they had to pay bills for new seasonal stocks before the actual selling season got underway. It always seemed like they needed the cash when it wasn't there. And it seemed like something unanticipated would always come up at home, like needing a new refrigerator, at exactly the wrong time. They usually relied on short term loans from the bank to get through seasonal cash cycles. They felt like "heroes" if they could make it through a season without borrowing money. As the business grew, working capital demands only increased.

In 1953 the boom continued, and an all time birth record was set: 10,880 births/day, or eight a minute.[1] That autumn, a stock market high was reported. As a result of a strong economy, hard work, and conservative business practices, Singleton's Shoes prospered. The families were outgrowing their little cracker boxes on South Eastland Drive, where the kids had to double-up in single bedrooms. They decided to spring for larger, more contemporary homes in Manheim Township, which was considered a "high rent" suburb. The township was burgeoning as a result of a new by-pass around the city, industrial expansion, modern housing developments, and an enduring reputation for excellent schools. Bob and Norm worked with a local contractor to build a three-bedroom ranch house on 201 Murry Hill Drive in a subdivision called Beverly Estates, where the streets—dirt construction roads at the time—were named after the builder and his family. Mollie and Ed's new house was less than a mile away in a subdivision called Bloomingdale.

The Murry Hill Drive house was a blend of flagstone, redwood siding, and brick, with shutters and garage door painted a coral color. Norm and Bob gave friends directions to their home by telling them to look for the pink shutters. The color selection was probably influenced by memories of the tropical hues in Fort Myers and Miami. But it was also very 1950s-contemporary. Each room was painted in a designer color—patiently selected from stacks of tiny paint chips—and illuminated with a trendy ceiling light fixture activated by low-voltage touch switches that the kids couldn't leave alone. The main living area featured an interior flagstone wall that covered the span of an adjoining living and dining room. It had a built-in raised-hearth fireplace, back-lit mantle, and cantilevered flagstone shelves. The flagstone served as a stunning backdrop for Norm's elegant holiday decorations and the traditional family Christmas photos. The basement had colorful vinyl acetate tile and raised plywood paneling finished in an unusual black-and-white-wash scheme. It was perfect accommodations for, among other things, roller skating, piano practice, a pool table, the Christmas train yard, and big parties for every occasion.

After they moved in the summer of 1953, Sandy transferred to Milton J. Brecht Elementary School from East Lampeter Elementary, where she had completed first and second grades. Brecht was a small, Tudor-style school building on the Lititz Pike halfway between downtown Lancaster and Beverly Estates. Bobby entered first grade that year and tagged along with Sandy on the two-mile commute in a yellow *Blue Bird* bus driven by Chris Hess, who picked them up at the end of their construction road. However, more often than not in the beginning, the kids were driven to school by Norm, who also chauffeured Bob back and forth to work every day. The family car was now a flashy, chartreuse-yellow 1952 Ford convertible, which Bob and Ed had purchased on dual trade-ins for their gray '49 models.

Bob's and Norm's lives revolved around Sandy and Bobby, the shoe business, relatives, and church. It was an *Ozzie and Harriet, Leave it to Beaver, Father Knows Best* kind of world, with the added dimension of a large, extended family living in the same town. Holiday gatherings— Easter, Memorial Day, Independence Day, Labor Day, Thanksgiving, and Christmas—always included some combination of grandparents, brothers, sisters, cousins, aunts, uncles, nieces and nephews. Bob and Ed each had two children; so did sister Marian (Linda and Curt Medsger) and sisters-in-law Becky (Diane and Barbie Powl) and Audrey (Mickey and Debbie Hauser). Boomers abounded. Birthday parties, usually organized as a surprise, included kids from school and the neighborhood. Naturally, it was all recorded in home movies. Norm did most of the work, but, despite long store hours, Bob was usually there to take the pictures and participate in the fun.

Outside immediate family their social life revolved around church activities, Optimist Club, and "card club." Bob was a regular usher at First Church and, in the footsteps of his father, volunteered to count and deposit cash from Sunday worship service collections. He and Norm were regular members of the Married Couples Sunday school class, where they nurtured lifelong frindships. The kids and Nanny Sing were always part of the Sunday ritual, which consisted of morning worship services, a fancy after-church meal, and a variety of all-day family leisure activities. The routine was an unchallenged, Singleton family tradition, despite subtle pressure by the kids to modify the routine during their teen years.

The Optimist Club was Bob's community service club. Most men of his generation, especially businessmen, belonged to a service club like Kiwanis, Rotary, Lions, or Sertoma. These clubs were different than the old fraternal organizations that were popular before the war. They usually gathered for a weekly luncheon or breakfast meeting to enjoy camaraderie, fellowship, and to some extent networking, but their primary function was service to the community. The Optimists' service mission focussed on youth; they labeled themselves "friend of the boy" while that label was still politically correct. Student public speaking competitions and youth appreciation awards were sponsored in the local schools. Midget baseball tournaments and bicycle safety courses were manned by enthusiastic Optimists. They also sponsored and organized the popular annual Lancaster Hobby Show. They were serious about their mission. Attendance was taken, and points were given for meetings attended and services volunteered. Bob would rarely leave the store for anything but a bite to eat at Bob Johnson's or a meeting of the Optimists. In reciprocity Ed covered for him; he was a Kiwanian. Bob chose a club which suited his personal philosophy. Optimists recited a prayer and the Optimist Creed at every meeting. The Creed was a simple, but eloquent statement of the principles by which he lived his life.[2] They even had an Optimist song, which Bob taught his kids and sang no less passionately than the George Ross pep song. It became so imprinted on his son that, as a 4-year-old, he belted out the song for an audience at his proud father's beckoning, standing tall atop a picnic table at the Optimist clam bake.

The card club was a group of four couples who got together about four times a year to have dinner and play pinochle. The group consisted of Bob and Norm, Clayt and Glo Sweigart, Henry and Arlene Ebersole, and Dick and Pat Lichty. Glo was Norm's cousin by way of her Aunt Nellie as were both Dick Lichty and Arlene (Lichty) Ebersole by way of another of Vi's sisters. The Saturday night card club gathering was one of those rare events where Bob and Norm left the kids at home with a babysitter, usually one of the grandmothers. Like Bob and Norm, the other card club couples had boomers and made postwar lives for themselves in various ways. Clayt, a former tank officer in Patton's army, became a salesman and post office worker; Henry was a manager at Armstrong; Dick was an independent trucker of raw milk. Their spouses lived traditional roles in homes that were kept meticulously—even by Lancaster County standards. Initially, card club gatherings consisted of a fancy dinner at one of their homes followed by pinochle, but were scaled back to just elaborate desserts and cards when the men agreed that the wives were working too hard. Card club was a tradition that continued for decades, ceasing only after its members started passing away.

OUTSIDE THE SHELTERED, MIDDLE-CLASS existence of the mid-'50s the Cold War was roiling, and racial tensions in the South were coming to the forefront. While the population boom continued, the economy cooled in 1956. Downtown retail trade was affected not only by dips in the economy, but also by the sprouting of suburban shopping centers. But even with the emergence of the centers, which promoted convenience and free parking, Singleton's Shoes continued to do well due to an emphasis on service and maintaining full inventories of shoe sizes and widths. This required rigorous attention to detail and a lot of extra work, but it paid off. Bob and Ed celebrated their success by trading in the yellow Fords for identical, two-tone 1956 Buick Specials. You couldn't miss them; they were black-and-white "three-holers" with black and red-trimmed interiors.

Success of their business was also due to the loyal and faithful service of long-time employees. Charlie Adams had the most seniority. He was like a member of the family. He pitched in during tough times, shared in successes, and occasionally took the brunt of practical jokes, which the Franklin Street boys were famous for. One morning Charlie was on the telephone in the back office, absent-mindedly fiddling with the heavy bag of church money that was set on the desk, ready for Bob's weekly deposit. Charlie heard someone coming into the office, and suddenly aware of his harmless, but guilty-looking behavior, grabbed the bag of cash and placed it out of sight—in the waste basket under the desk—planning to return it to its proper place at a less conspicuous moment. But a convenient time never presented itself, and Charlie simply forgot about it.

Bob was sitting at the desk shortly afterwards and detected the unusually heavy weight of the wastebasket when his foot brushed against it. Discovering the bag of cash, he deduced what had occurred and decided to play a joke on Charlie. Later that afternoon, when no customers were present, he walked out from the office, and in a strained voice asked if anybody knew what happened to the church money. Poor Charlie turned red with embarrassment, apologized, and dashed back to retrieve the booty. Unfortunately, the wastebasket was empty. He was flabbergasted. His merciless boss didn't help matters by reminding Charlie that their trash had already been picked up that day and suggesting that he figure out how to retrieve the money.

Charlie got on the phone to the trash collector, found out where they dumped it, called that location, and made a plea for help. He was told that all incoming paper was ground up in a shredder. "Will it grind up metal?" Charlie asked. The voice on the other end assured him that their big crusher would grind up anything and that his only hope would be a manual search through unprocessed deliveries. Charlie was in a sweat by the time he hung up and announced that he was heading for the dump. That would have been the natural time for Bob to divulge his little prank, but, astonishingly, he let Charlie make the trip. When Charlie ran out the door, Bob called the dump to let them in on the joke, suggesting that they play along but not stretch it out too far. Charlie was finally let in on the scheme after a brief but filthy search. He returned to a store full of devilish grins. The incident provided a source of laughs at Charlie's expense for many years. But he took it in good humor and remained with Singleton's for his entire career.

Other career employees at Singleton's were Norman Shaub, known as Shaubie, Bill Johnson, and Aunt Ruthie. These folks gave Singleton's a distinctly mature, if not old-fashioned image, but the business was fortunate to have a core group of elderly employees from a generation which still viewed a job in retail sales as a career. In the late 1950s it became increasingly difficult to retain young employees. Their first promising upstart was Johnny Beyers, who left after a few years to pursue a career in commission-based insurance sales. Vernon Shirk, known as Shirky, never had Johnny's potential, but resigned to become a traveling salesman for a wholesaler. Bob never forgot the Sunday afternoon when nervous Shirky came to the house to deliver the news and crashed into the mail box at the end of the driveway as he made a self-conscious exit. Bob always found humor in awkward situations, but accepted those resignations graciously, with sincere best wishes.

Singleton's retained a slate of part-time employees to help with seasonal peaks and irregular retail hours, which in the 1950s included all-day Saturdays, closed Mondays, and open Friday nights. As more shopping centers were built, downtown hours went through a series of expanded schedules to compete with their six-day, open-every-night hours. Singleton's adamantly resisted extended hours for as long as they could, using part-timers to fill the gaps.

One of their more colorful part-timers was an elderly gentleman named Ralph Heickes. Ralph was a retired widower who lived on West King Street. Many years earlier he had managed the women's shoe department at Garvin's, but more recently worked at Hannover's, a men's shoe store. Ralph was recommended by his friend Chauncey Hall, a cigar-chewing downtown tailor who often stopped by the shoe store on Friday evenings to enjoy an after-dinner smoke with Charlie. At Chauncey's suggestion, Bob called Ralph and invited him in to talk. Ralph was pleased to get the call and said that he would accept an hourly wage under the condition that—he rubbed his thumb against his fingertips—"it's under the table." He didn't want earned income to undermine his Social Security benefits. Bob worked out some kind of accommodation, because Ralph was experienced in the shoe business and had a likeable personality. He made people smile with colloquial expressions, like "wheat in the bin," when referring to salable merchandise. And he turned out to be a reliable employee. He would come and go, early or late in the day, whenever requested.

Although Ralph was funny, he could sometimes be a little coarse with his language. Singleton's was a family shoe store. At Hannover's Ralph was accustomed to working with only men. He had a presumptuous habit of welcoming customers by putting his arm over their shoulders and saying, "Greetings! What's on your mind?" He told Charlie about the time a customer walked into Hannover's, received Ralph's signature greeting, but wasn't favorably impressed. When asked what was on his mind, the customer replied, "Pussy...but it's none of your damn business!" Ralph facetiously pledged to Charlie that he would never again ask what was on a customer's mind. Singleton's decided to keep him in the men's department.

In early 1957 Todd Anthony, the salesman from Jarman Shoe Company, passed the word that a little shoe store in the nearby farm community of New Holland was for sale. It was called Martin's Store. Martin's was a family store with basic brands like *Jarman* for men and *Enna Jetticks* for women. They also did a lot of business in *Wolverine* work shoes and had a small, but outdated, selection of men's clothing. The proprietor was Jack Martin. He had just turned 65 and was ready to retire, but his son-in-law wasn't interested in the business. Bob and Ed had never planned for a second store, so they didn't follow up on Todd's lead. Shortly afterwards, Frank Murphy, another good friend and very respected salesman from Schawe-Gerwin Shoe Company, also mentioned the opportunity to the Singletons, and even discreetly offered to personally help with any needed financing. But again, they chose to ignore it.

A few weeks later Jack Martin walked into Singleton's, introduced himself, confirmed his plans, and asked the brothers if they would be interested. Their response was still negative. They explained that they were preoccupied with an uncertain future for their own store. The city had recently announced plans for the complete demolition and redevelopment of the second block of North Queen Street, which was becoming seedy and abandoned as businesses either closed, moved to shopping centers, or found other premises. Bob was concerned, and Ed was worried. Neither wanted the burden or complication of a second store.

Their attitude changed slightly when Jack called Bob at home one Sunday afternoon. Jack said that he hated to admit it, but he hadn't taken an inventory in three years and would pay the brothers to help him make a complete count of his stock on a day the store was closed. Jack would handle the clothing; the Singletons would count the shoes. Bob and Ed figured they had nothing to lose. Jack even offered to buy them lunch. They though it would be "sort of fun."

On the following Sunday they drove 12 miles to New Holland, met Jack at the store, and dug right in. Their inventory-taking process involved pulling shoe boxes part way out on the shelves until each box was counted, after which it was pushed back to avoid double counting. Shortly after they began pulling boxes, Bob noticed a problem with outdated cost codes on the boxes: Martin's didn't take mark-downs. Three- and four-year-old styles were still on the shelves labeled with original codes. Bob pointed this out to Jack, stating that at Singleton's these items would be either "out of inventory or marked way down." Jack responded by asserting that he never ran his business that way, so they compromised by keeping the boxes pulled out until after the full count to highlight the scope of the issue.

A third or more of the boxes were sticking out when they finished. The brothers gave each other a concerned look. Jack was shocked and deflated. Bob broke the ice: "Look, Jack, I'm just giving you the facts. If these had been in our inventory they'd be marked down at least two dollars a pair." Roy had always taught his sons that "your first loss is your greatest loss." They always made sure that end-of-season stocks were put on sale immediately, when the most value can be recovered—and money can be banked to help pay for the next season's styles. Jack couldn't argue with that logic. He made note of their assessment and said he would be in touch, although Bob and Ed continued to express no sign of interest. Jack insisted right up until they left that Martin's would be a good opportunity for them to consider. They parted on friendly terms.

A few weeks later Jack telephoned to ask if they would make an offer. Bob politely, but firmly, responded in the negative. By this time Jack was frustrated; he practically pleaded: "Look, I'll give you a good deal!" Bob reluctantly said that he would discuss it with his brother, but that Jack shouldn't be encouraged. The brothers were getting tired of the whole thing. Taking another look at the situation, they figured that Martin's inventory was worth about $28,000, but knew they could get it for less. Under the circumstances, Ed couldn't resist suggesting, "Let's offer him twenty thousand and see what happens." It was a long shot, bordering on an insult. But they thought, Why not?

Jack was upset, of course, when he received their aggressive offer. But he got back in a couple of days with his response: "I shouldn't do this, but I've taken a liking to you and Ed. You guys know the business. If you want it for twenty thousand, you got it."

Suddenly, the monkey was on Bob's back. "Jack, I've got butter-flies!" he admitted. He and Ed were indeed concerned about their Lancaster store at the time and never expected Jack to accept their offer. It was March, they were in the process of paying bills for spring merchandise, and cash was tight. But it was an opportunity that might be too good to pass up. Upon further consideration, Bob figured that in the worst case he and Ed could always hold a "going out of business" sale at Martin's, unloading the inventory for more than they paid for it. But Ed was still worried, so Bob suggested that they make a deal contingent on obtaining a bank loan for the entire purchase price. Somewhat to their amazement the bank agreed to the idea. The only condition was that they make their first payment on September 1st.

By the end of May 1957 Singleton's had two shoe stores. Ed would manage the New Holland store. Jack agreed to stay on for a few months to help with the transition, and Martin's only employee, Earl

Hoover, stayed on permanently. Earl was originally a farmer who had
hurt his back in a serious accident and was now working at Martin's as
a full time shoe repair man and occasional back-up salesman. He was
happy to stay under the condition that he continue to be allowed to
take vacation during deer hunting season. Deer season was at a busy
time of year for the shoe business, therefore non-hunters Bob and Ed
weren't particularly understanding. But Jack convinced them that the
repair business was a money-maker and it would be a mistake to lose
Earl by interfering with his annual rite of autumn.

The business prospered under new ownership. Singletons used
the larger Lancaster store to their advantage by coordinating stocks
and consolidating purchases. They maintained visibility in the community by continuing Martin's sponsorship of the annual Pet Parade,
where the local kids showed off their favorite animals and won prizes
for various categories of competition. During the first several months
Bob spent extra time at the New Holland store to become familiar
with the local trade so that he could more effectively do the merchandising for both stores. Over time they discontinued outdated brands,
like *Enna Jetticks*, and replaced them with more fashionable lines from
Lancaster, like *Naturalizer*. The pace of conversion was moderated out
of consideration for the impacted manufacturers' salesmen.

THE NORTH QUEEN STREET SITUATION was still unresolved in 1957.
Shopping centers had affected the downtown trade in Lancaster but
had not yet attracted any big name department stores or prominent
retail establishments. Leaving downtown was not considered a viable
option by the Singletons. But, unfortunately, they had few alternatives
at the time. Their premises would eventually be demolished, and all
desirable retail space in the first block of North Queen was occupied
by property owners or tenants with long-term leases.

A year after buying the New Holland store Bob heard a rumor
that the *Kinney* shoe franchise might not return to their premises at 32
North Queen Street, which had been destroyed by a major fire in
November 1956.[3] Kinney's was temporarily occupying rented space
across the street from their burned-out premises but had reportedly
decided to relocate to the Lancaster Shopping Center.

Bob contacted the bank to find out who owned the gutted
building, which was in the process of being reconstructed. The bank
referred Bob to an elderly, semi-retired Realtor named Bart Lynch,

who worked out of his home in East Petersburg. Bart confirmed the rumor, and a series of discussions that would stretch out over many months began in earnest. The complicating issue was timing: the renovated space would be ready for occupancy before the lease expired on their current premises. But the Singletons didn't want to double up on burdensome rental payments. Their current landlord, Benny Barr of Barr Nurseries and Flower Shop, was making it very difficult for them. He wouldn't give any consideration to shortening their lease term for even as little as a month, regardless of the fact that Singleton's had been a loyal tenant for over 35 years.

It was a frustrating and anxiety-laden experience. Bart, a wiry old gentleman with perfectly groomed gray hair under his ever present fedora, was also tougher than he looked. Just when it appeared that an accommodation could be reached, discussions would break off. Bart was most likely talking to other interested parties. It was one of the more trying times in the business for Bob and Ed. They discussed purchasing a commercial property rather than renting space. But the national economy had slipped into another recession by the summer of 1958, and the Singletons didn't want to risk investing more money in an uncertain downtown environment. With no suitable alternatives, the prospect of possibly having to close the business was not completely out of the question. Ed was very worried. Bob's concern was also apparent, thus Norm worried.

In the car on the way home after work, Bob usually discussed his day and vented frustrations in conversations with Norm. Thankfully, she was a good listener. Their conversation was typically a monologue, which rambled non-stop until they came to a stop in the driveway and continued with engine idling until Bob completed his unloading and got out to raise the garage door. But once inside the house, business talk ended. While the kids were aware of the events at the shoe store, they were insulated from business-related stress. After unburdening himself in the car—and often giving Norm a headache, which she tried hard to conceal—Bob managed to shift quickly into his domestic role. It was an immediate transformation as he entered the warm, inviting atmosphere of Norm's soft-lit world, redolent of fresh baking, unfailingly enriched by non-contingent love, and welcoming of the naïve but amusing perspective of developing adolescents. Except for Friday nights, when the shoe store was open, the family always enjoyed dinner together; and, except for evenings when little league baseball or lawn mowing was scheduled, dinner was usually a full-course ritual, conversationally engaging, and illuminated by candlelight.

Business challenges were never be so great that Bob would let them interfere with the life that he and Norm had planned. And their need for material things was never so great as to preclude realization of their dreams. On the other hand, with increasing business success, an optimistic outlook, and an uncompromising zest for the present, Bob made sure that his family was never lacking in necessities or comforts. Despite the demands of the business, the family always enjoyed holiday festivities that consistently exceeded expectations and went on family vacations that got better with each year that went by.

Fortunately, things were going well with the New Holland store. Under Singleton's ownership and merchandising methods the country store quickly developed into a robust little business. They paid off their bank loan in two years. Bob continued to press forward on the Lancaster relocation issue, but the situation didn't take a positive turn until Bart came back with a proposal in 1959. Despite his shrewdness the old guy seemed to favor the Singleton boys. After a few more discussions, they worked out a convenient arrangement on timing and negotiated a five-year lease with a couple of five-year renewal options. Singleton's also committed to making substantial leasehold improvements, including not only fully decorated interiors, but also a new, granite-floored entryway with an attractive marquis and modern signage overhead. It was all meant to be: the building they were moving into had housed the original Wilbur & Martin's store before it had relocated to 118 North Queen 35 years earlier.

The grand opening of the new store was on April 6, 1960 during the height of the spring season. Detailed planning preceded the move, which took place on a Sunday and Monday, days when the store was closed. It rained both days. Shoes were transported by sidewalk on borrowed four-wheel industrial dollies pushed by hired members of the Pequea Valley High School basketball team—whose employment was enlisted through Chuck Ebersole, Henry and Arlene's oldest son and leader of the team. But everything was set to go when the doors opened on Tuesday morning. Dozens of congratulatory plants and floral arrangements sent by suppliers, competitors, and friends adorned the lobby and central area of the store. In addition to well-wishers was a mob of customers. Singleton's recorded as many sales during their first two days at 32 North Queen as they did in a week at their old store a block away. It was a milestone for the business. Bob was particularly proud of their accomplishment and his role in making it happen. The next year he celebrated by trading in the two-tone Buick Special for a new, but more conservative, 1962 Buick Le Sabre—which Ivy jokingly called his "Lee Sabree"—and he took the family, accompanied by the three grandparents, on a vacation cruise to Bermuda.

MANY BUSINESSES IN LANCASTER never made it through the first downtown redevelopment cycle, which peaked in the early 1960s. Singleton's continued to prosper, however. Bob's love of his work and wonderful life at home were a constant source of stability and refuge in a world that was becoming confused and unstable. The insidious terror of a nuclear arms race contrasted with the excitement of a high profile space race. A torch was passed to a new generation, who in 1963 saw it swiftly extinguished in a televised assassination. Civil rights were finally being legislated, but school prayer was barred. The Beatles invaded the U.S.; the U.S. invaded Vietnam.

By the mid-1960s, surrounded by mutating baby boomers, international turmoil, and a downtown metamorphosis, Bob probably began to feel middle-aged for the first time—even though this reality had been long preceded by prematurely graying hair. When the kids gave him a hard time about it, he facetiously reminded them where the gray hairs came from. Sandy began her freshman year at Duke in 1964, and tested her parent's patience by overextending herself on the social scene, which impacted her health, exacerbated her mother's anxiety, and required her dad to put up additional tuition for summer school make-up credits. Business was strong, but new challenges always seemed to present themselves.

Singleton's premier employee, Charlie Adams, decided to retire at age 65. He might have worked longer, but perhaps sensed his mortality after suffering a bad accident a few years earlier. At the end of a long, hard day during Lancaster Sales Days, during his walk home to North Franklin Street, he was struck by a car. When Bob got the call from Charlie's wife Marian, he rushed to the hospital, where Charlie was being treated for a broken arm and collar bone. Bob could always be counted on in an emergency. Five years after Charlie retired, Marian would call him again to report that Charlie had died in his sleep. As before, Bob would get there right away. He and one of Charlie's other lifelong buddies carried the body downstairs.

Shaubie, whose health was failing, retired six months after Charlie and died not long after that. His wife Dorothy, known as Dot, was kind enough to leave her job in Hager's shoe department to help out part-time at Singleton's. With years of experience in retail shoe sales she was a tremendous asset. It was too bad she could only work part-time. Experienced full-time help was difficult to find. Without Charlie and Shaubie the daily customer load on Bob was enormous. That situation improved somewhat with the addition of Ed's son Bill, who joined Singleton's after graduating from high school in 1965. Bill was a natural. He had a knack for selling, which he had learned as a kid hawking generic bar soap door-to-door to earn money for summer camp. But the void left by Charlie and Shaubie remained.

Another void was created in 1966—this one closer to home. The family's jolly matriarch, Iva Cathrine, died on February 8th after a several month bout with colon cancer. She had not been her normal, robust self since the spring of that year, and by the time the problem was diagnosed, little could be done about it. Her physical condition deteriorated inexorably, and her final weeks were spent in misery. The family moved her from Louise Avenue to an extra bedroom in Marian's home, where she would receive constant care and attention. It was a sad and unpleasant task—even for a devoted daughter. For the proud, but modest matriarch, the stigma of cancer and loss of physical independence was so embarrassing that death would come as a relief. Her last time outside the house was a visit to Murry Hill Drive on Christmas Eve to witness her grandson Bob Jr. raising the pink garage door to discover a new car—a sporty, canary yellow Karmann Ghia—in a surprise carefully staged by his dad. At the family's most cherished time of the year, this thrilling event for the grandson undoubtedly stirred poignant memories of Roy and the tan Chrysler. It came as no surprise to anybody that Ivy would participate in this event, even "with one foot in the grave."

The manning issue at the store was unresolved until the spring of 1966 when the partners decided to sell the New Holland business and bring Ed back to Lancaster. The business was ripe for harvesting; in nine years they had tripled the sales of Martin's Store. But, while the timing was appropriate, they agreed not to sell the business outright. They didn't want to create the impression that they were motivated by

the announced opening of Lancaster's newest and largest shopping
center, the mammoth Park City Mall. Instead they organized a
methodical going-out-of-business sale directed at New Hollanders.
Ads were placed in the *New Holland Clarion* announcing the sale and
explaining the need for both partners in Lancaster. They had flyers
printed and hired some kids to distribute them in the neighborhoods.

Prices were slashed on shoes that wouldn't do well in Lancaster,
and the going-out-of-business sale was a smashing success. They sold
all but about $5,000 worth of marketable stock, which was trucked to
Lancaster in a Hertz rental van by Bill and Bob Jr. It only took a few
months for those items to turn over. Their net gain on Martin's Store
ended up being much greater than what they had paid for the business.
Ed bought a nice boat with his share and would enjoy long, relaxing
weekends on the Chesapeake Bay for years to come. Bob's share went
toward construction of a backyard, in-ground swimming pool and
college tuition payments for Sandy and Bob Jr., who was entering
Princeton that fall.

PUTTING TWO KIDS THROUGH COLLEGE was a financial load, but
their father never complained about it. As always, he relied on good
standing with the banks to manage seasonal cash flows. His loan appli-
cations consisted of simple verbal requests for funds applied to an
informal, open line of credit established after years of reliable and
trustworthy business dealings. Cash demands didn't end with college
expenses. He splurged on a lavish wedding for Sandy, who married
Dr. Jackson F. Lee after she graduated in 1968; replaced the Le Sabre
with a larger '69 Buick Limited; and that summer took Norm, adult
kids, and son-in-law on a fabulous vacation to Hawaii.

In 1971 Bob Jr. finished graduate school and got married to
"Scotty" Wilkerson. Shortly afterwards they left for the southwest,
where young Bob, in the footsteps of his dad, would enter Air Force
pilot training. With both kids far away, Norm's nest was now truly
empty; but her appetite for children would not go unsatisfied for long,
as granddaughter Erin Elizabeth was born to Sandy and Jeff that year.
Michael Jackson Lee came along two years later. Through Bob and
Scott's military stint and regular visits with Sandy and Jeff's kids, Bob
and Norm could relive some cherished memories, but this time conveniently, comfortably, and on their own terms.

By the time he reached a half-century in age Bob had successfully lived his dreams and achieved the life goals he had set down in writing during those bleak days in Great Yoho, including his personal vow to get back in the cockpit. His urge to fly had resurfaced in 1969 when, at the peak of the war in Southeast Asia, Bob Jr. signed up for an ROTC program at Princeton which included a deferment for grad school and flying lessons. Not to be outdone, the aging Sad Sack signed up for lessons with Lancaster Aviation, soloed after nine hours, and obtained his Private Pilot certificate a few months before his son did likewise. The senior Robert relished his triumph in this implicit familial competition. But without it ever having to be stated, he was the greatest supporter of his son's successful pursuit of U.S. Air Force pilot's wings in 1972. During the limited time father and son were together during those years, some of their most precious hours were spent in the cockpit of a single engine Cessna, flying over the magnificently quilted landscape of Lancaster County.

BY THE MID-1970s the future of downtown Lancaster was uncertain. Park City Mall was blooming, but demolition of the vacant buildings on the west side of North Queen Street had only just begun. Land-lords of Singleton's shoe store premises—two old ladies who were beneficiaries of the Lebzelter Estate—announced that their five-story building at 32-34 North Queen was for sale. Investing in downtown real estate was the last thing Bob and Ed were seeking, but they had no choice but to consider it. They briefly looked into the option of moving to Park City, but the rental rates there were more than triple those of downtown and the retail hours were intolerable. Shopping centers didn't fit into Singleton's business plan or lifestyle. They had to make it work downtown.

Purchasing the building was a risky proposition. Despite the fact that portions of the structure had been repaired and electrical wiring completely replaced after the 1956 fire, 32-34 North Queen Street effectively remained as one of the oldest buildings in the city, with parts of the first two floors dating back to the 1700s and the upper floors to the 1800s. It was a large building, extending almost a half-block to the rear along West Grant Street, which bordered the north side of Lancaster's famous Central Market. Over the years the building housed a series of prominent businesses, including Wilbur & Martin's, Bell Telephone, Singer (sewing machine store), Kinney Shoes,

Beneficial Finance, and the Community Gallery of Lancaster County. During the 1950s parts of the second floor were occupied by a dance studio and weight-loss salon. Each of the top three floors were configured as apartments. They hadn't been occupied since the 1930s and were in a state of disrepair exacerbated by the 1956 fire, which luckily was contained to the lower floors. Through negotiations with the sellers' attorney and an independent appraisal, the parties arrived at a reasonable selling price. Nevertheless, with tuition loans not yet fully paid, Bob had to go back to the bank again. He would also have to put off buying the Cadillac he always wanted; instead he waited a couple of years and traded in his old Buick for a new one of the same model, but with an updated name, Electra.

Investing in the building turned out to be a prudent decision regardless of the fact that they had no better alternatives at the time. Well-managed businesses survived even though downtown was aging. Nevertheless, of Lancaster's three major department stores, Garvin's had closed, and Hager's had moved to Park City. Watt & Shand also opened a store at the mall, but, under pressure from downtown merchants and the Chamber of Commerce, they continued to operate their prominent Penn Square store as an anchor for downtown trade. City and business leaders realized that redevelopment efforts beyond projects on the second block of North Queen were needed. In 1977 an Economic Development Company was created to make low-interest loans available to property owners and businesses who would upgrade their aging downtown buildings.

The façade of the Singleton building was designated by architectural historians as one of the prime candidates for restoration.[4] Less than three years after buying the property, mostly out of a sense of loyalty to the downtown district, Bob and Ed decided to do their part. They retained the architectural firm of deVitry, Gilbert & Bradley to come up with a proposal and hired Wholsen Construction Company to execute a restoration in 1978. The project received rave reviews and gave the business a little boost as well.

THE LATE 1970S WERE SUNSET YEARS for Singleton's Shoes. As a result of the revitalization efforts, downtown businesses continued to attract some carriage trade and traditional customers who weren't enamored of discount outlets or the supposedly convenient parking lots of the massive shopping centers. But it was hardly a growth environment. Their best employee, Ed's son Bill, probably perceived this. Despite assurances from his dad and uncle that the business would someday go his way, he resigned to pursue an attractive offer from his father-in-law, Les Eshelman, owner of a successful bricklaying business in town. Bob hated to see Bill leave and was tempted to convince him to stay, but over Ed's objections decided not to get in the way. He didn't want to feel responsible for holding back his nephew. As such, the business found itself without a succession plan and a less-than-ideal mix of regular and part-time help. The brothers managed to keep sales from declining by working a little harder and sticking to their time-tested service and stocking practices.

Bob and Ed made a lifestyle choice when they recommitted to the downtown in 1974, and it was probably the best thing they could have done for themselves. They were finally able to take more time off for vacations and leisure activities. Bob and Norm took a few trips out west and made regular winter trips to their favorite islands by air or cruise ship. Bob also continued his flying hobby, which was facilitated by a good friend from church, Joe Webber, who owned a Cessna 182 and made it available to Bob at a very friendly rate. Bob used it as an opportunity to fly with Norm on short overnighters to the shore or on weekend trips to visit the grandchildren in South Carolina. Summers were generally spent at home, where Bob loved swimming his daily laps before and after work. Norm, through her delightful preparations, resplendent with fresh fruit and floral trimmings, always made their treasured time spent by their backyard pool a truly romantic, albeit vicarious, island experience.

By 1979 shoe sales reflected the transformation of downtown trade and dominance of the shopping centers, which were now open on Sundays. Sales of children's shoes at Singleton's became very weak as youth flocked to sneaker franchises at the mall. And shoe sales to adults were reflecting mainly mature styles. It appeared that, like its owners and employees, Singleton's shoes were graying. Sales began to slip a little bit. Bob was in his late 50s, recognized the situation, and decided that they should develop a business plan in anticipation of retirement in about five years.

It was a good time to plan for the future. The general economic and political climate looked ominous. The Three Mile Island Nuclear Generating Station, located less than 20 miles from Lancaster, and dedicated just one year earlier, experienced the "biggest radiation leak ever from a commercial nuclear plant."[5] Just when the nation was thought to have emerged from an energy crisis—the White House reported that there was no energy emergency despite continued loss of Iranian oil production—gas stations were closed in Pennsylvania as worried citizens stocked up on gas. At the end of 1979 inflation was reported at 13.3%, and by May 1980 "unemployment skyrocketed to 7.8%, the highest since President Carter took office…in a deepening recession."[6]

As always, Bob took these events in stride and let Norm do the worrying. During a card club gathering, in a lighthearted jab at her hubby, Norm commented, "he makes me so mad!…he never worries about anything!" With a characteristic chuckle Bob defended himself: "That's right, Hon, I don't worry. But I do get *concerned* at times." Without a doubt he was the consummate optimist and pride of positive thinkers. Perhaps it was a result of his loving childhood environment, good fortune, fortuitous survival under enemy fire, abiding faith, and complete confidence that any problem can be solved through action. He was always vindicated. A few years later an era of doubt and stagflation came to an end, thanks in large part to the vision of an ex-actor-turned President who shared Bob's optimistic outlook.

DURING THE 1980s Bob and Ed followed their long term plan to exit the business. Inventories were rationalized to concentrate on the most profitable lines. The children's business was discontinued. By 1982 they planned for the sale of the building. High inflation, a weak stock market, and tax incentives were stimulating development of historical properties. Nearby buildings were being snapped up by developers. Bob and Ed were approached by a developer who was eager to acquire one of Lancaster's best locations near Penn Square. The shoe store had always been used by pedestrians as a short cut from North Queen Street to the popular Central Market area. No sooner had they been approached, than a second developer made a competing bid. Both offers were reasonable but required seller-financing at interest rates significantly below the double-digit rates that were commonplace in the '80s. To complicate matters, Bob Jr. entered the fray. He had recently settled into a new job after taking two years off to complete business school. He saw an attractive investment opportunity for himself and a better deal for his dad. He sweetened the best offer on the table with more attractive financing terms, and a deal was closed in

September 1982. Both Bobs were thrilled to keep the family name on the building. Ed was a little tentative until it became obvious that they had opted for the most reliable stream of mortgage payments, which continued beyond the point when shrewd developers would have exercised their option to refinance at much lower rates.

In 1983, a year before Bob turned 62, he and Ed decided to begin seeking potential buyers of the business, anticipating that the process might take as long as a year. Considering the state of the downtown, Bob had reason to be concerned. He quietly put out word of their intentions through their most trusted manufacturers' salesmen, Todd Anthony, Frank Murphy, Pete McGann of Brown Shoe Co., and Mel Feidel of Sebago. Their confidants were surprised by the news; they had always presumed that Bob would work until he died. But they were familiar with the business and Singleton's reputation: a successful enterprise that paid its bills early. Bob and Ed knew they could rely on this band of loyalists to identify interested parties in the area without stirring the downtown rumor mill. They were assured that a buyer could be found.

For a few weeks they didn't hear anything. Then calls started coming in from nearby towns of Camp Hill, Landsdale, Harrisburg, Coatesville, and York. They came in such rapid succession that Bob began to get cold feet. All prospective buyers were invited to visit, and they were permitted to see the books, which confirmed the financial strength of the business. It clearly wasn't a distress sale, although some of the suitors might have been put off by that. Most of the prospective out-of-town buyers dried up, except for an interested party who was not in a position to close the transaction for another year. The partners wondered how it would all turn out.

Later that spring, the bookkeeper from Shaub's, their next-door competitor, walked into the back office of Singleton's. His name was Delbert Denlinger. Bob was seated at his desk, eating his lunch. "Is it true you're going to sell your store?" asked the unexpected visitor.

Bob was shocked. "Who told you a thing like that, Del?"

"Pat," answered Del. Pat Herr was the owner and manager of Shaub's. "He was at a shoe show and heard the rumor." Trade shows were a natural clearinghouse for industry gossip. Clearly, the cat was out of the bag.

"Frankly, Del, if we can find a buyer at the right price, we're thinking about it, but we're not in any hurry."

"Well, I'm interested," said Del. He explained his situation: in addition to drawing a paycheck at Shaub's, he was collecting rentals from a small apartment building he had purchased in Strasburg a few years earlier. And he had recently gotten married to Sally Krill, whose father, a local doctor, had agreed to back him for any needed funds that he couldn't obtain from the bank.

While Bob and Ed were both surprised that young Del—more of an accountant than a shoe salesman—would be up to the challenge, they said that they would be willing to discuss it, but only at night, outside regular hours, to maintain confidentiality. That was no problem for Del. He admitted, "If Pat knew I was talking to you, I'd be fired." That was no surprise. At best Pat was a cordial competitor; at worst he was aloof and arrogant—completely the opposite of the Singleton brothers.

One evening later that week Del and his father-in-law came into the store to meet with Bob and Ed. Their personal chemistry was good, so they got right into it. The partners had established a selling price for the business that was slightly higher than the marked-down value of the inventory. Bob demonstrated how Singleton's took markdowns by pulling a shoe box from the shelf, translating its penciled cost code, and explaining how that item would have been coded at a higher cost a season earlier. Del wasn't familiar with the technique, but understood Bob's assertion that the inventory's book value might be higher under a more conventional technique. While it made sense to the prospective buyers, they still wanted to discount the small amount of goodwill that had been figured into the asking price. Bob and Ed would have none of that. Indeed, the value of the family name and customer following was probably worth more than the brothers had priced it. The parties all felt that a deal could be arrived at, but before working out the details they agreed to "sleep on it" over the upcoming Memorial Day weekend. As he left, Del reminded the Singletons to keep their discussions quiet.

Del had reason to be concerned about confidentiality. Bob would later learn that Pat Herr played golf that weekend with an officer from Delbert's bank, who must have asked if one of Shaub's employees was attempting to buy a competitor's business. On the next workday Pat confronted Delbert, confirmed the rumor, and fired him on the spot. Shell-shocked Del was practically in tears when he fled next door to Singleton's. Bob and Ed, shocked by the ethics displayed by their competitor, came to Delbert's rescue. They said they would honor their commitment to sell him the business and offered to put him on the payroll until a mutually agreeable closing date could be arrived at.

Del returned that night with his father-in-law to finalize general terms of an agreement that would be turned over to the lawyers. It was a congenial meeting and for all practical purposes a done deal. Dr. Krill announced that he would host a celebratory dinner with their wives at the Lancaster Country Club. And the business would end up being sold sooner than any of them had expected. As the meeting was breaking up Dr. Krill pulled Bob aside to ask if, in addition to helping Delbert with the fall and spring buys, he would mind "stepping aside" immediately after the closing, rather than working until the end of the year as originally planned. Bob knew that the business couldn't afford excess overhead, Delbert would need to establish his own authority, and, as a condition of the sale, Ed would stay on for another year until reaching age 62. The others knew that Bob was the partner who was most ready to retire, but, with the accelerated time frame, may not be prepared to stop working right away. But Bob had already considered that. Before they left he gave his answer: "You know what, Dr. Krill? I'm ready...O.K."

Singleton's Shoes was the family business for 55 years. Suddenly, it was no more. Norm was out by the pool when Bob came home early with the news. She was surprised by the rapid turn of events. Friends and neighbors were shocked. They couldn't believe that Bob would just walk away from it after all those years. He had spent so much of his time there—at nights after regular hours, on his day off, sometimes even on Saturday nights. But like departing Great Yoho, he had no regrets. This was just the end of a grand chapter and the beginning of a new life with his beloved Norma. True to form, he never looked back.

# CHAPTER 18

# SUMMER SOLSTICE

IT FELT STRANGE TO HIM at first, but retirement was something to which Bob quickly adjusted, especially during the height of summer—his and Norm's favorite season of the year. His deeply-rooted bond with her made it relatively easy to transition to a modified daily routine, which would now include more daytime hours in her space. Incredibly, after 40 years of marriage, they seemed to love each other more every day, still liked the same things, and genuinely enjoyed doing things together. Other than swimming, tennis was their regular physical recreation, usually mixed doubles with friends.

They also frequently ventured out on short day-trips. They were finally in a position to purchase the Cadillac Bob always wanted, a sporty, white 1985 DeVille with a chrome luggage rack on the trunk. Their little trips were frequently as laid back as picking strawberries at a local farm, enjoying soup and sandwiches at a country restaurant, and coming home for freshly baked strawberry shortcake in their screened-in porch by the pool. The pace of summer was always manifest in the passing sequence of the local seasonal fare, highlighted by strawberries and sweet peas in June, peaches and blueberries in July, Silver Queen corn and black raspberries through mid-September, and green cooking apples and neck pumpkins into October.

They stretched their warm weather pleasures well into autumn, until frost imparted its daily soft patina on the morning landscape and cotton gloves were needed for sunrise tennis appointments. Norm hated to see the onset of fall, which evoked subconscious thoughts of kids leaving for school and the passing away of parents; but, by the time their porch furniture was placed into winter storage, she would already be in the thick of preparations for holidays and family visitations, knowing that in retired life those good times would be followed, not by the endless gray spells of mid-Atlantic weather, but by a winter retreat in Florida.

Through the Fort Myers tourist bureau Bob located a condo-minium rental on the southern end of Fort Myers Beach. The nearby town of old Fort Myers had totally changed in four decades—the Bradford Hotel was barely recognizable, and Buckingham Field was now home to a municipal mosquito control unit—but the remote location in their "Island's End" condominium overlooking the Gulf provided the island-like atmosphere that they had always enjoyed. Days were filled with tennis, long walks on the beach, socializing with new friends by the pool, and short trips to visit Lancaster friends then in Florida: Sis and Harry, who years earlier had relocated to the Orlando area; Mollie and Ed, who frequently stopped at RV parks in the panhandle; Miley Ament, who had moved to Fort Myers Beach in retirement; and Stan and Margie Miller, their Murry Hill Drive neighbors and tennis pals who often went south in winter.

By and large the mid-1980s were golden years. But as travel and leisure became a greater part of their lives, the increasing demands of an aging house, nagging lawn, overgrown shrubs, sprawling trees, and a leaf-besieged swimming pool became more of a burden. Thus, in reasoned anticipation of old age, and prompted by enticing ads in the real estate section of the newspaper, Bob and Norm visited a new townhouse development at Willow Valley, located in a beautiful part of southern Lancaster County next to a small resort complex and retirement community of the same name. They liked what they saw. After several weeks of investigating other communities, they settled on Willow Valley and listed for sale their Murry Hill Drive home of 33 years. Perfectly maintained and attractively priced, their beloved home was sold almost too quickly, as they were not prepared for the dislocation of temporary living in a tiny apartment until their new townhouse was built. That complication prevented them from fitting Florida into their winter plans for 1987. Bob maintained his cheerful attitude; but under cramped, albeit temporary, circumstances, Norm struggled to keep a stiff upper lip. As always, she made the best of it—Christmas decorations and all—but worried if they could ever adjust to living in a two-bedroom condo.

As usual, her worrying was wasted energy. That spring they moved into beautiful, bright, and airy new quarters. The townhouse had a vaulted ceiling in the living room, tall windows on three sides, a study loft, inviting kitchen, and modern bathrooms and appliances. The interiors were nicely decorated with the help of their long time friend Marvin Shearer, who had also done several interior projects for them on Murry Hill Drive. It didn't take long to get settled. Norm was thrilled. More than anything else, her delight is what made Bob happy. They quickly returned to a contented retired life, and their time spent at Willow Valley turned out to be more precious than they could ever imagine.

In 1988 they returned to Fort Myers Beach, this time to a small house a block away from the beach. At first, they weren't as keen for this location as they were for the Island's End high-rise-condo-with-a-view, but they grew to like it enough to return again the next year. But when 1989 arrived Norm was not herself. She was much quieter than usual. Her eyes weren't their normal bright sparkling blue. During walks on the beach, she complained a little about a nagging ache on one side of her back. It had also bothered her earlier that fall, and she had casually mentioned it to her doctor, who attributed it to normal aches and pains of age and tennis. On the Friday morning of their second week in Florida Norm came out of the bathroom in an unusual state of distress. You could see it in her eyes. She knew something was wrong; the blood that she had just discovered was more than a tell-tale amount. Bob could attest to that.

He immediately took her to a local clinic. The physician ran some tests and recommended that a colonoscopy be scheduled as soon as possible. They set it up for Monday morning. Unexpected gloom descended upon their world that weekend, but they did their best to keep the faith, bolster each other's spirits, and pray for the best. After Monday morning's procedure their worst fear was confirmed; Norm would indeed need surgery to diagnose the extent of and, with luck, eradicate the cancer. The doctor advised them that they could choose to have the surgery performed locally or safely elect to return home for the operation. Norm wanted to go home; Bob felt the same way. That evening they cried together. Then Bob packed the car, and they left for Lancaster in the morning.

All the arrangements were made before they arrived home. As always, Bob could be counted on to exercise good judgement and take action in a time of crisis. The kids were notified, and Norm checked into the hospital shortly after they got back. Son Bob, who was on business in Europe at the time, managed to arrive at the hospital soon after Norm came out of surgery. He found his dad seated by her bedside in the intermediate care unit. She was in a sedated sleep, attached to tubes and wires. Her mate sat in a daze, just staring at her—and looking more tired, gaunt, and alone than his son had ever witnessed.

The doctor's report wasn't encouraging. A portion of Norm's colon had been removed, but the cancer had metastasized to the liver. It was the aggressive, fast-moving kind. A range of conventional and experimental treatments were discussed. But the doctors were sure of their prognosis; non-conventional treatments would be pointless. A program of conventional chemotherapy was said to be worth trying, but false hope was discouraged. The cancer had spread too far and was moving much too fast. Norm would have no more than six-months-to-a-year to live. Bob was in shock. It was like somebody had pulled the rug out from under him.

He quickly made up his mind that he would be strong for both of them. Indeed, he was, and amazingly, so was she. Because they had always been so close—and shared everything—they were able to talk openly about their grim reality. They talked a lot. Initially they tried to maintain a routine, and she was able to go out a few times. One of those times was their 50th high school reunion, which, although nobody told her, was scheduled a year early to ensure her attendance. At home she insisted on continuing her duties in the kitchen until it became impossible due to chemical-induced weakness and nausea. Slowly but surely, she began to share tips with her hubby about how to function in her space, something that he never had to do before. He was spoiled and knew it. Six months earlier he would have laughed and resisted. Now he didn't, although he downplayed the need for his tutoring.

In June Norm made the decision to end the debilitating and ineffective chemotherapy treatments. Emotionally, it was the most painful moment for both of them, because it signaled loss of hope and the beginning of the end. At the doctor's recommendation Bob called in the Hospice people. Norm wanted to spend her final days at home in her beautiful townhouse. She loved the space so much, but worried that Bob would decide not to remain there after she died. She had always assumed that he would be the first one to go, based on the fact that his father had died so young from a coronary condition and all his siblings had inherited an excessively high cholesterol condition. Norm had spent the last 20 years of her life monitoring her mate's diet and tailoring her culinary delights to suit his condition, worrying about him right up to the end. More than anybody, she knew how much he loved and needed her. In her last conversations with family members and the minister she affirmed that she had no regrets in life and that she had done everything she wanted to do, gone everywhere she had wanted to go, and had loved it all. That was her final gift to Bob. She died on July 28th in the prime of her favorite season of the year.

Reverend Kerr was with the family at the end. Charles Scott Kerr had been the senior minister of First United Methodist Church through most of the 1960s and '70s. He was one of the most loved and revered pastors in the church's history. He officiated at Bob's mother's funeral and both of the kids' weddings. Charles was like a member of the family. Suffering from a chronic heart condition, he had to step down from his duties as full-time senior pastor of First Church. But as fragile as his health was, he spent many long days with Norm and Bob during her infirmity and was present continuously to offer comfort during the all-day vigil on her final day of painkiller-induced semi-consciousness. He lovingly mustered all his strength to officiate at Norm's funeral, which was attended by several hundred people. His powerful message and robust delivery betrayed his frail condition. He told Bob that it was one of his most heavily attended funerals. That was no surprise. Everybody loved Norma.

This was without a doubt the most difficult time in Bob's life. He needed to draw upon his greatest strengths—faith, optimism, courage, and friendships—to deal with the unbearable loss. Every week after Norm's death, Reverend Kerr joined him for lunch at the Willow Valley Restaurant. These weekly meetings continued for over a year. Bob would be forever thankful for Charles's friendship, support, and counsel during his long grieving and healing process. A magnificent network of friends, neighbors, and relatives was also a rich blessing. He knew that he was fortunate in this regard and never took them for granted. Everybody seemed to know exactly what to do. Caring people went out of their way to laugh and cry with him, and, having known how he was treated by Norm, constantly kept his refrigerator stocked with healthy preparations and fresh seasonal bounty from Lancaster County's prolific farmlands.

# CHAPTER 19

# BACK AGAIN

IF HE PREVIOUSLY HAD ANY mixed feelings about retiring early, those thoughts evaporated when Norm died. A delayed retirement decision only would have deprived him of golden years with her that had been mercilessly cut short. He was truly thankful for the seven wonderful years they were able to share together in retirement. But it didn't make her death any easier to accept. It took a long time until he could walk through the front door without feeling her presence, or calling out "Hi Hon!" before realizing that his greeting would go unrequited.

As a realist, he knew that he had to get over the grief. His strength of character would never permit succumbing to a depressed existence. His proven recipe for success and happiness had always been a blend of staying busy, working hard, being with friends, and keeping the faith. It worked before and would serve him well again as a widower in retirement. He immediately forced himself into an Army-like routine. He was up by sunrise every day to execute his jogging ritual or make an early court time. He got more involved in his downtown activities, not only as supervisor for the Singleton Building, but by helping out part-time at Larry Helicher's TMB clothing store next door. He also increased his generous level of participation in volunteer activities, which included giving time for Optimist youth programs, organizing Christmas bell ringers for the Salvation Army, serving on the homeowners' association board, or preparing tax returns for the IRS's Volunteer Income Tax Assistance program, established for the benefit of people unable to pay for tax help. In recognition of his contributions he received Optimist of the Year Award in 1995.

Tennis was his favorite recreation when Norm was living; now it became his regular therapy and genuine passion. His new life revolved around his tennis schedule, which included play every day but Sunday. He always played with enthusiasm and competitiveness. His agility on the court betrayed his biological age and occasional bouts of arthritis.

He rarely complained about the pain; he simply dealt with it through a disciplined program of stretching exercises and compensated by means of a modified playing style, featuring side-arm serves, left-hand volleys, and underhand smashes. He enjoyed trouncing most guys his own age and many younger. Like his father and bowling, when he set out to do something, he did it well. And always with enthusiasm.

Also like Roy, he was always well-known in town. Except for the war years, he lived in Lancaster his entire life, had more relatives in the area than he could easily keep track of, and for nearly four decades operated a retail establishment in the center of town. By the time he retired, there weren't many places he could go without running into or being recognized by an old friend, neighbor, classmate, church colleague, business associate, or customer. If he didn't always remember their names, which was rare, he usually remembered their shoe sizes. He would often say, "There goes an eight-double," referring to size 8AA. He especially liked the "trips, quads and quints," because other shoe stores wouldn't consider stocking those extra-narrow widths. There were a lot of skinny feet in Lancaster County, and they were usually his customers. If anybody needed an introduction to, or reference on a Lancastrian they didn't know, they could rely on Bob. He could be counted on to always speak about a person's positive attributes. The fact is, he saw positive attributes in everybody he knew.

Retirement years provided him with more opportunities to renew and strengthen old friendships. Dick Kreider, one of his regular tennis buddies, was a classmate from Manheim Township who went on to become a Navy aviator. Dick continued to fly after the war and until recently maintained his proficiency on a classic, single-engine wood-and-fabric Aeronca. Bob frequently went with him on low-level sorties over the farmlands. They made an odd couple in the cockpit: Dick had bad eyes; Bob had a bad ear. Between them, they somehow managed to return intact, except for occasional loose screws in their wooden wing struts. Common sense ultimately prevailed, and the plane was eventually sold. Bob also got better acquainted with Brame Witmer, a Willow Valley condominium neighbor, fellow-Optimist, and regular tennis crony until his health began to decline. Brame's health deteriorated quickly, preventing his ability to function independently; but thanks to his reliable club mate, he never failed to miss Optimist meetings on Tuesdays and eagerly looked forward to regular lunchtime outings on days when he would have been otherwise abandoned in the retirement center by busy friends or distant family. Bob was always there for his friends, right up to the end.

Over the years Bob never made an effort to stay in touch with wartime acquaintances, although he managed to cross paths with a few. Bake from Quarryville used to stop by the shoe store just to say hello. Before leaving, one of them invariably reminded the other, "Go out and get something to eat...then you'll feel more like working." It always produced a hearty laugh. When Norm was still living, Deat and Mary Deaton, who lived in the Midwest, stopped by to visit during a cross-country vacation one year. Dick Crippen from Hut 18 and his wife also looked up Bob on a summer trip that brought them through town. For years they exchanged Christmas cards with the Deatons, Crippens, and neighbors from Zaragoza Street. For 45 years Norm faithfully corresponded with Gwen Parsons, the young mother she met on the train to Laredo. They felt like they knew each other's families from their annual letters and photo exchanges that chronicled their respective life stories. Communicating the sad news of Norm's death in Gwen's Christmas card was one of the hardest notes for Bob to write.

By the mid-1990s World War II 50th anniversary events became popular as aging vets faced increasing evidence of their gradual, inevitable, and final reduction in force. Some sought to clarify the record; most just wanted to share untold experiences before they went unremembered. Bob was invited to several of these gatherings, and the reminiscing stimulated him to reconnect with his past. Through the internet he located a web site set up by an organization of members of his old bomb group, the 381st Bomb Group Memorial Association (BGMA). One of the association's founders was a gentleman by the name of "Pax" Sherwood, who lived nearby in York, Pennsylvania. Bob arranged a trip to meet his fellow Ridgewell alumnus and explore the profuse collection of Triangle L memorabilia in Pax's basement.

As a result of that visit, Bob was motivated to attend the next 381st Bomb Group reunion. But first he would attempt to locate his old pal Johnnie Rutherford, who might also be interested. Surprisingly, Bob had run into Johnnie only one time after the war, and it was a complete coincidence. He was with Norm and the kids on vacation, touring the Blue Ridge Mountains in their yellow Ford convertible. They had just pulled into one of the scenic overlooks on Skyline Drive, when he noticed a familiar face in the adjacent parked car. It was Johnnie!—accompanied by his wife Thelma. What a place for a chance reunion—several hundred miles away from home in a remote area—but, how appropriate, considering their incredible first meeting in a Nissen hut in Great Yoho. Their meeting on Skyline Drive was the last time Bob saw Johnnie before attempting to make contact more than 40 years later. Luckily, John was listed in the Lancaster directory; and, astonishingly, his address was shown as the retirement center at Willow Valley, directly across the highway from where Bob lived. In excited anticipation Bob reached for the telephone to dial the number, but was interrupted by the phone's ringing. He picked up the receiver only to be shocked out of his wits by the voice on the other end: it was Johnnie! Another coincidence?…or part of a greater plan? Perhaps every person's life is just a story which cries out for a hopeful opening, healthy development, unique climax, fulfilling denouement, and neat closure. Certainly, Bob's would have no loose ends. He and John attended their first bomb group reunion together.

In 1995 Bob decided to take a trip to England with his friend and neighbor from Willow Valley, Anne Kruse, whose son lived in London and whose late husband Dick, a former B-17 pilot and retired Pan Am captain, had passed away not long after Norm's death. Norm never had an interest in going abroad, but Bob had a suppressed desire to return to the scene of his wartime exploits. So did Bob Jr., who arranged to meet them for an expedition to the site of his former air base at Ridgewell. Very little remained of the base, which was dismantled soon after the war, but with little hesitation Bob recognized the Kings Head pub in Great Yeldham and the Ashen church, which hadn't changed much in a half-century. A framed photo of Pax Sherwood in the pub's hallway also confirmed that he was in the right place. Across from the church was another old property called the Red Cow, the name of a beer house which once occupied the premises. Today it is the private residence of Mike Williams, a retired gentleman who warmly received at least three unexpected visitors on a nostalgic tour. Mike has a wonderful collection of photos, maps, and records of the old air base and continues to share correspondence with at least one gray-haired toggalier who came back for a visit.

While tracing the remains of the old base perimeter, Bob had a chance to speak to an elderly woman who emerged from a farmhouse on the east side. She confirmed that the dilapidated block and stucco storage shed at the foot of her driveway was originally part of the base.

She was a young teenager when the Yanks lived there and remembered the terrible days when bombers crash-landed in wheat fields and doodle bugs droned overhead. She also remembered how the kids ran for cover when the buzzing sound of the missile's pulse jet went silent, signaling that it had begun its final, gravity-powered trajectory. With tears in her eyes she recalled the time she was riding her best friend's bicycle and they had to dive for cover in the ditch alongside the road. She remembers being afraid that she would cause damage to her friend's most prized possession.

The trip to the American Military Cemetery at Cambridge was an unexpectedly special part of the trip to England. It was difficult not to be overwhelmed by the beauty and peacefulness of this burial place, which starkly contrasts with the horrible fate of the thousands resting there. Bob was disappointed not to find the grave of his friend and supervisor, Lieutenant Hart, who perished in the Isle of Man incident during the final days of the war. But, he was relieved to learn from the park supervisor that the remains of many servicemen originally buried there had been returned to America by families who wanted loved ones on home soil. Months after Bob returned from England he saw a notice posted in the 381st BGMA newsletter from a Lester Hart of Ohio, seeking any information about his deceased brother Wayne. Bob was pleased to help a family he never knew bring closure to a tragic episode in their lives; he responded with consoling words about his respected friend from Ashtabula and specific details about Wayne's high spirits as he raced to catch a coveted seat on the ill-fated bomber.

In the first year of the new century Bob returned overseas again, but this time to the country he had bombed. His primary mission was to visit grandson Mike, who was stationed near Frankfurt and serving as pilot-in-command of an Air Force C-21A Learjet transport, an air-craft used to chauffeur American military leaders, government officials and VIPs between various countries in that part of the world. A 1992 graduate of the U.S. Air Force Academy, Captain Mike Lee is the youngest of a bloodline imprinted with his grandfather's attraction to flying. Together, they visited the beaches at Normandy and toured a modern, rebuilt Germany. Needless to say, it was a special trip for the proud grandfather and reluctant toggalier.

Returning to the past is a privilege reserved for elders with the wisdom to supplant sentimental nostalgia with insightful reflection. Bob has the ability to do this with good humor, honest objectivity, and a generous attitude. He doesn't dwell on the past and doesn't yearn to repeat it; he's clearly comfortable that he got it right the first time. He remains very busy and active, and he continues to look to the future with enthusiasm and cheerful optimism. He has confidence that his legacy will live through his children and grandchildren, which with great feeling he claims to be his greatest accomplishment.

Grandson Mike finished his C-21 assignment in 2001, after which he got married to his fiancée Ryann Tomlin, a Registered Nurse and University of South Carolina graduate. Mike's next assignment will be flying MC-130E's for the USAF Special Operations Squadron. Granddaughter Erin graduated from Davidson College and went on for her M.D. at the University of North Carolina. She is currently completing her residency in pediatrics at Rush-Presbyterian St. Lukes Medical Center in Chicago while her fellow Davidson alumnus and husband of three years, Dr. Steven Brackbill, is completing his residency in internal medicine at Northwestern Memorial Hospital. With caring young men and women like Erin, Mike, Steve and Ryann, Pappy Singleton has good reason to be optimistic about our collective futures.

Each generation of the Singletons has been privileged to live full lives and pursue ever greater opportunities thanks to a secure foundation built upon the love, hard work, generosity, and ingrained values of their parents. In modesty characteristic of his parents—a trait similarly attributed to his generation—Bob claims that he will most likely be remembered for practical attributes like "dependability" and "always being on time." When prompted, he acknowledges that he will also probably be remembered for running a successful shoe business. That's sort of like saying he had to "work" today in his wartime letters from Great Yoho. His modesty can only reflect the perspective of a truly grateful man and genuine believer who so deeply loves his family, friends, and land where he grew up, that he only wants to give more. The evidence is in the enriched lives of the people he has touched and the way he has lived his life.

# AFTERWORD

IN THE PROCESS OF WRITING ABOUT DAD'S LIFE I learned a great deal about our ancestors and his wartime experiences. I also picked up some colorful details about his past that provide insight into the way he thinks, acts, and lives his life. Frankly, there were no surprises. I have been fortunate to have a father who speaks openly about his personal experiences—not in a way that dwells on intimate details or evokes syrupy emotions, but in a manner that typically generates laughter and stirs happy sentiments.

He was never one to philosophize or become too introspective. And he didn't preach. He instilled values through simple, personal anecdote and the example of his consistent daily behavior. I learned through a generous amount of unambiguous positive reinforcement— or the simple withdrawal of same, which due to its infrequency seemed harsh and humiliating. Probably like most fathers and sons of our generations, we didn't spend much time talking about the soft stuff. We went to church regularly and always strove to be good Christians but didn't talk much about that either.

As part of the research for this book I conducted several taped interviews with Dad and used that medium for addressing some normally untouched personal topics like success and failure, triumphs and regrets, and heaven and hell. His thoughts on these concepts are mostly integrated into the preceding chapters. However, now that he is an octogenarian and many of his generation are gone, his comments about the afterlife deserve some further elaboration. Just as I had expected, he doesn't view those entities literally. His concept of the afterlife is completely embodied in how a person is thought of after they are deceased. He says, "Wouldn't it be hell to leave the world and have people think badly of you?" Good point.

But his next point was lost on me. Perhaps because I am a generation younger, I found it both odd and interesting that he was concerned about "how many people would show up at the funeral."

Granted, in his robust physical state, there's a good probability that he will outlive most of his contemporaries. It would be just like him. However, knowing how favorably he is regarded—and genuinely loved—by people of more than just his own generation, it's difficult for me to believe that he would not have a big crowd show up for his final event. One thing I do know for sure: if there is a heaven, he'll go by first class. And Mom will have dinner waiting.

# MISSION LOG

## LIST OF SORTIES FLOWN

*MISSION #1*

| | |
|---|---|
| TARGET - | *Soest (Rail Yards)* |
| DATE - | *Dec. 4th, 1944* |
| SHIP - | *#538* |
| PILOT - | *Sweetland* |
| POSITION - | *Waist* |
| LENGTH - | *7½ hrs.* |
| REMARKS - | *Flak- light; No fighter opposition; No ships lost.* |

*MISSION #2*

| | |
|---|---|
| TARGET - | *Stuttgart (Rail Yards)* |
| DATE - | *Dec. 9th, 1944* |
| SHIP - | *#590 "IN LIKE ERROL"* |
| PILOT - | *Roebuck* |
| POSITION - | *Tail* |
| LENGTH - | *7½ hrs.* |
| REMARKS - | *Flak- medium, accurate; No fighter opposition; Oxygen casualty in crew; Temperature -55°.* |

*MISSION #3*

| | |
|---|---|
| TARGET - | *Mannheim (Railroad Bridge)* |
| DATE - | *Dec. 11th, 1944* |
| SHIP - | *#553 "FEATHER MERCHANT II"* |
| PILOT - | *Malleus* |
| POSITION - | *Tail* |
| LENGTH - | *8¼ hrs.* |
| REMARKS - | *Flak- heavy; No fighter opposition; One ship blew up, due to direct hit by flak.* |

*MISSION #4*

| | |
|---|---|
| TARGET - | *Merseburg (Oil Refinery)* |
| DATE - | *Dec. 12th, 1944* |
| SHIP - | *#018 "LOS ANGELES CITY LIMITS"* |
| PILOT - | *Malleus* |
| POSITION - | *Tail* |
| LENGTH - | *8¼ hrs.* |
| REMARKS - | *Flak- medium; No fighter opposition* |

MISSION #5
TARGET -      Cologne (Marshalling Yards)
DATE -        Dec. 18ᵗʰ, 1944
SHIP -        #313 "THE COLUMBUS MISS"
PILOT -       Biene
POSITION -    Tail
LENGTH -      6¼ hrs.
REMARKS -     Flak- light, inaccurate; No fighter opposition; Altitude 31,500'.


MISSION #6
TARGET -      Ettinghausen (Air Field) Near Frankfort
DATE -        Dec. 24ᵗʰ, 1944
SHIP -        #313 "THE COLUMBUS MISS"
PILOT -       Greenspan
POSITION -    Waist
LENGTH -      6 hrs.
REMARKS -     Greatest air armada ever assembled; Support to ground troops fighting
              Rundstedt in the Ardennes break-thru; Mission highly successful; Jet-
              propelled fighters seen; Seen V-2's being launched; Visual bombing- seen
              ground battles.


MISSION #7
TARGET -      Paderborn (Marshalling Yards)
DATE -        Jan. 17ᵗʰ, 1945
SHIP -        #102 "JULIE LINDA"
PILOT -       Stevens
POSITION -    Toggalier
LENGTH -      6½ hrs.
REMARKS -     My first mission as toggalier…10x500 RDX; No trouble at all…
              everything went O.K. for me; a PFF bombing; I had camera in nose of ship,
              so snapped some pictures of our formation, etc; Flak- light; Seen another
              rocket being launched.


MISSION #8
TARGET -      Mannheim (Rail & Highway Bridge)
DATE -        Jan. 20ᵗʰ, 1945
SHIP -        #809 "PFC's LIMITED"
PILOT -       Clark
POSITION -    Toggalier (5 x 500 RDX)
LENGTH -      7 hrs.
REMARKS -     PFF bombing; camera turned on at "bombs away;" Temperature -54°C;
              Flak- moderate; Came back with one engine feathered (#3); Lost the

*formation, and thought we would have to land in France; Weather, very bad! No instruments for landing "blind"...really sweat it out!*

MISSION #9

TARGET -       *Aschaffenburg (Tank Assembly Plant) Near Frankfort*
DATE -          *Jan. 21ˢᵗ, 1945*
SHIP -           *#265 "HELL'S ANGEL"*
PILOT -         *Peters*
POSITION -    *Toggalier (6 x 500 RDX – 6 x 500 Incend.)*
LENGTH -      *7½ hrs.*
REMARKS -    *PFF bombing; Results unobserved; My coldest mission yet...-60°C; Terrible fog during assembly; Two ships collided just before landing ("EGG HAID"); Flak- light.*

MISSION #10

TARGET -       *? Last Resort Target (Rail Yards)*
DATE -          *Jan. 28ᵗʰ, 1945*
SHIP -           *#590 "STAGE DOOR CANTEEN"*
PILOT -         *Malleus*
POSITION -    *Toggalier (5 x 1000 GP's)*
LENGTH -      *7 hrs.*
REMARKS -    *Bombed last resort target...Cologne was our primary target; We went over the primary, but "mickey" ship went out...even had bomb bay doors open; PFF bombing; Flak- very heavy!*

MISSION #11

TARGET -       *Coblenz (Marshalling Yards)*
DATE -          *Jan. 29, 1945*
SHIP -           *#127 "PAIR O' QUEENS GEE & BEE"*
PILOT -         *Stevens*
POSITION -    *Toggalier (10 x 500 G.P.'s  2 x 500 Incend.)*
LENGTH -      *7 hrs.*
REMARKS -    *Flak- light; PFF bombing; A routine mission.*

MISSION #12

TARGET -       *Mannheim-Ludwigshaven (Rail Yards)*
DATE -          *Feb. 1ˢᵗ*
SHIP -           *#127 "PAIR O' QUEENS GEE & BEE"*
PILOT -         *Williamson*
POSITION -    *Toggalier (2 x 500 Incend.  10 x 500 RDX)*
LENGTH -      *7 hrs.*

REMARKS - *Flak- medium; First group over target; Had best view yet of rocket being launched; 28,000' most of mission, except for bomb run; Turned on camera at bombs away; PFF bombing.*


## MISSION #13 (12b)

TARGET - *Last Resort...town unidentified.*
DATE - *Feb 6*[th]*, 1945*
SHIP - *#265 "HELL'S ANGEL"*
PILOT - *Malleus*
POSITION - *Toggalier (10 x 500 RDX  4- M47 Incend.)*
LENGTH - *8 hrs.*
REMARKS - *Primary target was Lutzendorf, near Merseburg. Our formation got "screwed-up", so we bombed a target of opportunity; I bombed by instinct, and luckily hit a German town, somewhere nearby; Some fun! (What a bombardier I am?) The crew was betting on me...what a time we had! Flak- light; Got first good view of Zuider Zee; The "Jerries" even threw "flak" up at us there.*


## MISSION #14

TARGET - *Nuremberg (Nazi Capital) Rail Yards*
DATE - *Feb. 20*[th]*, 1945*
SHIP - *#590 "IN LIKE ERROL"*
PILOT - *Cotea*
POSITION - *Toggalier (10 x 500 RDX)*
LENGTH - *8½ hrs.*
REMARKS - *Weather broke up our formation...fell in with the 398*[th] *(Triangle W); All the 8*[th] *Air Force went to this target; Planes everywhere!! Flak- medium-accurate; PFF bombing; Camera in ship today.*


## MISSION #15

TARGET - *Kobbelitz (Rail Yards)*
DATE - *Feb. 22*[nd]*, 1945*
SHIP - *#265 "HELL'S ANGEL"*
PILOT - *Williamson*
POSITION - *Toggalier (10 x 500 RDX)*
LENGTH - *8 hrs.*
REMARKS - *A "pin-point" job...bombed from 9,700'. A tactical Air Force job; Visual bombing; Hit target perfect; E/Fighters in area...seen one shot down; No "flak"...(fortunately); Seen another V2 launched; the 535*[th] *was lead squadron today; Formation perfect.*

MISSION #16
TARGET -       Hamburg (Sub Pens)
DATE -         Feb. 24th, 1945
SHIP -         #170 (New ship…its 3rd mission)
PILOT -        Springmeyer
POSITION -     Toggalier (12 x 500 Navy bombs)
LENGTH -       8½ hrs.
REMARKS -      Bombed from 26,500'; Flak- heavy, not accurate; Flew #2 position, high
               element, low squadron; Went in on Zuider Zee again; Seen one B-17 go
               down over the North Sea; Scattered clouds…PFF bombing.

MISSION #17
TARGET -       Neckarsulm (Marshalling Yards)
DATE -         March 1st
SHIP -         #590 "IN LIKE ERROL"
PILOT -        Stevens
POSITION -     Toggalier (8 x 500 RDX  4 M17 Incend.)
LENGTH -       9½ hrs.
REMARKS -      Bombed from 21,000'; PFF bombing; No flak; Did get some flak going
               over bomb line; Got one hole in ship; Took off around 9:30 and didn't get
               back until 7 P.M.

MISSION #18
TARGET -       Chemnitz (Marshalling Yards)
DATE -         March 2nd, 1945
SHIP -         #590 "STAGE DOOR CANTEEN"
PILOT -        Bowler
POSITION -     Toggalier (18 x 250 G.P.'s)
LENGTH -       9½ hrs.
REMARKS -      Took off in darkness…6 A.M; Briefing 3:15 A.M; No flak; Group
               ahead of us was hit by fighters; Came back with about 20 gal. of
               gas…thought we were going to land in Brussels; Had a little trouble with
               my oxygen mask.

MISION #19
TARGET -       Rheine (Air Field containing ME 262's)
DATE -         March 21st, 1945
SHIP -         #693 (New Plane)
PILOT -        Smith
POSITION -     Toggalier (38 x 100 Frags. in Cluster)
LENGTH -       6 hrs.
REMARKS -      Altitude 22,000'; Visual bombing; Flak- medium; Seen V2 being
               launched over Zuider Zee; Good results…seen many fires burning.

*MISSION #20*

TARGET -    BERLIN *(Arms Factory)*
DATE -      *March 28th, 1945*
SHIP -      *#809 "PFC's LIMITED"*
PILOT -     *O'Neil*
POSITION -  *Toggalier (4 x 1000 Navy bombs 2 M17 Incend.)*
LENGTH -    *8½ hrs.*
REMARKS -   *Only had 45 minutes from briefing until takeoff...took off at 6:15; Tail*
            *gunner put in my guns; We assembled over France; Weather worst yet!!*
            *Flew by instruments most of time; Flak- heavy, but inaccurate; H2X*
            *bombing; One of our ships was badly damaged; We flew home alone, from*
            *France to base, due to bad weather...flew at 500' most of time; What fun!!*


*MISSION #21*

TARGET -    *Fassberg (Near Hannover)*
DATE -      *April 7th, 1945*
SHIP -      *#538*
PILOT -     *O'Neil*
POSITION -  *Toggalier (38 x 150)*
LENGTH -    *8½ hrs.*
REMARKS -   *Wakened at 2 A.M; Take-off delayed 4 hrs...took-off at 10:15; Really*
            *"sweat out" the take-off today! Visual bombing; No flak; Bandits reported,*
            *but we didn't see any E/A; Luftwaffe really up strong today; #3 ship in*
            *lead element, lead squadron; High and low squadrons bombed the secondary*
            *target.*


*MISSION #22*

TARGET -    *Dresden*
DATE -      *April 17th, 1945*
SHIP -      *#025*
PILOT -     *Robinson*
POSITION -  *Toggalier (12 x 500 G.P.'s)*
LENGTH -    *8½ hrs.*
REMARKS -   *Seen oil tanker on fire when crossing over channel; flew new type formation*
            *today; Very hazy all the way, however bombing was visual; Our group led*
            *the entire 8th Air Force; Was in low squadron; Group following us was hit*
            *by fighters; Had one bomb hang up on me today...finally salvoed it; Good*
            *bombing results!!*


*[MISSION #23- not recorded in log. Probable mission flown: Munich, April 21, 1945.]*

# NOTES AND SOURCES

## PREFACE

1. Tom Brokaw, *The Greatest Generation* (Random House, 1998).

## CHAPTER 1. SCOTCH AMBROSIA

1. John Ward Willson Loose, *Lancaster County: The Red Rose of Pennsylvania* (CCA Publications, Inc. 1994).
2. Ibid.
3. Author cannot confirm whether John was in fact William's son. He was not mentioned in Ambrose's obituary as a survivor. He could have been deceased when Ambrose died, because John was listed as a Quarryville cabinetmaker in 1875 (when he was probably in his 20s) and was no longer listed after 1910 (when he was probably in his 60s). The connection is made based on family references to Ross and Eva Singleton as Roy's cousins. They were both listed as children of a John Singleton living in homes at 326 N. Mary Street and 212 E. New Street.
4. *Biographical Annals of Lancaster County, Pennsylvania: Biographical and Genealogical Sketches of Prominent and Representative Citizens and Many of the Early Settlers* (J.H. Beers & Co., 1903), 1239.
5. "Death of James McMichael," *The Quarryville Sun*, November 22, 1901.
6. *Annals*, 1239.
7. *Annals*, 1333.
8. Douglas Harper, "Our Century," *Sunday News*, Lancaster, Pa., 1st ser., March 7, 1999, A-12.
9. Evelyn Thom, telephone interview by author, January 16, 2000.
10. Marian Medsger, telephone interview by author, January 8, 2000.

11. Harper, "Our Century," *Lancaster (Pennsylvania) New Era,* 1st ser., March 9, 1999, A-6.
12. "Death of James."
13. Harper, "Our Century," March 7, 1999, A-13.
14. Medsger interview.
15. Ibid.; quote attributed to Ivy by Marian.
16. Harper, "Our Century," *Lancaster New Era,* March 8, 1999, 1.
17. Harper, "Our Century," March 7, 1999, A-12; and Rieker advertisement in *Lancaster City Directory,* 1903-04.
18. Medsger interview; quote attributed to Ivy by Marian.
19. Harper; "Our Century," March 9, 1999, A-6.
20. Obituary, Ambrose A. Singleton, *Lancaster Daily Intelligencer,* February 15, 1926, and *The Quarryville Sun,* February 16, 1926.

## CHAPTER 2. WILLYS KNIGHT

1.  Thom interview.
2.  Ibid.
3.  Medsger interview.
4.  Marty Crisp, "Our Century," *Lancaster New Era,* 2nd ser., March 15, 1999, 1.
5.  Richard Rhoads (Elwood's son), family genealogy chart, June 21, 2000.
6.  Medsger interview.
7.  Wibur & Martin Shoe Co. advertisement, *Lancaster Daily Intelligencer,* March 9, 1916.
8.  Ibid.
9.  Medsger interview.
10. Crisp, "Our Century," *Sunday News,* 2nd ser., March 14, 1999.
11. Medsger interview.
12. Crisp, "Our Century," *Sunday News,* 2nd ser., March 14, 1999.
13. Maria Coole, "Our Century," *Sunday News,* 3rd ser., May 2, 1999, A-13.
14. Ibid.
15. Ibid.

## CHAPTER 3. MRS. SMITH'S NOODLES

1. Inferred from letter written to Wilbur & Martin Shoe Co. by Great Western Shoe Company, Milwaukee, Wisconsin, March 15, 1933.
2. Medsger interview.
3. Ibid.

## CHAPTER 4. CALIFORNIA TAN

1. "Countdown to the Millennium: Pages from the Past," *Lancaster New Era*, May 26, 1999, AA-3.
2. Ibid., AA-4.
3. Loose, *Lancaster County*, 50.
4. Victor Goehring letter to Tom Brokaw in Brokaw, *An Album of Memories: Personal Histories from the Greatest Generation* (Random House, 2000), 187-88.
5. "Countdown to Millenium," June 2, 1999.
6. Ibid., June 6, 1999.
7. Ibid., June 9, 1999.
8. Obituary from post-war news report: "2,198 Lancaster Casualties Reported in World War II," *Intelligencer Journal*, Lancaster County Heroes Edition of World War II, December 7, 1945, 10.

## CHAPTER 5. SAD SACKS

1. Bob insists that this is the song they were singing, even though the popular version of "How Much is that Doggie in the Window" wasn't recorded by Patti Page until 1952. Either it was a different song that slipped from his memory, or it was a different, earlier version of the same song.

## CHAPTER 6. ZARAGUZIE STREET

1. Norm's father Martin Zimmerman Diffenbach was one of five siblings: Mary, Fanny, Lizzy, and Henry. Dot and Becky Mellinger were daughters of Mart's deceased sister Mary. After Mary died at

Becky's birth, her two daughters were raised by Mart's mother Rebecca and sister Lizzy. Lizzy married Weaver Martin, who ran the Ezra Martin & Co. butcher business. Their daughter Ruth, married to Landis Hershey, was the source of this information. Landis worked for his father-in-law and eventually took over operations of Ezra Martin & Co., which no longer exists. Mart's mother Rebecca J. Diffenbach, known as Grammy Diff, lived beyond the century mark and was honored during and after her lifetime by huge family reunions held in her name, which were often attended by Mart and Vi, their daughters, and their daughters' families.

2.   "First U.S. Patrols Enter Germany, Mass for Assault on West Wall; Army Plans Slow Demobilization: War in Pacific Gets First Priority When Germany Surrenders," *Lancaster New Era*, September 6, 1944.

3.   "Countdown to Millennium," June 16, 99, AA-4.


## CHAPTER 7.  GREAT YOHO

1.   John Rutherford interview, March 14, 2000.
2.   Ibid. John said that the number of missions required for his tour completion was 30. According to Chaplain James Good Brown in *The Mighty Men of the 381st: Heroes All* (Publishers Press, 1994), 489, in the fall of 1944 the Eighth Air Force had raised the required number of missions to 30 from 25. Bob does not recall his tour requirement having changed from 25.


## CHAPTER 8.  TRIANGLE L

1.   Roger A. Freeman, "The Mighty Eighth Air Force," *World War II*, March 2001, 30.
2.   Ibid., 36.
3.   Chaplain James Good Brown, *The Mighty Men of the 381st: Heroes All* (Publishers Press, 1994), Chapter IX.
4.   Freeman, 40.
5.   Brown, 215.
6.   Ibid., 218.

7. Ibid., 219.
8. Ibid., 221.
9. Ibid., 291.
10. Freeman, 42.
11. Brown, 421.
12. Ibid., 162.
13. Ibid, 550.
14. Ibid., 425; although Osborne (below) attributes "61⁺" missions to *Mizpah*.
15. David R. Osborne, *They Came From Over the Pond* (381ˢᵗ Bomb Group Memorial Association, 1999), 204.
16. Ken Keller, *43-37910: The Last Day of a B-17, As told by the Crew of Nine Ten to Ken Keller* (TRIAD, Inc. Website, 1999).
17. Ibid.; Keller makes reference to description of the air battle in *Flying Fortress, The Boeing B-17*, by Ernest R. McDowell.

CHAPTER 9. GREASE MONKEYS

1. Rutherford interview.
2. Ibid. John didn't say, but the author assumes, perhaps incorrectly, that Boston Blackie is the same person as Toby Tobias, because both were into photography. Apologies to all if this is incorrect.
3. Ibid.
4. Ibid.
5. Brown, 489.
6. "Countdown to Millennium," June 16, 1999.

CHAPTER 10. MILK RUN

1. Composite of recollections from Singleton, Rutherford, Keller, and Eddie S. Picardo, *Tales of a Tail Gunner: A Memoir of Seattle and World War II* (1996).
2. Rutherford interview.
3. Possible formation structures are described in "The real B-17 Flying Fortress," *The B-17 Flying Fortress* (Bombs-Away.Net, 2000); the article points out that formations were modified

throughout the war to respond to the changing nature of the threat.

4. Throughout this book brackets around ellipses ("[...]") are used to distinguish a deletion by the author from Bob's other frequent uses of ellipses in his correspondence.

## CHAPTER 11. FEATHER MERCHANT

1. "Allied Bombs Seek to Sever Nazi Rail-to-Ruhr Arteries," *The Stars and Stripes*, December 5, 1944. All quotations listed from this source are assumed to have been taken from issues dated the day after the mission, based on the mission number written on a clipping posted in mission log.

2. Ibid. "1,200 Heavies Hit Nazi Rails", *Stars and Stripes*, December 5, 1944.

3. Ibid.

4. Ibid.; *Stars and Stripes*, December 10, 1944.

5. The name of pilot was probably misspelled as "Roebuck" in his mission log. According to Brown and Osborne, there is only one Robuck in the 381st, a Mead K. Robuck of the 535th Squadron, although his service dates, listed by Osborne as 5/44 - 8/44, do not overlap Bob's. Jim Tennet, Curator of Ridgewell Airfield Commemorative Association, confirms that microfilm records show Mead K. Robuck as pilot on the December 4th mission.

6. Mission log insert, "GAF Tactics 19 Mar," *Tactics Report No. 11* (HQ 8th Air Force).

7. Rutherford interview.

8. Contrails on this mission reported by Osborne, 156.

9. "Heavies Renew Attack on Rails," *Stars and Stripes*, December 11, 1944.

10. Osborne, 156 describes reported losses. Bob had no knowledge of official losses until the day after the mission. Flak intensity was an official post-mission assessment. The description of flak in his mission log is generally consistent with Osborne's characterization, derived from official sources. For example, the December 9th mission log entry describes flak as "medium, accurate" while Osborne's description is "moderate and accurate."

11. Ibid.

12. Brown, 481.
13. "1,600 Heavies Hit Reich," *Stars and Stripes*, December 12, 1944.
14. Mission log.
15. Osborne, 157.
16. "1,250 U.S. Heavies Hit Reich Again," *Stars and Stripes*, December 13, 1944.
17. Freeman, 42.
18. Excerpt from "Daily Bulletin No. 283, Headquarters AAF Station 167, Monday 9 October 1944," quoted in Brown, 478.
19. Brown, 477.
20. "1,250 U.S. Heavies," *Stars and Stripes*, December 13, 1944.
21. Date of newspaper clipping showing aerial photo of Cologne is undocumented, but, based on its sequence in the mission log, is believed to have been after the raid of December 18th. Results of the bombing were unobserved on the day of the raid, according to Osborne, 157.

## CHAPTER 12. CHANGE OF PLANS

1. Mission log.
2. Osborne, 157.
3. "Record Bomb Blow 8th AF's Yule Gift to Nazis," *Stars and Stripes*, December 25, 1944.
4. Brown, 502; Bob refers to the festival as a "carol service" in his letter of December 24, 1944.
5. Brown, 504.
6. In his January 18th letter he listed who sent him cards: *"Mr. & Mrs. Brackbill (the ones on Franklin St.); Uncle Vince & Aunt Ella; Uncle Sam & Pauline; Mrs. Worrest; Charlie Adams & wife; the Preacher and wife; Aunt Ruthie and Amos; Emma Rhoads (seemed funny not seeing it signed, "the twins"); Donnie Harsh; Sis & Harry; Uncle Weaver & Aunt Lizzie; Uncle George; Eva Singleton (of all people, her. I never expected it. She works at Garvins...Dad's cousin.); Charles & Lizzie Miller; Ruth & Bill Feller & baby; the Aments; Mollie & Ed; Harriet & Bob & baby; Mom & Dad; and, best of all, YOU."*

## CHAPTER 13. TOGGALIER

1.  "Conduct of a Combat Bombing Mission," *Toggalier Checklist* is-
    sued by Capt. Thomas J. Hester, Acting Group Bombardier, 381st
    Bomb Group. Bob also had in his possession a more official-
    looking *Bombardiers Check List,* which included bombsight
    operating procedures, and a *Checklist for Bombardiers on All-Electric
    Bombing Equipment,* with which he would have had to be familiar
    to drop bombs in different modes, like salvo or train.

2.  Rutherford interview; it's not clear whether all or some of the
    loading crews were black, but it's common knowledge that troops
    were usually segregated during WWII. Bob may have noticed, but
    never commented about it.

3.  *Checklist.*

4.  Ibid.

5.  Ibid.

6.  Ibid.

7.  Ibid.

8.  "V-2 Like a Big Bullet, Reports Mustang Pilot," *Stars and Stripes,*
    January 2, 1945.

9.  Rutherford interview.

10. Osborne, 161.

11. Ibid.

12. Ken Stone, *Hot Seat on a Bomber,* videotape (1985, rev. 1991).

13. Rutherford interview.

14. This cockpit incident occurred on one of Bob's missions; how-
    ever, he cannot recall if it was on the January 20th mission.
    Author assumed it was on this mission based on the comment,
    "one engine feathered (#3)," in his mission log.

15. Incident pieced together by author from records in Osborne and
    Brown.

16. On our 1999 visit to Ridgewell a lady who lives on the neighbor-
    ing farm told us that she still remembers this incident, which
    occurred when she was a teenager.

17. Osborne, 162.

18. It's not clear if this was the mission where Bob had his closest call
    with flak; it could have been on the March 1st mission, where he
    reported a "hole in ship" in his mission log. But, based on the

relative flak intensity reported on these two missions, author has made the assumption that the close call occurred on January 28th.

19. Osborne, 163. Author uses the description "hangar queen," which was then, and is now, a term commonly used by air crews when referring to a ship that spends a lot of time under repair.

20. Ibid.

## CHAPTER 14. FRESH EGGS

1. Lutzendorf is the primary target listed in Osborne and in Bob's mission log. Osborne also lists Lutzendorf (spelled incorrectly) as the primary and Berlin as the secondary. But Brown lists Ohrdruf as the target, and official records found by Tennet also show Ohrdruf as the primary target of Bob's 535th ship. These towns are all in the same vicinity, southwest of Leipzig. Since the group formation got broken up, it's not clear who received the brunt of the attacks. Despite its isolated location in the foothills, Ohrdruf would have been a strategic, well-defended, and hard-to-destroy target. Col. Robert S. Allen, in his book *Lucky Forward: The History of Patton's 3rd US Army:* the underground bunker at Ohrdruf was fifty feet below the surface consisting of multi-story structures, connected by several miles of tunnels, and encased in reinforced concrete. It contained "paneled and carpeted offices, scores of large work and store rooms, tiled bathrooms with bath tubs and showers, flush toilets, electrically equipped kitchens, decorated dining rooms and mess halls, giant refrigerators, extensive sleeping quarters, recreation rooms, separate bars for officers and enlisted personnel, a moving picture theater, and air-conditioning and sewage systems." It was built by slave labor from nearby concentration camps.

2. Bob spells Zuider Zee according to the way it was shown on his maps at that time; a more contemporary spelling is Zuyder Zee.

3. Osborne, 165.

4. Brown, 538.

5. "8th Pummels Luftwaffe's Airfields," *Stars and Stripes,* March 20, 1945.

6. Rutherford interview.

7. Brown, 541.

8. Brown, 545.
9. Brown, 576.
10. "March Record Month for 8th," *Stars and Stripes*, April 1, 1945.
11. *Stars and Stripes*, April 14, 1945.
12. Because no notes were recorded on this mission, Bob cannot recall whether he flew on the mission to Munich or Pilsen, the final mission flown by the 381st on April 25, 1945.
13. "Luftwaffe Still Numerous, Arnold Says, But Out of Gas," *Stars and Stripes*, April 8, 1945.
14. Information contained in Hall's comments, according to Osborne, 174.
15. Freeman, 44.
16. Osborne, 174.

## CHAPTER 15. GOING HOME

1. John completed 30 combat missions, which comprised the length of his tour. It's likely that Bob also needed 30 missions for tour completion, but his best recollection is that he went overseas on an arrangement that required 25.
2. Magazine clipping in Rutherford's scrap book from *Saturday Evening Post*, June, 1945.
3. Rutherford interview.
4. CMSgt Wesley C. Weaver, "War Story: Lt. Col. Robert A. Bennett, April 8, 1923-May 17, 1995," *381st Bomb Group (H) Memorial Association Newsletter*, February, 1998, and Osborne, 213. On his January 21st mission in *Hell's Angel* Bob flew for the first time with two of the three crew members who were killed on March 30th: 2nd Lt. Alexander D. Nelson, copilot and T/Sgt. Chester M. Sloimczenski, engineer/top turrett gunner. He had flown with two others who were also on the March 30th mission; they had been part of Malleus's regular crew but ended up being captured: S/Sgt. Charles L. Majors, radar jammer (top turret gunner) and Sgt. Guy Stubblefield, waist gunner.
5. "8th Air Force to Go Back to School," *Stars and Stripes*, circa. June, 1945.

6.  Letter of September 7, 1945 from Acting Adjutant General, Maj. Gen. Edward F. Witsell to W. Roy Singleton, quoted in letter from Roy to Bob, October 1, 1945.

CHAPTER 16. BOOMERS

1.  "Countdown to Millennium," June 23, 1999.
2.  Ibid., June 27, 1999.
3.  Ibid., June 23, 1999.
4.  Ibid., June 30, 1999.
5.  Ibid., July 4, 1999.
6.  "W. Roy Singleton Dies, Operated Shoe Store," *Intelligencer Journal*, November 4, 1952.

CHAPTER 17. SHOE PILOT

1.  "Countdown to Millennium," June 23, 1999.
2.  *Optimist Creed* (Optimist International®), quoted in its entirety on the last page of this book.
3.  "Mid City Blaze Fells 50 Firemen: Historic Building At 32-34 N. Queen Swept By Flames," *Intelligencer Journal*, November 15, 1956.
4.  Brochure published as companion to exhibit at Community Gallery of Lancaster County coordinated by John J. Snyder, Jr., *Lancaster's Architecture: The Past's Gift to the City's Future*, October 17-November 28, 1976.
5.  "Countdown to Millennium," October 17, 1999.
6.  Ibid., October 20, 1999.

# THE OPTIMIST CREED

*Promise Yourself* —

To be so strong that nothing can disturb your peace of mind.

To talk health, happiness and prosperity to every person you meet.

To make all your friends feel that there is something in them.

To look at the sunny side of everything and make your optimism come true.

To think only of the best, to work only for the best and expect only the best.

To be just as enthusiastic about the success of others as you are about your own.

To forget the mistakes of the past and press on to the greater achievements of the future.

To wear a cheerful countenance at all times and give every living creature you meet a smile.

To give so much time to the improvement of yourself that you have no time to criticize others.

To be too large for worry, too noble for anger, too strong for fear, and too happy to permit the presence of trouble.

OPTIMIST INTERNATIONAL®